Leasehold disputes

Francis Davey is a practising barrister. He has been a fee-paid judge of the First-tier Tribunal (Property Chamber) since its inception.

Justin Bates is a barrister at Arden Chambers. He is the deputy editor of the *Encyclopedia of Housing Law* and is recommended in both *Chambers and Partners* and the *Legal 500* for his leasehold property work. He regularly appears in the FTT(PC), LVT and Upper Tribunal (Lands Chamber) and recent significant cases include *Burr v OM Property Management Ltd*; *Avon Estates Ltd v Sinclair Gardens Ltd*; *Avon Freeholds Ltd v Regent Court RTM Co Ltd*; *Fairhold Mercury Ltd v HQ (Block 1) Action Management Co Ltd*; *Assethold Ltd v 7 Sunny Gardens RTM Co Ltd* and *Ninety Broomfield Road RTM Co Ltd v Triplerose and other appeals.*

Available as an ebook at www.lag.org.uk/ebooks

Leasehold disputes

THIRD EDITION

Francis Davey and Justin Bates

Legal Action Group
2014

This third edition published in Great Britain 2014
by LAG Education and Service Trust Limited
3rd floor, Universal House, 88–94 Wentworth Street, London E1 7SA
www.lag.org.uk

First edition 2004
Second edition 2008

While every effort has been made to ensure that the details in this text are correct, readers must be aware that the law changes and that the accuracy of the material cannot be guaranteed and the author and the publisher accept no responsibility for any loss or damage sustained.

British Library Cataloguing in Publication Data
a CIP catalogue record for this book is available from the British Library.

This book has been produced using Forest Stewardship Council (FSC) certified paper. The wood used to produce FSC certified products with a 'Mixed Sources' label comes from FSC certified well-managed forests, controlled sources and/or recycled material.

Print ISBN   978 1 908407 10 8
ebook ISBN   978 1 908407 11 5

Typeset by Regent Typesetting, London
Printed in Great Britain by Hobbs the Printers, Totton, Hampshire

Justin dedicates this book to Olachi and Lucie,
with hope that neither ever needs to read it.

Francis dedicates this book to his mother,
Elizabeth Davey.

Foreword

Siobhan McGrath, President of the Property Chamber
of the First-tier Tribunal

I am pleased to have been asked to write a foreword to this third edition of *Leasehold Disputes*. The law and practice governing leasehold management and leasehold disputes is far from simple. It affects many thousands of landlords and lessees across England and Wales. It is therefore gratifying that Francis Davey and Justin Bates have been able to distil the essential principles into an accessible and comprehensive text.

The popularity of the first two editions of the book was apparent to me in the tribunal hearing rooms where copies of the book were used by both practitioners and litigants in person as a ready reference tool. I imagine therefore, that this third edition has been eagerly awaited. In the last six years, the law has moved on apace. In particular there have been significant developments in the jurisprudence governing section 20 consultation and section 20ZA dispensation and in the exercise of the right to manage.

For the tribunal and its users in England, 2013 saw the LVT move into the First-tier Tribunal (Property Chamber). Chapter 16 of the book deals succinctly and well in outlining the procedures and new case management powers afforded to the tribunal following this change. Importantly, the contrasting LVT regime that has been retained in Wales is given separate treatment.

Several other new chapters reflect the increasing sophistication in practice in this area and include an important consideration of the recoverability of a landlord's legal costs both as service charges and as administration charges as well as summarising judicial guidance on the tribunal's exercise of its discretion under section 20C. For the first time a chapter has been included on freehold service charges. This is a sensible move. Freeholders will often have to contribute to the same estate charges as are paid by leaseholders and yet lack the protection of sections 18 to 30 of the 1985 Act.

The leasehold sector includes private landlords, public landlords, tenant management companies, owner-occupiers and right to buy vii investors. Each may have different priorities and there will be wide divergence of resources. I have no doubt however, that for all of those involved, *Leasehold Disputes* will be an invaluable source of essential knowledge and information.

Siobhan McGrath
President of the First-tier Tribunal (Property Chamber)
February 2014

Preface

This book is intended to give advice for residential tenants in a dispute with their landlord that might bring them before the First-tier Tribunal (Property Chamber) (FTT) (in England) or a leasehold valuation tribunal (LVT) (in Wales).

Outline of this book

Chapter 1 deals with what is currently the most important – and common – area of dispute between tenants and landlords, namely service charges. It discusses the existing case-law on when such charges are payable and in what sum. Chapter 2 then explains how service charges are to be held and protected by landlords.

When landlords undertake large works, or enter into contracts lasting longer than a year, to which their tenants will have to contribute in their service charges, landlords are required to go through a relatively elaborate consultation process concerning the works. Should landlords fail to consult properly, the amount they are allowed to recover from their tenants may be capped. The law on consultation is covered in chapter 3.

In considering whether and how to challenge a service charge demand, it is important for a tenant to have as much information as possible. Chapter 4 explains what information landlords must give to leaseholders, both with demands for payment and more generally.

Insurance disputes are dealt with in chapter 5, while chapter 6 deals with certain miscellaneous charges, called administration charges, that might be recovered by a landlord from a tenant and that may not be covered by the definition of service charges.

Sometimes the root of a dispute between landlord and tenant is a poorly drafted lease. Any party to a lease can apply to a tribunal to have the lease altered (varied) on various grounds. Chapter 7 explores the situations when such a variation can be ordered, and the process by which variation takes place.

Chapter 8 describes the power of the tribunal to appoint a manager where there has been some failure of management of a property; and also the ways in which the tribunal supervises the manager once appointed.

Chapter 9 discusses the alternative route by which tenants may force the appointment of their own management company, a so-called 'right to manage' (RTM) company, regardless of any preceding fault.

Chapter 10 explains the various powers open to landlords to attempt to recover their costs of leasehold disputes – powers which are rarely available to tenants.

Chapter 11 gives a very brief sketch of the power that a landlord has to take back the property they have leased if the tenant is at fault in paying the rent or complying with a covenant in the lease. This is a process known as forfeiture, and would be quite severe for residential leases if the law did not curb the power of landlords to forfeit in various ways which are discussed in the chapter.

Chapter 12 deals with special considerations applicable where the lease was acquired under the 'right to buy'.

Chapter 13 gives a thumb-nail sketch of the various ways in which a tenant might attempt to secure and fund legal representation before the tribunal.

Chapter 14 explains about situations in which freeholders might be required to contribute to shared costs in a similar way to leaseholders and the limited role that the tribunal can play in such cases.

Chapters 15, 16 and 17 deal with procedure in the LVT, FTT and Upper Tribunal, respectively.

Tenants involved in the purchase of their freehold, or an extension or renewal of their lease, should expect to have legal advice (since they are involved in a process of conveyancing). This book does not attempt to deal with the LVT's jurisdiction over leasehold enfranchisement, or the other statutory rights of tenants to purchase the freehold of their property. These matters will be largely ignored hereafter.

And finally

It is now just over ten years since we wrote the first edition of this work and we are grateful to all those who have bought copies of the previous editions and offered constructive feedback on how to improve the third edition.

In particular, we (jointly) owe thanks to Esther Pilger at LAG, for putting up with our 'relaxed' approach to deadlines.

In addition, Justin would like to thank Andrew Arden QC, both for teaching him basic grammar and for giving him seemingly endless opportunities to develop as a lawyer and legal writer. Further thanks are due to all those people who have been kind enough to read parts of this work or comment on ideas and arguments over the years, including Gusta Glover, Tilly Rubens, Philip Parkinson, Andrew Bailey, Janice Northover, Roger Hardwick, Shaun Jardine, Lorraine Scott, Geraldine Haden, Michael McCrone, Neil Maloney, Charmaine McQueen-Prince and Eyvind Andresen. Most importantly, thanks are due to his wife, Elizabeth, for her patience, love and support.

Francis would like to thank the team at the Nearly Legal blog who allow him to chew over points of law that would otherwise be obscure to him; also for the useful training and discussion organised by Bruce Edgington and David Brown of the Eastern Region of the First-tier Tribunal; and most of all his wife, Helen Snape, who untiringly supports him in all he does.

The book is accurate to 17 January 2014, although we have tried to incorporate any subsequent developments at proof stage.

Francis Davey
Justin Bates
London, January 2014

Contents

Table of cases

Table of statutes

Table of statutory instruments

Abbreviations

ARHM	Association of Retirement Housing Managers
ASI	Architects and Surveyors Institute
CLRA 2002	Commonhold and Leasehold Reform Act 2002
CPR	Civil Procedure Rules
DCLG	Department for Communities and Local Government
FTT	First-tier Tribunal
FTT(PC)	First-tier Tribunal (Property Chamber)
FTT Rules	Tribunal Procedure (First-tier Tribunal) (Property Chamber) Rules 2013 SI No 1169
HA 1996	Housing Act 1996
IA 1986	Insolvency Act 1986
ICAEW	Institute of Chartered Accountants for England and Wales
ISVA	Incorporated Society of Valuers and Auctioneers
LA 1980	Limitation Act 1980
LASPO Act 2012	Legal Aid, Sentencing and Punishment of Offenders Act 2012
LPA 1925	Law of Property Act 1925
LRHUDA 1993	Leasehold Reform, Housing and Urban Development Act 1993
LTA 1985	Landlord and Tenant Act 1985
LTA 1987	Landlord and Tenant Act 1987
LVT	Leasehold valuation tribunal
LVT Fees Regs	Leasehold Valuation Tribunals (Fees) (Wales) Regulations 2004 SI No 683
LVT Procedure Regs	Leasehold Valuation Tribunals (Procedure) (Wales) Regulations 2004 SI No 681
PEA 1977	Protection from Eviction Act 1977
PTR	Pre-trial review
QLTA	Qualifying long-term agreement
RA 1977	Rent Act 1977
RICS	Royal Institution of Chartered Surveyors

RTA	Recognised tenants' association
RTB	Right to buy
RTM	Right to manage
SC Consultation (England) Regs	Service Charges (Consultation Requirements) (England) Regulations 2003 SI No 1987
SC Consultation (Wales) Regs	Service Charges (Consultation Requirements) (Wales) Regulations 2004 SI No 684
UT	Upper Tribunal
UT(LC)	Upper Tribunal (Lands Chamber)
UT Rules	Tribunal Procedure (Upper Tribunal) (Lands Chamber) Rules 2010 SI No 2600

CHAPTER 1

Service charges

continued

Key points

- A service charge is any variable sum of money paid by the tenant which is payable, directly or indirectly, for services, repairs, maintenance, improvements, insurance or management of the property. It may or may not be included in the tenants rent.
- The starting point is always what the lease says. Is there a contractual obligation on the tenant to pay for each and every item of expenditure? Has the demand been made in accordance with the lease? Has the correct amount (or proportion) been demanded?
- Then consider whether the demand complies with the statutory requirements, both as to information to accompany demands, timing of demands and any statutory consultation
- Finally, is the sum demanded reasonably incurred and/or reasonable in amount?
- The tribunal can resolve disputes about variable service charges, including whether there is any contractual obligation to pay, whether the statutory conditions have been complied with and what amount is due. It cannot, however, re-write the lease obligations.

Advice for tenants

- Most leases of flats place the landlord under an obligation to do works and provide services for the benefit of the tenants, with a corresponding obligation on the tenants to pay for those works or services. These 'service' charges can be a source of contention between the landlord and tenant. Tenants often feel that they have a greater stake in the property than the freeholder and resent being presented with bills for works which they either did not support or would have wished to have done differently.
- Sometimes – particularly where the landlord is a tenant-owned company – these disputes will break out between individual tenants. Works may need to be done urgently, but one or two tenants may be unwilling to contribute to the costs of the necessary works.

continued

- The tribunal can now deal with almost all such disputes. Some of these disputes will be purely question of law, some will be entirely questions of fact and many will be a mixture of the two.
- It is vital for any tenant who wishes to challenge the reasonableness of a service charge to obtain comparable evidence to bolster their case. The vast majority of service charge cases that fail do so for lack of evidence and failure to appreciate the principles of reasonableness.

Introduction

1.1   Service charges are sums of money paid by tenants to landlords for services and works provided or done by their landlord. The tribunal has long been able to adjudicate on whether or not service charges are reasonable and, since the commencement of the Commonhold and Leasehold Reform Act (CLRA) 2002, has also been able to decide any question of payability of service charges. This chapter addresses both the general law on recovery of service charges (construction of the lease; statutory controls; reasonableness) and then considers the role of the tribunal in these matters.

What are service charges?

1.2   Leases have a multitude of names for service charges, eg 'the maintenance charge', the 'block charge', the 'estate charge' etc. The name given to the particular charge by the lease is irrelevant. For the purposes of the rights and liabilities discussed in this book, service charges are those defined in Landlord and Tenant Act (LTA) 1985 s18 as: 'an amount payable by a tenant of a dwelling as part of or in addition to the rent which is payable directly, or indirectly, for services, repairs, maintenance, improvements or insurance or the landlord's costs of management and the whole or part of which varies or may vary according to the relevant costs'.

Payable

1.3   The service charge will normally be said to be payable because of an obligation in the lease. The principles of lease construction are discussed below. It is, in principle, possible for a service charge to arise under an agreement other than the lease, if, eg, the landlord and tenant had agreed that the landlord should do certain work or provide a specific service, subject to reimbursement by the tenant.

1.4   The term 'landlord' is given an extended meaning. It is defined as any person with the right to enforce payment of a service charge. For example, it includes management companies in tripartite leases, and could even extend to other tenants where the lease imposes a duty of repair on one tenant which is to be paid for by others.[1]

By a tenant

1.5   This includes a statutory tenant and a leaseholder who has sublet their flat as well as the sub-tenant.[2] The fact that a tenant is also a tenant of more than one flat or of additional (non-residential) parts of the building does not exclude a charge from being a service charge.[3]

1.6   The money must, however, have been demanded from (and payable by) the tenant in their capacity as tenant.[4] If, for example, a lessee-owned freehold company demanded money from its members as members, even if the money was to be used for works that would otherwise be service charge works, the charge would not be a service charge as it would not arise from a landlord–tenant relationship.

Of a dwelling

1.7   Originally, the definition in the LTA 1985 applied only to flats. This was changed to 'dwelling' by the LTA 1987,[5] so as to bring leasehold houses within the scope of the definition.

1.8   A 'dwelling' is defined as a building or part of a building occupied or intended to be occupied as a separate dwelling, together with any yard, garden, outhouse or appurtenance belonging to or usually enjoyed with it.[6] This is a very broad definition:

a) There is no requirement that the tenant actually lives in the property (ie if it is sublet, even on a short tenancy, it is still a dwelling).[7]

1 LTA 1985 s30: *Cinnamon Ltd v Morgan* [2001] EWCA Civ 1616.
2 LTA 1985 s30.
3 *Oakfern Properties Ltd v Ruddy* [2006] EWCA Civ 1389; [2007] 3 WLR 524; approving *Heron Maple Court v Central Estates* [2002] 1 EGLR 35.
4 *Di Marco v Morshead Mansions* [2008] EWCA Civ 1371; [2009] HLR 33.
5 LTA 1987 s41.
6 LTA 1985 s38.
7 *Oakfern Properties Ltd v Ruddy* [2007] Ch 335.

b) The fact that the tenant holds more than one dwelling or other property under one lease does not matter either. For example, in the case of person who has a lease of a whole building, out of which has been granted individual flat leases, both the head leaseholder and the occupational leaseholders are tenants of dwellings.[8] This remains so even if the lease includes extensive other, non-residential property. The most extreme example of this known to the authors is found in *Oakfern* – in which it was suggested that a person holding a lease of a shopping centre with a resident caretaker was a tenant of a dwelling.

1.9   There are conflicting decisions as to whether or not holiday homes (ie properties let on long leases under which the tenant is only permitted to occupy the property for part of the year) are 'dwellings' for these purposes. In *King v Udlaw*,[9] the Lands Tribunal held that they were not, while in *Phillips v Francis (No 1)*,[10] the High Court held that they were.

Whole or part of which varies or may vary according to relevant costs

1.10   This part of the definition has caused real difficulties. In order to come within the scope of the definition, there has to be a direct relationship between the amount of costs as a cause and the amount of the service charge as a consequence.[11]

1.11   Thus, a charge that is fixed in amount under the lease cannot be a service charge as it cannot be said to vary in any way, let alone by reference to the costs of the landlord. Likewise, a charge which is initially fixed but which then increases according to an external index (eg Retail Prices Index (RPI)) does vary, but not in relation to the costs of the landlord and, hence, is not a service charge.[12] Similarly, a charge which is fixed but then increases in accordance with a formula in the lease is not a service charge.[13] Where the lease provides for a fixed charge to be paid, which can be increased (to another fixed charge) if the landlord serves a notice, it is a question of construction

---

8   *Oakfern Properties Ltd v Ruddy* [2007] Ch 335. See also *Buckley v Bowerbeck Properties Ltd* [2009] 1 EGLR 43.

9   [2008] 2 EGLR 99.

10   [2010] 2 EGLR 31.

11   *Home Group Ltd v Lewis* LRX/176/2006.

12   *Coventry City Council v Cole* [1984] 1 WLR 398.

13   *Arnold v Britton* [2013] EWCA Civ 902.

of the agreement in each case to see whether there is anything linking the alteration to the costs of providing the services; if there is no such link, then the charges are not service charges.[14]

1.12   By contrast, a charge which is a fixed percentage of a variable sum is a service charge; for example, in *Longmint Ltd v Marcus*[15] the management fee was set in the lease at 15 per cent of the service charge expenditure; since the service charge expenditure varied from year to year, it followed that the management fee must also vary. Similarly, where the lease provides for recovery of one sum of money as a service charge, comprising individual elements, then, so long as the total demand varies, it does not matter that some of the individual elements are fixed.[16]

Relevant costs

1.13   These are defined as costs or estimated costs incurred or to be incurred by or on behalf of the landlord or a superior landlord in connection with the matters for which the service charge is payable.[17] 'Costs', for these purposes, include overheads.[18]

Exclusions

1.14   The statutory regime over service charges does not apply to service charges paid by tenants of local authorities, national park authorities or new town corporations unless the tenancies are long leases.[19] Nor do the charges apply to a rent payable by a Rent Act 1977 tenant where the rent is registered, unless it is entered as a variable amount.[20]

---

14 For examples of charges which were found not to vary with the relevant costs and hence were not variable service charges, see *Home Group Ltd v Lewis* LRX/176/2006; *Chand v Calmore Area Housing Ltd* LRX/170/2007 and *Minister Chalets v Irwin Park Residents Association* LRX/28/2000. For those which were, see *Re: Appeals by (1) Southern Housing Group Ltd and (2) Family Housing Association (Wales) Ltd* [2010] UKUT 237 (LC).

15 LRX/25/2003; [2004] 3 EGLR 171.

16 *Warwickshire Hamlets Ltd v Gedden* [2010] UKUT 75, in which the lease provided for the recovery of one charge comprising both fixed and variable elements; the Upper Tribunal rejected an argument that the fixed elements could not be considered, and focused instead on the total charge.

17 LTA 1985 s18(2).

18 LTA 1985 s18(3).

19 LTA 1985 s26.

20 LTA 1985 s27.

1.15   In practice, tenancies under short leases – ie those of less than seven years[21] – are unlikely to be paying significant service charges because in such leases the landlord is given the responsibility for the majority of repair and maintenance,[22] although sometimes landlords do re-charge for the costs of externally provided services – such as gas or electricity – and such charges would be service charges.

Contractual restrictions on recovery of service charges

1.16   There are three issues which arise. First, does the lease provide for a payment of a service charge at all? Second, has the demand been properly calculated in accordance with the lease? Third, have any pre-conditions for payment specified in the lease been complied with?

Contractual entitlement

1.17   This book is not the place for a full treatment of the entire law relating to contractual interpretation.[23] Rather, it attempts to describe the general approach taken to the interpretation of service charge clauses.

1.18   The starting point is that service charge provisions are construed restrictively and the courts/tribunals are unlikely to allow the recovery of costs which are not clearly included.[24] Further, in the event of any ambiguity, the issue is resolved against the landlord.[25]

---

21 LTA 1985 s13.

22 LTA 1985 s11.

23 See eg Lewison, *The interpretation of contracts*, 2011; *Chitty on Contracts*, 31st edn. The leading cases are *Investors Compensation Scheme v West Bromwich Building Society* [1998] 1 WLR 896; *Chartbrook Ltd v Persimmon Homes Ltd* [2009] UKHL 38; and *Rainy Sky SA v Kookmin Bank* [2011] UKSC 50.

24 *Gilje v Charlegrove Securities Ltd* [2002] 1 EGLR 41; *Norwich City Council v Marshall* LRX/114/2007; *Leicester City Council v Master* LRX/175/2007; *Paddington Basin Developments Ltd v Gritz* [2013] UKUT 338 (LC); *Wembley National Stadium Ltd v Wembley London Ltd* [2007] EWHC 756 (Ch); *McHale v Cadogan* [2010] EWCA Civ 14; [2010] HLR 24; compare *Arnold v Britton* [2012] EWHC 3451 (Ch) and *Universities Superannuation Scheme Ltd v Marks & Spencer plc* [1999] 1 EGLR 13.

25 *Gilje; Cadogan v 27/29 Sloane Gardens Ltd* LRA/9/2005; for leases granted after the commencement of the Unfair Terms in Consumer Contracts Regulations 1994 (now Unfair Terms in Consumer Contracts Regulations 1999 SI No 2083), this approach is also required by reg 7. See generally *R (Khatun) v LB Newham* [2005] QB 37. This restrictive approach would not necessarily apply to a management company under a lease: *Seacon Residents Co Ltd v Oshodin* [2012] UKUT 54 (LC).

1.19   Thus, where a lease contained a provision which allowed recovery of repairs and a provisothat the landlord could make any alteration in the services at any time, it was held that this did not cover repairs to external walls.[26] Likewise, a provision entitling a landlord to recover the cost of providing and maintaining additional services or amenities did not permit the landlord to recover the cost of installing double-glazed windows.[27] Similarly, a clause permitting the recovery of 'the cost of all other services which the lessor may, at its absolute discretion, provide or install' did not cover legal fees relating to an action against the tenants.[28] Further, where the lease obliged the landlord to take out insurance in the name of both the landlord and tenant, an insurance policy taken out only in the name of the landlord was insufficient, such that the costs were not recoverable as a service charge from the tenant.[29]

1.20   There is no rule of law or presumption that a landlord should always recover their whole expenditure; it may well be that the lease puts obligations on the landlord which are not to be reimbursed by the tenants.[30] Further, in the absence of clear wording to the contrary, a lease will not be read so as to enable the landlord to make a profit.[31]

1.21   In appropriately worded leases, it may also be possible for a landlord to include notional costs in the service charges; a common example is the notional rent for accommodation provided to a warden or caretaker.[32]

1.22   In practice, there is often a more generous approach taken with lessee-owned or controlled companies, eg by implying a term into the lease to ensure that there can be proper recovery by the company.[33]

---

26 *Jacob Isbicki v Goulding* [1989] 1 EGLR 236.

27 *Mullaney v Maybourne* [1986] 1 EGLR 70.

28 *St Mary's Mansions v Limegate Investment* [2002] EWCA Civ 1491; [2003] HLR 24; [2002] 43 EG 161.

29 *Green v 180 Archway Road Management Co Ltd* [2012] UKUT 245 (LC).

30 *Rapid Results College Ltd v Angell* [1986] 1 EGLR 53; *Campbell v Daejan Properties Ltd* [2012] EWCA Civ 1503.

31 *Jollybird v Fairzone* [1990] 2 EGLR 55 as explained in *Arnold v Britton* [2012] EWHC 3451 (Ch). If the lease did provide for more than 100 per cent of expenditure to be recovered, it is very likely that an application could be made to the tribunal to vary the lease: see chapter 7.

32 *Lloyds Bank plc v Bowker Orford* [1999] 2 EGLR 44; *Earl Cadogan v 27/29 Sloane Gardens Ltd* [2006] L&TR 18; *Gilje v Charlesgrove Securities Ltd* [2001] EWCA Civ 1777; *Agavil Investments Ltd v Corner and others* (unreported, 3 October 1975, Court of Appeal).

33 *Embassy Court Ltd v Lipman* (1984) 271 EG 545.

While understandable, it is difficult to justify as a matter of law unless the company was the original landlord. If there has been a subsequent purchase of the freehold by the leaseholders or the formation of a Right to Manage (RTM) company, that is not something which would normally be admissible evidence when construing the meaning of a lease granted prior to the acquisition of the freehold or management by that company.[34]

Calculation of the amount payable

1.23   In blocks of flats, most service charge clauses apportion the total expenditure of the landlord amongst the tenants. Service charges are only recoverable to the extent permitted under the lease, hence the apportionment between tenants is governed by the terms specified in the lease.

1.24   Typically a lease will apportion service charges in one of four ways:
1) by floor area;
2) by rateable value;
3) by fixed proportions; or
4) by a duty to pay a 'fair proportion' or words to that effect.

1.25   Apportionment by floor area or fixed proportions is unlikely to pose any significant difficulties.

1.26   Many older leases apportion costs according to rateable value. The difficulty with this is that domestic rateable values were almost completely abolished from 31 March 1990,[35] such that the proportions would appear to be frozen as at that date.[36]

1.27   Where a lease obliges the tenant to pay a 'fair proportion' (or similar words) of the costs of works or services, it will be a question of fact and degree in each case whether the resulting charge meets these conditions.[37] The phrase 'due proportion' is usually taken to mean a reasonable or fair proportion of the relevant charges.[38] On any such wording, it is clear that the landlord has a broad discretion.[39]

---

34   *Wilson v Lesley Place RTM Co Ltd* [2010] UKUT 342 (LC).
35   Local Government Finance Act 1988 s117.
36   Although, for an alternative view, see *Furlonger v Lalatta and others* [2014] EWHC 37 (Ch).
37   See, among many possible examples, *Sutton (Hastoe) Housing Association v Williams* (1988) 20 HLR 321; [1988] 1 EGLR 56; *Re Rowner Estates Ltd* LRX/3/2006.
38   *Hackney LBC v Thompson* [2001] L&TR 7.
39   *Shersby v Greenhurst Park Management Ltd* [2009] UKUT 241 (LC).

Contractual pre-conditions

1.28 The provision of a certificate from a surveyor or accountant is a common feature of modern residential leases. The certificate will usually give a definitive figure of the service charge expenditure and, in many cases, is a condition precedent for payment of those charges. If it is a condition precedent for payment then, until the certificate is provided, the service charges are not payable.[40] It is unlikely, however, that a failure to comply with the condition precedent would mean that the money was never due;[41] rather, the money is likely to become due once the condition is satisfied.[42] If the lease does not specify a time for provision of a valid certificate, then it is likely that a requirement would be implied that it be provided within a reasonable period of time.[43]

Statutory restrictions on the recovery of service charges

1.29 There are a series of statutory restrictions on the recovery of service charges.

Information requirements

1.30 Service charge demands must comply with LTA 1987 ss47 and 48, and must be accompanied by a summary of rights and obligations. These requirements, and the consequences of non-compliance, are discussed in chapter 4.

Consultation

1.31 The consultation process and the consequences (in terms of irrecoverable service charges) of failing to consult are discussed in chapter 3.

---

40 See eg *Finchbourne Limited v Rodrigues* [1976] 3 All ER 581; *CIN Properties Limited v Barclays Bank* [1986] 1 EGLR 59; *Rigby v Wheatley* LRX/84/2004.

41 *Warrior Quay Management Company and another v Joachim and others* LRX/42/2006.

42 *Southwark LBC v Woelke* [2013] UKUT 349 (LC).

43 *Redrow Homes (Midlands) Ltd and others v Hothi and others* [2011] UKUT 268 (LC).

Stale service charges

1.32   The problem of 'stale' or late service charge demands was noted in the Nugee Report[44] and LTA 1985 s20B attempts to meet it.[45] The landlord must, within 18 months of incurring the cost, either:

a) demand it from the tenant as a service charge;[46] or

b) notify the tenant in writing that the cost had been incurred that the they will subsequently be required under the terms of his lease to contribute to them by the payment of a service charge.[47]

1.33   For these purposes, costs are incurred not when the service is provided to the landlord, but when the liability to pay has crystalised, either by presentation of an undisputed invoice or actual payment.[48]

What is a demand for these purposes?

1.34   Any demand must be contractually valid[49], so that a demand based on estimated costs when the lease required a demand to be based on an actual cost was insufficient for the purposes of LTA 1985 s20B(1). The demand need not, however, comply with the various statutory provisions on information to accompany demands, eg LTA 1987 ss47 and 48 (see chapter 4), as these requirements may be satisfied retrospectively.[50]

Notification

1.35   In order to be a valid notification under LTA 1985 s20B(2), the notice must be in writing and state the total costs which had been incurred by the landlord, together with a statement that the tenant will be required under the terms of the lease to contribute to those costs

---

44 *Management of privately owned blocks of flats*, 1985.

45 Interestingly, not in the way that the Nugee Report suggested; the report recommended that service charges be demanded within 12 months of the underlying cost falling due, failing which, recovery would be barred; to ameliorate any potential unfairness, the court should be given power to disapply the 12-month limit in any case.

46 LTA 1985 s20B(1).

47 LTA 1985 s20B(2).

48 *Burr v OM Property Management Ltd* [2013] EWCA Civ 479.

49 *Brent LBC v Shulem B Association* [2011] EWHC 1663 (Ch).

50 *Johnson v County Bideford* [2012] UKUT 457 (LC); *MacGregor v BM Samuels Finance Group plc* [2013] UKUT 471 (LC).

by payment of a service charge.[51] There is no requirement to detail the proportion of those costs that the tenant will subsequently be required to pay and/or inform the tenant what the resulting service charge demand will be.[52]

1.36 It has been suggested that, if the landlord is – within 18 months – unable to calculate their total costs accurately, it is acceptable to err on the side of caution and include a (reasonably) generous estimate in the notice.[53] This is now unlikely to arise in practice, since it has been established that costs are not 'incurred' until an invoice has been received (or possibly paid) by the landlord, such that it should always be clear what has been incurred at any given date.

On-account payments

1.37 These provisions have limited application where, as in most modern leases, service charges are paid in advance, as the 'on account' payments do not relate to any costs which have been incurred; rather, they relate to costs which *will be* incurred.

1.38 It follows that, if the on-account demands exceed the actual expenditure, then LTA 1985 s20B has no application.[54] It is only if the on-account demands are insufficient and a balancing payment is required that section 20B arises.[55] In such cases, the correct approach is to:

a) identify the date at which the on account payments were exhausted;

b) identify the date of the demand for the balancing payment; and

c) disallow only those charges that were both incurred after the date in a) and more than 18 months earlier than the date in b).[56]

Grant aided works

1.39 Where service charges have been incurred in respect of which a grant has been or is to be paid under Housing Act 1985 s523, Housing

---

51 *Brent LBC v Shulem B Association* [2011] EWHC 1663 (Ch); earlier cases discussed in the first and second editions of this work should no longer be followed.

52 *Brent LBC v Shulem B Association* [2011] EWHC 1663 (Ch).

53 *Brent LBC v Shulem B Association* [2011] EWHC 1663 (Ch).

54 *Gilje v Charlesgrove Securities Ltd* [2003] EWHC 1284 (Ch); [2004] HLR 1; [2004] 1 All ER 91.

55 *Holding and Management (Solitaire) Ltd v Sherwin* [2010] UKUT 412 (LC).

56 *Holding and Management (Solitaire) Ltd v Sherwin* [2010] UKUT 412 (LC).

Grants, Construction and Regeneration Act 1996 Part 1 or Regulatory Reform (Housing Assistance) (England and Wales) Order 2002 SI No 1860 art 3, the amount of the grant must be deducted from the costs and the amount of the service charge reduced accordingly.[57] The same applies in relation to external works under the Local Government and Housing Act 1989, where the landlord is an assisted participant in a group repair scheme.[58]

1.40   Even if another source of public funding is used, it appears that credit must be given by the landlord so as to ensure that there is not double recovery.[59]

Reasonableness

1.41   There is no general 'reasonableness' requirement for service charges. Rather, where service charges are payable for works which have been done or services which have been performed, then they are only payable to the extent that they are reasonably incurred[60] and to the extent that the services or works are of a reasonable standard.[61] Where service charges are payable before the costs are incurred, only a reasonable amount is payable, with any necessary adjustment (whether by repayment, reduction or subsequent charges or otherwise) afterwards.[62] There is no presumption either for or against reasonableness[63] but, on any appeal, it is for the party who is appealing to show that the first-instance decision on reasonableness was wrong.[64]

Reasonably incurred

1.42   Whether a cost is reasonably incurred involves consideration of two related questions. First, was the decision to incur the cost a reasonable one? Second, did the landlord take appropriate steps to

---

57 LTA 1985 s20A(1).

58 LTA 1985 s20A(2).

59 *Craighead v Islington LBC* [2010] UKUT 47 (LC), where the argument was accepted, but there was no double recovery on the facts.

60 LTA 1985 s19(1)(a).

61 LTA 1985 s19(1)(b).

62 LTA 1985 s19(2).

63 *Yorkbrook Investments v Batten* (1986) 18 HLR 25; [1985] 2 EGLR 100.

64 *Veena SA v Cheong* [2003] 1 EGLR 175; *Wellcome Trust v Romines* [1999] 3 EGLR 229.

test the market?[65] Whether and to what extent this was done in any case is a question of fact for each case, but there are certain general principles:

a) There is no requirement that the landlord obtain the lowest price in the market.[66]

b) There may be a range of reasonable decisions which could be reached as to whether or not a particular cost should be incurred; the decision is for the landlord rather than the tenants (or tribunal) and, so long as the decision falls within that reasonable range, the cost will be reasonable incurred.[67]

c) The fact that something is contemplated in the lease does not automatically make it reasonable to incur costs for that item.[68]

d) Costs incurred pursuant to professional advice are more likely to be reasonable; conversely, failing to take relevant advice is evidence of unreasonableness.[69]

e) When examining the method of repair (or provision of services) chosen by the landlord, the level to be reimbursed by the tenant will be assessed with reference to whether the landlord would have chosen this method of repair (or provision of services) if they were to bear the costs themselves.[70]

f) The nature and location of the property is a relevant consideration as to what level of services is reasonable, with, for example, a luxury block in Mayfair having different demands to a converted house on the Old Kent Road.[71]

g) Costs in respect of works carried out by or on behalf of public authorities after a public procurement exercise are likely to be reasonably incurred.[72]

h) The fact that tenants may suggest that they could, acting individually, provide services cheaper than those provided by the landlord, is irrelevant. Landlords are entitled to use qualified personnel

---

65 *Forcelux v Sweetman* [2001] 2 EGLR 173.

66 *Forcelux v Sweetman* [2001] 2 EGLR 173; *Havenridge Ltd v Boston Dyers Ltd* [1994] 2 EGLR 73.

67 *Regent Management Ltd v Jones* [2011] UKUT 369 (LC); *Southall Court (Residents) Ltd v Tiwari* [2011] UKUT 218 (LC).

68 *Veena SA v Cheong* [2003] 1 EGLR 175.

69 *Fernandez v Shanterton Second Management Company Ltd* LRX/153/2006.

70 *Hyde Housing v George Williams* LRX/53/1999.

71 *Veena v Cheong* [2003] 1 EGLR 175.

72 *Camden LBC v Auger* LRX/81/2007; *Lewisham LBC v Luis Rey-Ordieres and others* [2013] UKUT 014.

and any comparisons by the tenant must be on a 'like-for-like' basis.[73]

i) Where it is possible for works to be done at no charge to the tenant (eg under a guarantee), to carry out works at a cost to the tenant will render the whole of those costs unreasonable unless there is some good reason not to have invoked the guarantee.[74]

j) It is irrelevant whether or not the tenant will benefit from the works, so long as the tenant is obliged to pay for them under the lease.[75]

k) The fact that it is 'reasonable' to have a service provided does not automatically mean that the costs associated will be 'reasonably incurred'.[76]

l) The fact that tenants have a time-limited interest in the property may be a material factor when considering 'reasonableness'.[77]

m) The financial impact of major work on lessees, and whether the work should therefore be phased, is something which should be considered by the landlord.[78]

n) How the need for the work arose is not a relevant factor, even if the repair works are only required because of the landlord's breach of a repairing covenant.[79]

o) There is nothing objectionable to a landlord managing a property through a connected company (or providing other services through such a company) and recovering the costs as such, so long as the arrangement is not a sham.[80]

---

73 *A2 Airways Housing Group v Taylor and others* LRX/36/2006.

74 *Continental Property Ventures v White* [2007] L&TR 4.

75 *Broomleigh Housing Association v Hughes* (1999) EGCS 143; *Billson v Tristrem* [2000] L&TR 220.

76 *Veena SA v Cheong* [2003] 1 EGLR 175. While it may be reasonable to have a cleaner provided for a block of flats, that will not necessarily mean that the particular cleaner in question represents costs 'reasonably incurred'.

77 A tenant with a three-year lease could not be required to pay for roof replacement works which would fulfil the landlord's repairing obligations over 20 years or more when such works were not necessary to fulfil the obligations over the shorter period of the tenant's lease: *Scottish Mutual Assurance plc v Jardine Public Relations* [1999] EGCS 43.

78 *Garside v RFYC* [2011] UKUT 367 (LC).

79 *Continental Property Ventures v White* [2006] 1 EGLR 85, although there could be a set-off in such circumstances.

80 *Skilleter v Charles* (1991) 24 HLR 421; [1992] 1 EGLR 73; *MacGregor v BM Samuels Finance Group plc* [2013] UKUT 0471 (LC); *Phillips v Francis (No 2)* [2012] EWHC 3650 (Ch); *Country Trade Ltd v Hanton* [2012] UKUT 67 (LC).

1.43 Tenant advisers should also check that the service charge does not include any taxes or charges which are not properly recoverable from a tenant, eg VAT should be charged at five per cent on utilities and the Climate Change Levy is not payable.[81]

1.44 One argument which *cannot* succeed is that a fixed apportionment (fixed percentage; floor area; rateable value, etc) set down in the lease is 'unreasonable' for the purposes of LTA 1987 s19.[82] If a lease gives a landlord a discretion as to what proportion to charge (eg a 'fair' or 'reasonable' proportion), it can be argued that this has not been met in the given case, although there is considerable deference paid to the decision of the landlord.[83]

Reasonable standard

1.45 This is, in effect, a 'value for money' test. If the standard of works or services is too low when compared with the sums charged, the service charge should be reduced by an appropriate proportion.[84] It is unlikely that this could ever result in a reduction to 'zero' however.[85]

Reasonable amount in advance

1.46 Where service charges are payable before works are done or services are provided, only a reasonable amount may be charged. This might arise both with 'on account' payments and with contributions towards a reserve fund or sinking fund. What is a reasonable amount is clearly a question of fact in each case, but it should be noted that the landlord has a broad discretion.[86]

1.47 Interestingly, LTA 1987 s19(2) appears to provide for a statutory balancing mechanism, regardless of the lease terms. It expressly provides that where service charges are paid before costs are incurred, only a reasonable amount is payable *and* after the costs have been incurred, any necessary adjustment *shall be made*, whether by

---

81 *MacGregor v BM Samuels Finance Group Ltd* [2013] UKUT 471 (LC).
82 *Schilling v Canary Riverside Development Ptd Ltd* LRX/26/2005; *Re Rowner Estates Ltd* LRX/3/2006; *Warrior Quay Management Co Ltd v Joachim* LRX/42/2006.
83 *Shersby v Greenhurst Park Management Ltd* [2009] UKUT 241 (LC).
84 *Yorkbrook Investments Ltd v Batten* [1985] 1 EGLR 100; *Country Trade Limited v Noakes* [2011] UKUT 407 (LC).
85 *Yorkbrook Investments Ltd v Batten* [1985] 1 EGLR 100; *Country Trade Limited v Noakes* [2011] UKUT 407 (LC).
86 *Southall Court (Residents) Ltd v Tiwari* [2011] UKUT 218 (LC); *Hyde Housing Association v Lane* [2009] UKUT 180 (LC).

repayment, reduction or subsequent charges. This certainly appears to *require* parties to conduct a balancing exercise once costs have been finalised.

Role of the tribunal

1.48   Both a court and the tribunal have jurisdiction to deal with service charge disputes[87] but, in most cases, it will be preferable for the case to be dealt with in the tribunal, given its expert knowledge and common practice of conducting a site visit.[88] If the case raises complex issues of law, however, the matter may be best dealt with in the court.[89]

1.49   An application may be made to the tribunal to determine whether a service charge is payable.[90] Anyone may make the application, although most applications are made by a landlord or a tenant.[91] A managing agent that is not a party to the lease should not normally, however, be the respondent in a service charge case; rather it would normally be appropriate for the landlord (their client) to be named as respondent should be their client.[92]

1.50   Whether a service charge is payable involves consideration of the lease terms and compliance with the statutory pre-requisites, both of which the tribunal has jurisdiction to decide.[93] The tribunal can also consider whether the service charge is not payable for any other reason, eg a set-off,[94] an estoppel[95] or because the lease is void for mistake, forgery or misrepresentation.[96] The more complex the point

---

87   LTA 1985 s27A(7).

88   *Phillips v Francis (No 1)* [2010] L&TR 28.

89   *Phillips v Francis (No 1)* [2010] L&TR 28; *Continental Property Ventures Inc v White* [2007] L&TR 4.

90   LTA 1985 s27A(1).

91   *Oakfern Properties Ltd v Ruddy* [2006] EWCA Civ 1389; [2007] Ch 335. A person subject to a vexatious litigant order may, however, be prevented from issuing proceedings in the tribunal: *Attorney-General v Singer* [2012] EWHC 326 (Admin).

92   *Barton v Accent Properties Solutions Ltd* LRX/22/2008.

93   *Southend-on-Sea BC v Skiggs and others* LRX/110/2005; [2006] 2 EGLR 87.

94   *Continental Property Ventures v White and White* [2006] 1 EGLR 85; [2007] L&TR 4; LRX/60/2005.

95   *Havering LBC v Smith* [2012] UKUT 295 (LC).

96   *Canary Riverside Pte Ltd v Schilling and others* LRX/65/2005 (Lands Tribunal).

of law, however, the more likely is it is that the tribunal will decline jurisdiction and transfer the case to the court.[97]

1.51 The power to determine what is payable does not, however, allow the tribunal to re-write the terms of the lease by eg setting terms for payment which allow the tenant to pay over a longer period than the lease permits.[98] Nor does it allow the tribunal to consider allegations of breach of trust unless it is necessary to resolve that issue in order to determine an issue which is within the scope of the tribunal's jurisdiction.[99]

1.52 If any such application is made, the tribunal may also determine:[100]

a) the person by whom it is payable;
b) the person to whom it is payable;
c) the amount which is payable;
d) the date at or by which it is payable;
e) the manner in which it is payable.

1.53 An application may be made whether or not the service charge has been paid[101] unless the amount due has been admitted by the tenant, but the mere fact that a tenant has paid does not, without more, amount to an admission.[102]

1.54 In addition, an application may be made for a determination as to whether, if costs were incurred for services, repairs, maintenance, improvements, insurance or management of any specified description, a service charge would be payable in respect of those costs.[103] If any such application is made, the tribunal may also determine:[104]

a) the person by whom it would be payable;
b) the person to whom it would be payable;
c) the amount which would be payable;
d) the date at or by which it would be payable, and
e) the manner in which it would be payable.

---

97 *Canary Riverside Pte Ltd v Schilling and others* LRX/65/2005 (Lands Tribunal).
98 *Southend-on-Sea BC v Skiggs and others* LRX/110/2005; [2006] 2 EGLR 87.
99 *Solitaire Property Management Co Ltd v Holden* [2012] UKUT 86 (LC).
100 LTA 1985 ss27A(1)(a)–(e).
101 LTA 1985 s27A(2), overturning *R v London LVT ex p Daejan Properties Ltd* [2002] HLR 25; [2002] L&TR 5.
102 LTA 1985 s27A(5); *Shersby v Grenehurst Park Residents Co Ltd* [2009] UKUT 241 (LC).
103 LTA 1985 s27A(3).
104 LTA 1985 s27A(3)(a)–(e).

1.55   This jurisdiction clearly permits an application to be made in advance of costs being incurred. In practice, it is more likely to be useful where any dispute between the landlord and tenant can be resolved in its entirety before any work is done, for example where the dispute is one of construction of the lease.

1.56   While in principle it is possible to apply to an tribunal for a determination of the reasonable costs for carrying out building work in advance of the work being done if the costs subsequently prove to be considerably more (or less) than this figure, there is nothing to stop either party from applying back to the tribunal for a determination of the payability and reasonableness of the new sums.[105]

1.57   The tribunal may not hear any application concerning a service charge which:[106]

a) has been agreed or admitted by the tenant;
b) has been, or is to be, referred to arbitration pursuant to a post-dispute arbitration agreement to which the tenant is a party;
c) has been the subject of determination by a court; or
d) has been the subject of determination by an arbitral tribunal pursuant to a post-dispute arbitration agreement.

1.58   Any decision by the tribunal is only binding on the parties to that case.[107]

Burden of proof

1.59   A particular difficulty with service charge proceedings in the tribunal is the question of burden of proof.[108] It is unhelpful to approach the question by considering any burden of proof; the correct approach is to consider the matter in the round and only resort to any burden of proof in the event that there is not a clear answer.[109] In the event that it is necessary to resort to the burden of proof, the position appears to be that it is for the tenant to adduce some evidence to suggest that there might be a question mark over any service charges demanded. If this is done, then the landlord must provide sufficient evidence

---

105 *Compton Court, Victoria Crescent, London, SE19* LVTP/SC/008/091 and 092/01 (LVT).
106 LTA 1985 s27A(4).
107 *MacGregor v B M Samuels Finance Group Ltd* [2013] UKUT 471 (LC).
108 See, generally, Timothy Fancourt QC, 'Property law update', *New Law Journal*, 14 July 2006, p1132.
109 *Daejan Investments Ltd v Benson* [2011] EWCA Civ 38; [2011] 1 WLR 2330, at [86]; not affected by the appeal on this point.

to establish that the service charges are properly due. If the land-lord produces no evidence, then its case should fail.[110] The nature of the evidence will vary from case to case. In some circumstances, the quantum of the bills can be enough to suggest that something is amiss (eg leaking water pipe,[111] electricity being abstracted[112]). In others, like-for-like quotes will be needed.[113]

1.60   The situation may be different where one or more issues have been transferred to the tribunal by a court. There are strict rules on the burden of proof in court, and it is arguable that the party with the burden in court ought also to have the burden in the tribunal. For example, a landlord suing for payment of service charges would have to prove that the service charges were payable, and it would be strange if a transfer of that claim to the tribunal affected that burden.

Limitation periods and proceedings in the tribunal

1.61   There is nothing in the LTAs 1985 or 1987 or the CLRA 2002 which deals with the period of time which can be subject to challenge in the tribunal. Likewise, it is far from clear what (if any) provisions of the Limitation Act (LA) 1980 would apply to proceedings in the tribunal. This issue is exceptionally complex and is badly in need of resolution by the Upper Tribunal or a higher court.[114]

1.62   In principle, proceedings in the tribunal are an 'action' before a 'court of law' for the purposes of the LA 1980.[115] There are, there-fore, the following possibilities exist in respect of applications by tenants.[116]

---

110 *Yorkbrook Investments Ltd v Batten* [1985] 2 EGLR 100; (1986) 18 HLR 25; *Schilling v Canary Riverside Development Ltd* LRX/26/2005 & LRX/65/2005 (Lands Tribunal).

111 *Wallace-Jarvis v (1) Optima (Cambridge) Ltd (2) Khazai* [2013] UKUT 328 (LC).

112 *MacGregor v B M Samuels Finance Group Ltd* [2013] UKUT 471 (LC).

113 See para 1.45(h) above.

114 See the discussions in Roberts 'Service charges, *Daejan* and claims in restitution' Conv 2003, Sept/Oct 380–397 and Bates and Davey, 'Service charges and limitation periods – a timeless question' [2005] 8 JHL 3.

115 *Hillingdon LBC v ARC Ltd* [1999] Ch 139; *Warwickshire Hamlets Ltd and another v Gedden and others* [2010] UKUT 75 (LC).

116 As identified and discussed in *Re 3, 12, 23, and 29 St Andrew's Square etc* LON/00AW/LSL/2003/0027 (LVT).

a) The application is an application for recovery of a sum payable under an enactment and, hence, subject to a six-year limitation period.[117]

b) The application is a precursor to a claim for monies had and received and, as such, is treated as a quasi-contract with a six-year limitation period.[118]

c) The application is action on a specialty (ie a deed or statute) with a 12-year limitation period.[119]

d) The application is an action by a beneficiary under a trust such that no limitation period applies.[120]

1.63   Alternatively, no provision of the LA 1980 applies, such that the doctrine of laches will apply to limit the years in issue.[121]

1.64   If the claim is by the landlord and the service charges are reserved as rent, then there would be a six-year limitation period,[122] otherwise it would be 12 years.[123]

1.65   In practice, many tribunals avoid this difficult issue by using case-management powers to limit the years in dispute to those in respect of which there is likely to be any meaningful evidence within the control of the parties.

Effect of tribunal decisions

1.66   Closely linked to the limitation issue is the status and effect of a tribunal decision. The tribunal does not have power to order one party to pay money to another; it simply determines the rights and

---

117   LA 1980 s9, based on *Hillingdon LBC v ARC Ltd* in both the High Court ([1998] 1 WLR 174) and Court of Appeal ([1999] Ch 139; accepted by the LVT in *Paine v Wyndham HA* CAM/38UC/LSC/2011/0173).

118   LA 1980 s5, based on *R (Daejan Properties Ltd) v London LVT* [2000] 3 EGLR 44 (High Ct); [2001] EWCA Civ 1095; [2002] HLR 25 and accepted by the LVT in *Royal Borough of Kensington and Chelsea v Mezziani* LON/00AW/LSC/2009/0246.

119   LA 1980 s8, based on *Collin v Duke of Westminster* [1985] 1 QB 581; [1985] 1 All ER 463.

120   LA 1980 ss21(1), 42; LTA 1987. This was the case in *Warwickshire Hamlets Ltd and another v Gedden and others* [2010] UKUT 75 (LC).

121   See generally *Green v Gaul* [2006] EWCA 1124.

122   LA 1980 s19.

123   LA 1980 s8.

obligations of the parties.[124] If the tenant has not paid the money demanded, then no issue arises, as they need only pay what the tribunal has determined. If, however, the money has been paid, then it seems that there must be subsequent proceedings in the county court for a restitutionary remedy.[125] Such proceedings could be defended on any of the normal defences available for such a claim, including a good faith change of position (ie the landlord has spent the money as there was no reason to think it was not payable to the contractor). Such a defence would appear to present real difficulties for a tenant seeking to recover money.[126]

124 *Warrior Quay Management Co Ltd v Joachim* LRX/42/2006; *Holding & Management (Solitaire) Ltd v Dr Holden and others* [2012] UKUT 86 (LC); *R (Daejan) v LVT* [2001] L&TR 9 (HC). Indeed, there exists a statutory process for enforcement via the county court: see chapters 15 and 16.

125 *R (Daejan) v LVT* in both the High Court [2001] L&TR 9 and Court of Appeal [2001] EWCA Civ 1095; [2001] 3 EGLR 28.

126 See the discussion by Roberts in *The Conveyancer*, Sept/Oct 2003, 380 at 388. As to restitution defences generally, see *Lipkin Gorman v Karpnale Ltd*, [1991] 2 AC 548.

CHAPTER 2

Holding service charges

Key points

- Service charges are held on trust, which means that payments made by tenants should be protected against bankruptcy, insolvency or dishonest misuse.
- The trust arises automatically and without the need for any particular action by a landlord or tenant.
- Certain public sector landlords and buildings with resident landlords are, however, excluded.
- Disputes about whether a landlord is in breach of trust should be dealt with in the court, rather than the tribunal.
- There are, confusingly, two pending reforms to this area of law, but it does not appear likely that either will ever come into force.

Advice for tenants

- Service charges are held on a statutory trust. The purpose of this is to protect the money in the event that the landlord becomes insolvent or the bank holding the money collapses, or even if the money was stolen by a dishonest landlord or his or her employee. The statutory trust arises without the need for any action by a landlord or tenant.
- There is much scope for confusion in this area as there are two important reforming Acts, neither of which have been brought into force. Tenants and their advisers should take care to ensure that they are working from an accurate version of the statutory scheme.
- The tribunal has a limited role to play in disputes about the trust. If you believe that the landlord has wrongly applied trust monies, then your remedies are likely to be found in court by way of a civil claim for breach of trust or an action for an account.

Introduction

2.1   The Landlord and Tenant Act (LTA) 1987[1] imposes a statutory trust in respect of service charge payments made by most private sector tenants.[2] This has two significant benefits for those tenants. The first is to 'ring-fence' those funds and protect them against the insolvency[3] or bankruptcy[4] of the landlord or the collapse of the bank/building society holding the money.[5] The second is to impose all the general duties of trustee on the landlord, including as to investment of the money, remedies for misappropriation, etc.[6] The majority of the provisions apply to all leases, regardless of when granted,[7] and trump any other implied or express trust, insofar as the terms of the implied or express trust are inconsistent with the statutory trust.[8]

The trust

2.2   The trust arises in respect of any money actually paid[9] by a tenant as a service charge[10] where the tenant is required to do so under the terms of their lease[11] and two or more tenants are required to contribute to the same costs through the payment of service charges. Additionally, the trust arises if a tenant is required under the terms of the lease to contribute to costs which no other tenant is required to contribute to.[12]

1   Itself inspired by the work of the Nugee Committee (Committee on the Management of Blocks of Flats, 1984).

2   LTA 1987 s42.

3   In the case of individuals: Insolvency Act (IA) 1986 s283.

4   In the case of a corporate landlord: IA 1986 s145.

5   *Financial Services Compensation Scheme: Treatment of service charges for residential property*, Department for Communities and Local Government (DCLG), April 2009, explaining that the (then) £50,000 guarantee applied to each tenant, rather than to the fund as a whole.

6   See the discussion in *Warwickshire Hamlets Ltd v Gedden* [2010] UKUT 75 (LC). Permission to appeal was granted in that case but the appeal but not on an issue which cast doubt on the trustee aspect of the decision: [2010] EWCA Civ 1418. It does not appear that the appeal was pursued.

7   LTA 1987 s42(8).

8   LTA 1987 s42(9).

9   Thus, it does not apply to money demanded but not paid: *Maunder Taylor v Blaquiere* [2002] EWCA Civ 1633; [2003] 1 WLR 379.

10   As defined in LTA 1985 s18: LTA 1987 s42(1).

11   LTA 1987 s42(1).

12   LTA 1987 s42(1).

2.3   The person to whom the money must be paid, referred to in the LTA 1987 as 'the payee', must hold the money[13] in one or more funds. The money should be held in an authorised bank or building society account.[14] Unless the lease provides to the contrary,[15] tenants are deemed to be entitled to a share of the service charge fund which is proportionate to their liabilities to pay service charges.[16]

2.4   That does not mean that tenants can demand a specific sum of money be paid to them. Rather, the money is held:[17]

a) to defray costs incurred in connection with matters for which the service charges were payable; and

b) subject to that, on trust for the tenant or tenants for the time being.

2.5   Money received for a specific service charge item must be used to meet the costs of that service charge; an overpayment in respect of expenses actually incurred cannot (without a specific proviso in the lease to this effect) simply be applied for some other purpose or retained to off-set future expenditure.[18]

Exceptions

2.6   The statutory trust does not apply to 'exempt landlords' as defined in LTA 1987 s58. In substance, this excludes most tenants of public sector landlords (not just social landlords), fully mutual housing associations and resident landlords.

2.7   A landlord is a 'resident landlord' if:

a) the building was not a purpose-built block of flats, that is a building which contained when constructed and now contains two or more flats;

b) the landlord occupies a flat in the building as his or her own or principal resident; and

c) the landlord has done so for at least 12 months.[19]

---

13 Which includes any investments representing the money and any interest: LTA 1987 s42(2).

14 LTA 1987 s42(5); Service Charge Contributions (Authorised Investments) Order 1988 SI No 1284.

15 LTA 1987 s42(8).

16 LTA 1987 s42(4).

17 LTA 1987 s42(3).

18 *St Mary's Mansions Ltd v Limegate Investment Co Ltd and others* [2002] EWCA Civ 1491; [2003] HLR 24; see also *Redendale Limited v Modi* [2010] UKUT 346 (LC).

19 LTA 1987 s58.

2.8   In addition, the trust does not arise in respect of service charges payable by a tenant whose rent is registered under Rent Act (RA) 1977 Part 4, unless the amount is registered as a variable amount under RA 1977 s71(4).[20]

2.9   Given the wording of LTA 1987 s42, the trust will also not arise in the situation where there is a building comprising two flats, one of which is owned (even if not occupied) by the landlord who has merged the leasehold with the freehold.

Termination of the trust

2.10   If the lease of any tenant is terminated (eg by forfeiture), the tenant is not entitled to any part of the trust fund and the money continues to be held for the remaining tenants.[21] If all the leases are terminated, then the trust is dissolved as at the date of termination of the last lease and any monies are paid to, or retained by, the landlord, unless the lease provides for an alternative form of distribution[22] A tenant who sells his or her lease is not entitled to the return of any service charge monies paid but not yet expended, rather, the incoming tenant will have the benefit of the trust fund.[23]

2.11   While LTA 1987 s42 makes detailed provision on the distribution of the funds in the event that the leasehold interests all come to an end, there is no provision made at all in respect of what should happen if the freehold is transferred. In particular, there is no obligation on a landlord to transfer the trust fund to the purchaser upon a sale of the reversion.[24]

Disputes

2.12   Disputes in relation to these provisions are dealt with by the court, rather than the tribunal.[25] In particular, the tribunal has no jurisdiction to deal with breach of trust claims.[26]

20 LTA 1987 s42(1).
21 LTA 1987 s42(6).
22 LTA 1987 s42(7).
23 LTA 1987 s42(3).
24 Presumably the tenants could apply under the rule in *Saunders v Vantier* (1841) 1 Beav 115, put an end to the trust and distribute the assets between them.
25 LTA 1987 s52(2).
26 *Solitaire Property Management Co Ltd v Holden* [2012] UKUT 86 (LC).

Pending reforms

2.13   There are two pending reforms, neither of which is now likely to come into force, which have created considerable confusion as regards the statutory trust.

Commonhold and Leasehold Reform Act 2002 reforms

2.14   The Commonhold and Leasehold Reform Act (CLRA) 2002[27] introduced a new section 42A into the LTA 1987, under which service charges would continue to be held on trust, but would now be held in an 'authorised account', ie an account held with a specific financial services provider. A duty was to be imposed on the landlord to inform the financial service provider that the payments were being held on trust for the purposes of paying service charges and no other monies were to be held in the account. Tenants were to have the right to withhold payment where they had reasonable grounds for believing that the landlord was not holding the monies in an authorised account. A new power to inspect relevant documents related to the trust account was also introduced.

2.15   These provisions were not brought into force and, in 2007, the government announced that they would never come into force in their original form.[28]

Housing and Regeneration Act 2008 amendments

2.16   The Housing and Regeneration Act 2008[29] amended LTA 1987 s42A so as to give the appropriate national authority power to make regulations as to how service charge contributions are to be held and whether monies can be moved between one or more accounts. The automatic right to withhold service charges has been removed and replaced with a power for the appropriate national authority to specify the conditions under which service charges may be withheld. Again, regulations may make different provision for different cases, presumably so as to allow local authorities and registered social landlords to be excluded from the provisions.

---

27 CLRA 2002 s156.
28 *Commonhold and Leasehold Reform Act 2002 – a consultation paper on regular statements of account and designated client accounts*, DCLG, June 2007.
29 Housing and Regeneration Act 2008 Sch 12.

2.17   These provisions have not been brought into force and, as at November 2012, the government had no plans to do so.[30]

---

30 See Baroness Hanham, *Hansard*, HL Deb, 19 November 2012, col 307.

CHAPTER 3

Consultation

Key points

- There is a statutory consultation process which applies to 'qualifying work and 'qualifying long-term agreements'. Qualifying works arise where a landlord intends to carry out work which would require a tenant to contribute more than £250. A qualifying long term agreement is an agreement made on behalf of the landlord for a period of over 12 months.
- If the landlord does not follow the consultation requirements then the recoverable service charges are capped unless the tribunal grants dispensation.
- The nature of the consultation process varies depending on whether it is works or agreements and whether or not a public sector landlord is involved.
- In general terms, tenants should be consulted on the general idea of the works/agreement and given an opportunity to nominate contractors. Landlords must get at least two quotes, one of which must be from a company which is wholly unrelated to the landlord.
- Dispensation is likely in most cases; tenants should focus on why the works are either more extensive or more expensive as a result of the failure to consult.
- Dispensation can be granted on terms, eg as to payment of the tenants legal costs.

Advice for tenants

- It may be that the terms of the lease oblige the landlord to consult the tenants before incurring certain costs, and it is always worth checking for this. In most cases, however, it is the Landlord and Tenant Act (LTA) 1985 which provides the statutory basis for consultation.
- Tenants should play a full and active role in any consultation process, as failure to do so may subsequently be held against them on any dispute about the works or services.

- If the landlord does not consult in the statutorily prescribed manner, then, unless the landlord obtains dispensation, the recoverable service charges will be capped. While it is likely that dispensation will be granted in most cases, it will usually be granted on terms, including as to payment of legal costs incurred by the tenant in responding to the application. It may be that tenants can find solicitors or surveyors prepared to act on a contingency fee basis, whereby their fees are capped at those recovered from the landlord.
- If possible, tenants should try to establish a recognised tenants' association (RTA), as specific benefits accrue to such associations, including a right to be consulted on the choice of managing agent.

Introduction

3.1   While it is possible for the lease to prescribe a consultation procedure in respect of service charge expenditure,[1] in most modern leases only the statutory scheme will apply.

3.2   Landlord and Tenant Act (LTA) 1985 ss20 and 20ZA (and the regulations made thereunder) make provision for a landlord to consult leaseholders in respect of certain items of service charge expenditure, and impose a cap on recoverable service charges if the landlord has failed to consult and dispensation is not granted by the tribunal. Although lawyers commonly speak of 'the consultation requirements', LTA 1985 s20 does not prohibit a landlord from entering into whatever contract he or she pleases, whether for the carrying out of works or the supply of services. It merely prevents the landlord from passing on the costs of the works or services to the lessee unless the landlord has satisfied the statutory requirements.[2]

3.3   These provisions must be seen as part of a wider scheme in the LTA 1985 and are designed to ensure that leaseholders do not pay more than is reasonable.[3] There is no wider purpose to the consultation provisions, ie they are not designed to promote openness or

---

1 See, eg *CIN Properties Ltd v Barclays Bank plc* [1986] 1 EGLR 59; *Northway Flats Management Co (Camden) Ltd v Wimpey Pension Trustees Ltd* [1992] 2 EGLR 42.

2 *Paddington Basin Developments v West End Quay* [2010] EWHC 833 (Ch); [2010] 1 WLR 2735, at [26]–[27].

3 *Daejan Investments Ltd v Benson* [2013] UKSC 14; [2013] 1 WLR 854 at [41]–[43].

transparency, nor to give tenants a veto.[4] Leaseholders should, however, engage with any consultation process, as a failure to do so may be held against them when considering issues of the reasonableness of the costs,[5] and leaseholders may be able to force landlords to obtain at least one quotation from a provider of the leaseholders' choice, which may provide useful evidence if a service charge dispute arises.

'Old' consultation requirements

3.4   Statutory consultation in respect of service charges stems from the Housing Act 1974[6] and was amended, replaced and consolidated over the years, culminating in section 20 of the LTA 1985.

3.5   The old provisions were replaced by section 151 of the Commonhold and Leasehold Reform Act (CLRA) 2002 (repealing and replacing LTA 1985 s20), with effect from 31 October 2003 (England) or 31 March 2004 (Wales).[7]

3.6   The 'old' provisions are unlikely to be relevant to many, if any, cases and so are not discussed further. For commentary on the 'old' provisions and transitional provisions, readers are referred to the previous two editions of this work.

New requirements

3.7   The 'new' consultation provisions apply to two discrete types of service charge expenditure: qualifying works and qualifying long-term agreements. The details of the procedure to be followed for each type are different.

Qualifying works

3.8   Qualifying works arise where a landlord intends to carry out works to a building or any other premises and any tenant is required to

---

4 *Daejan Investments Ltd v Benson* [2013] UKSC 14; [2013] 1 WLR 854 at [46], [52].
5 *Southall Court (Residents) Ltd v Tiwari* [2011] UKUT 218 (LC).
6 Section 124, inserting section 91A into the Housing Finance Act 1972.
7 Commonhold and Leasehold Reform Act 2002 (Commencement No 2 and Savings) (England) Order 2003 SI No 1986; Commonhold and Leasehold Reform Act 2002 (Commencement No 2 and Savings) (Wales) Order 2004 SI No 669.

contribute more than £250 towards the costs of those works.[8] If the landlord fails to consult in the prescribed manner or fails to obtain dispensation from the tribunal, the recoverable costs are capped at £250.

3.9   'Qualifying works' are defined as 'works to a building or any other premises'.[9] In the county court, it has been held that this comprises 'matters that one would naturally regard as being "building works"', such that window cleaning was excluded.[10] Under the 'old' consultation regulations, it was held that qualifying works were restricted to 'physical works involved in repair or maintenance' and could not include professional services provided by an independent person as part of a scheme of works.[11] If, however, the professional services were provided by the same person or company which carried out the works, then the total cost of that work, including the professional costs, fell to be considered.[12]

3.10   It had previously been assumed that the £250 'threshold' applied on a 'project' or 'set of works' basis, with a 'common sense' test to avoid artificial 'splitting' of works so as to avoid the £250 threshold.[13] In *Phillips v Francis*[14] the High Court disagreed: the £250 is a cumulative figure to be applied to the total of all costs of qualifying works in each service charge year, such that every item of expenditure must be taken into account.

3.11   The decision in *Phillips v Francis* has proved controversial[15] and, at the time of writing, an appeal is listed for May 2014. Many landlords and managing agents appear to be ignoring the decision, regarding the consequences as unworkable; while a few have been seeking advance approval/dispensation for every item of low-value work. While it might be argued that the decision of the High Court is not

---

8   LTA 1985 ss20, 20ZA; Service Charges (Consultation Requirements) (England) Regulations ('SC Consultation (England) Regs') 2003 SI No 1987; Service Charges (Consultation Requirements) (Wales) Regulations ('SC Consultation (Wales) Regs') 2004 SI No 684 – reg 6 in each case.

9   LTA 1985 s20ZA(2).

10 *Paddington Walk Management Ltd v Peabody Trust* [2010] L&TR 6.

11 *Marionette Ltd v Visible Information Packaged Systems Ltd* [2002] EWHC 2546 (Ch); although such costs might now be subject to consultation as a qualifying long-term agreement.

12 *Marionette Ltd v Visible Information Packaged Systems Ltd* [2002] EWHC 2546 (Ch).

13 As was the position under the 'old' consultation requirements – see *Martin v Maryland Estates Ltd* (2000) 32 HLR 116, CA.

14 [2012] EWHC 3650 (Ch); [2013] 1 WLR 2343.

15 See, eg 'The meaning of qualifying works' [2013] L&TR 60.

– strictly speaking – binding on the tribunal,[16] the risks involved in departing from the decision of the High Court are obvious.

Qualifying long-term agreements

3.12   A qualifying long-term agreement (QLTA) is an agreement entered into, by or on behalf of the landlord or a superior landlord, for a term of more than 12 months.[17] If the landlord seeks to recover more than £100 from any tenant in any 'accounting period', then the consultation provisions are engaged.[18]

3.13   In identifying whether an agreement is a QLTA, the correct approach is to ask: (i) whether it is an agreement; (ii) made by or on behalf of the landlord; (iii) which is for a term of more than 12 months.[19]

3.14   If an agreement fails to specify its duration, it is a question of fact for the tribunal whether it is an agreement for a term of more than 12 months.[20] Provision for termination, even within the 12-month period, does not assist in determining the duration of the contract these circumstances.[21]

3.15   By contrast, an agreement for a fixed term of 12 months or less is not a qualifying long-term agreement, notwithstanding the possibility that it could continue for more than 12 months.[22]

3.16   The definition of 'accounting period'[23] is unnecessarily complex. All accounting periods are 12 months long, but if the service charge accounts are not produced on an annual basis, the regulations impose a fictitious 12-month accounting period which may create an

---

16 See *Secretary of State v RB* [2010] UKUT 454 (AAC); *Holding & Management (Solitaire) Ltd v Sherwin* [2010] UKUT 412 (LC).

17 LTA 1985 s20ZA(2).

18 SC Consultation (England) Regs; SC Consultation (Wales) Regs – reg 4 in each case.

19 *Paddington Basin Developments Ltd v West End Quay Estate Management Ltd* [2010] EWHC 833 (Ch); [2010] 1 WLR 2735. Note the extended definition of 'landlord' to include eg tripartite leases with management companies.

20 *Poynders Court Ltd v GLS Property Management Ltd* [2012] UKUT 339 (LC).

21 *Poynders Court Ltd v GLS Property Management Ltd* [2012] UKUT 339 (LC).

22 *Paddington Walk Management Ltd v Peabody Trust* [2010] L&TR 6.

23 SC Consultation (England) Regs; SC Consultation (Wales) Regs –reg 4 in each case.

awkward fit between the system of accounts described in the lease and the 'accounting period' required under the regulations.[24]

3.17　The regulations exclude certain kinds of agreement from being QLTAs.[25] Excluded agreements include contracts of employment and contracts between a parent company and its subsidiaries (or between those subsidiaries).

3.18　In addition to those excluded by the regulations, agreements entered into before any agreements for leases were concluded are not QLTAs.[26]

Which consultation procedure applies?

3.19　There are five different procedures which might apply, depending on the nature of the landlord and the proposed contract:

1) QLTA where public notice is required;
2) QLTA where public notice is *not* required;
3) work under an existing QLTA;
4) work (not under a QLTA) where public notice is required;
5) work (not under a QLTA) where public notice is *not* required.

3.20　Whether or not public notice is required depends on whether the contract is governed by the Public Contracts Regulations 2006.[27] In general terms, contracts (whether for services or works) made by public authorities are (subject to costs thresholds), within the scope of the Public Contracts Regulations 2006. A full analysis of these matters is beyond the scope of this work.

3.21　Outlines of each of the five forms of consultation are provided at the end of this chapter. There are certain common features which are discussed below.

24　See the first and second editions of this work, in which we discussed various oddities in the drafting. Given the passage of time and the absence of any reported cases on the point, it seems unlikely that these oddities have caused any significant difficulties.

25　SC Consultation (England) Regs; SC Consultation (Wales) Regs – reg 3 in each case.

26　*BDW Trading Ltd v South Anglia Housing Ltd* [2013] EWHC B10 (Ch); it must be that an agreement for a lease which is sufficient, given the definition in LTA 1985 s36.

27　SI No 5, in effect, public sector contracts over prescribed values.

Common features

'Describe in general terms'

3.22   Whether a notice sufficiently describes in general terms the works to be carried out or contract to be entered into is a question of fact and degree.[28]

Relevant period

3.23   The relevant period is defined as 30 days from the date of the notice; this means 30 days from the date on which the notice is served on the recipients (whether actual service or deemed service).[29] Although the regulations prescribe a 'relevant period' of 30 days, there does not appear to be any objection to giving a longer period.[30] Given that most notices are sent by post[31] (and, hence, will take some time to arrive), it might be thought wise to give a longer period of, say, 40 days.[32] There is no need to specify a calendar date as the end of the consultation period, so long as that date is clear from the notice.[33]

Observations

3.24   In all five possible consultation procedures, leaseholders are invited to make observations to which the landlord must have regard and must summarise and provide answers for other leaseholders to see. To qualify as an 'observation', it must relate to the works or contract itself and not, for example, simply raise questions as to how lease-holders will be expected to make payment.[34]

Connection to the landlord

3.25   In some cases a landlord will need to obtain at least one estimate from a person wholly unconnected with them, and in other cases the

---

28 *Southern Land Securities Ltd v Hodge* [2013] UKUT 480 (LC).

29 *Trafford Housing Trust Ltd v Rubinstein and others* [2013] UKUT 581 (LC).

30 *Peverel Properties Ltd v Hughes* [2013] L&TR 6.

31 Although note that the Upper Tribunal indicated that registered or recorded delivery would be preferable: *Trafford Housing Trust Ltd v Rubinstein and others* [2013] UKUT 581 (LC).

32 Note that the RICS Service Charge Residential Management Code (2nd edn) appears to support this proposition, as it reminds readers that the statutory consultation provisions should be seen as the minimum standard required, not the optimum: para 18.1.

33 *Peverel Properties Ltd v Hughes* [2013] L&TR 6.

34 *Re OM Property Management* [2014] UKUT 9 (LC).

landlord will have to indicate if there is a connection (and what that connection is) between them and a party to an agreement. There is no exhaustive definition of what 'connection' means and a common-sense approach is likely to be taken by the tribunal.

3.26   Some relationships are deemed to be a connection:[35]

- a company is connected to its present or prospective directors and managers and their close relatives;
- a company is connected to any other company if any of its directors or managers is, or is to be, a director or manager of the other company;
- a company is connected to a partner in a partnership if any partner in the partnership is a director or manager of the company or is a close relative of such a director or manager.

3.27   For the purposes of the regulations, a person's 'close relative' is a person's spouse, cohabitee, parent, parent-in-law, son, son-in-law, daughter, daughter-in-law, brother, brother-in-law, sister, sister-in-law, step-parent, step-son or step-daughter. A person's 'cohabitee' is either a person of the opposite sex who is living with that person as a husband or wife or a person of the same sex living with that person in a relationship which has the characteristics of the relationship between husband and wife.[36]

Inspection of information

3.28   Many of the notices required as part of the consultation process require the landlord to supply detailed information, for example concerning estimates and details of work that needs to be done. The landlord has the option, rather than sending the information with the notice, to indicate a place where the information can be inspected and hours when inspection may take place.[37]

3.29   Both the place and the hours for inspection must be reasonable.[38] No charge may be made for the inspection.[39] The landlord must

---

35 SC Consultation (England) Regs; SC Consultation (Wales) Regs – Sch 1 para 5(6), Sch 2 para 4(3), Sch 4 Part 1 para 4(3), Sch 4 Part 2 para 4(7) in each case.

36 SC Consultation (England) Regs; SC Consultation (Wales) Regs – reg 2(1) in each case.

37 SC Consultation (England) Regs; SC Consultation (Wales) Regs – Schs 1–4 para 2(1) in each case.

38 SC Consultation (England) Regs; SC Consultation (Wales) Regs – Schs 1–4 para 2(1) in each case.

39 SC Consultation (England) Regs; SC Consultation (Wales) Regs – Schs 1–4 para 2(1) in each case.

enable copies to be taken or supply to the tenant on request, and for no charge, a copy.[40]

Service of the consultation notices

3.30   Care must be taken to ensure that the notices have been properly served on the tenant. Neither LTA 1985 s20 itself nor the regulations made thereunder make any provision for how or where to serve the notices, simply providing that they must be 'given' to the tenant. On the face of it, that might suggest personal service. However, there are two important qualifiers. The first is Interpretation Act 1978 s7, which provides for a rebuttable presumption that a properly addressed, stamped and posted envelope will reach the address it was sent to in the normal way (ie two clear days later for first class post).[41] Second, many leases contain contractual provisions allowing for service in a specified manner at a particular address (usually the flat in question).[42] Compliance with these contractual provisions will also amount to good service.

3.31   In addition, it is commonly the case that the tenant has given an alternative address for service. In those circumstances, the alternative address must be used.[43]

Estimation of costs

3.32   In order for the consultation process to be realistic, the landlord will have to give an estimate of the cost of the work. Where it is practical for the landlord to estimate the relevant contribution of each tenant's unit of occupation, then that estimate should be given. Where it is not practical to do that but it is practical to estimate the total amount of expenditure on the building or other premises to which either the agreement relates, or on which the work is being done, then that estimate should be given. Failing that, if it is practical to give the current unit cost or hourly or daily rate that would apply to any works to be done, then that rate should be given.[44]

40 SC Consultation (England) Regs; SC Consultation (Wales) Regs – Schs 1–4 para 2(2) in each case.
41 *Calladine-Smith v Saveorder Ltd* [2011] EWHC 2501 (Ch); [2012] L&TR 3, explaining how section 7 works and how to rebut the presumption.
42 In practice, the lease often attempts to incorporate Law of Property Act 1925 s196.
43 See *Akorita v 36 Gensing Road Ltd* LRX/16/2008.
44 SC Consultation (England) Regs; SC Consultation (Wales) Regs – Sch 1 para 5, Sch 2 para 4, Sch 4 Part 1 para 4 SC Consultation (England) Regs; SC

3.33   Where it is not practical for the landlord to give any of this information, they must explain why they are unable to comply and give a date by when they expect to be able to supply the estimated amount, cost, or rate as the case may be.[45]

3.34   All estimates must include VAT where applicable.[46]

Delays in the consultation process

3.35   There is commonly a delay in the consultation process, eg between the two notices owing to difficulties in obtaining quotes, etc. There is no 'expiry' date on an LTA 1985 s20 notice, but each stage should normally follow the other in a matter of 'months rather than years'.[47] If there has been a change in the scope of the works or the process, then this would also indicate that a new consultation process must be started.[48]

Prior certification of compliance

3.36   There is no explicit procedure which would enable a landlord to apply for a declaration that he or she has complied with the consultation requirements; in such circumstances, the landlord must apply for dispensation (see below) and ask the tribunal to dismiss the application for lack of jurisdiction (ie there is no need for dispensation as there has been compliance).[49] It may also be possible to make an application under LTA 1985 s27A(3) to have the tribunal determine that a service charge will be payable, although this was doubted by the Upper Tribunal in *Southwark LBC v Various Leaseholders*.[50]

Consultation (Wales) Regs – Schs 1–4 para 2(1) in each case. See *Southwark LBC v Various Leaseholders* [2011] UKUT 438 (LC) for a discussion of what is 'practical'.

45 This saving provision is only available in Schs 2 and 4 Part 1, SC Consultation (England) Regs; SC Consultation (Wales) Regs – Sch 2 para 4(7) and Sch 4 Part 1 para 4(7) in each case.

46 SC Consultation (England) Regs; SC Consultation (Wales) Regs – reg 2(2) in each case.

47 *Jastrzembski v Westminster City Council* [2013] UKUT 284 (LC).

48 *Jastrzembski v Westminster City Council* [2013] UKUT 284 (LC).

49 *Southwark LBC v Various Leaseholders* [2011] UKUT 438 (LC).

50 [2011] UKUT 438 (LC).

Dispensation

3.37   The tribunal has power to dispense with any or all of the statutory consultation requirements if it is reasonable to do so.[51] The tribunal has no power to dispense with any contractual consultation requirements.[52] An application for dispensation may be made before or after any works are carried out or any contract signed.[53] It appears that an application may also be made on the grounds that it would be difficult, if not unworkable, to apply the consultation regulations.[54] If there is an issue as to compliance with the consultation regulations and there is no formal application for dispensation, the tribunal should (at least if the landlord is unrepresented) ask the landlord whether he or she wishes to apply for dispensation.[55]

3.38   When considering whether to grant dispensation, the primary focus of the tribunal is to ensure that tenants are protected from paying for inappropriate works or paying more than is appropriate.[56] In particular, the tribunal should not ask itself whether the failure to consult was 'technical' or 'minor'.[57] It is for the tenants to establish that they have been prejudiced by the failure to consult,[58] but this is not a high threshold and the tribunal should be 'sympathetic' to the leaseholders on this point.[59]

3.39   If the extent, quality and cost of the works are not affected by any failure to consult, then dispensation should normally be granted.[60]

---

51   LTA 1985 s20ZA(1).

52   *Northways Flats Management Co (Camden) Ltd v Wimpey Pensions Trustees Ltd* [1992] 2 EGLR 42.

53   *Daejan Investments Ltd v Benson* [2013] UKSC 14; [2013] 1 WLR 854 at [41], [56]; *Auger v Camden LBC* LRX/81/2007.

54   *Paddington Basin Developments Ltd v West End Quay Estate Management Ltd* [2010] EWHC 833 (Ch); [2010] 1 WLR 2735l but compare *Southwark LBC v Various Leaseholders* [2011] UKUT 438 (LC).

55   *Warrior Quay v Joaquim* LRX/42/2006.

56   *Daejan* at [44]. See also the re-statement at [51] of *Jastrzembski v Westminster City Council* [2013] UKUT 284 (LC). But in *Re OM Property Management Ltd* [2014] UKUT 9 (LC), the Upper Tribunal cautioned against applying a gloss to the statutory text.

57   *Daejan* at [47]. It follows that the earlier cases of *Stenau Properties Ltd v Leek* [2011] UKUT 478 (LC); *Newham LBC v Hannan* [2011] UKUT 406 (LC); *Auger v Camden LBC* LRX/81/2007; *Re: 30–40 Grafton Way, London, WC1E 6DX* LRX/185/2006; *Eltham Properties Ltd v Kenny* [2008] L&TR 14 should be treated with some caution.

58   *Daejan* at [67].

59   *Daejan* at [68].

60   *Daejan* at [45].

3.40 Dispensation may be granted on such terms or conditions as the tribunal thinks appropriate.[61] If, for example, a landlord sought dispensation to enable works to be carried out urgently, the tribunal could require the landlord to arrange a meeting with the leaseholders to discuss the works and could shorten the 30-day consultation periods.[62]

3.41 If dispensation is sought retrospectively, the terms may include a reduction in the recoverable service charge to reflect any additional and unreasonable costs incurred as a result of the failure to consult.[63]

3.42 Regardless of whether dispensation is sought in advance or retrospectively, the tribunal may also order the landlord to pay the tenants' reasonable costs incurred in connection with the application for dispensation.[64]

3.43 The authors consider that the effect of the *Daejan* decision is to make dispensation (albeit on terms) likely in the vast majority of cases.[65]

Consultation about managing agents

3.44 Additionally, recognised tenants' associations (RTAs) have the right to be consulted about managing agents.[66]

3.45 The RTA may, at any time, serve a notice on the landlord requesting the landlord to consult the association in relation to the appointment or employment of a managing agent.[67]

3.46 If such an agent is employed, the landlord must, within a month of service of the notice, reply by service of a further notice on the RTA specifying the obligations which the manager discharges on the

---

61 *Daejan* at [54]–[55].
62 *Daejan* at [56].
63 *Daejan* at [57].
64 *Daejan* at [59]. This was subsequently said to include the costs incurred 'in reasonably investigating and establishing non-compliance with the Regulations, investigating or seeking to establish prejudice, and investigating and challenging [the] application for dispensation': [2013] UKSC 54 at [7]–[8].
65 See *Voyvoda v (1) West End Properties (2) 32 Grosvenor Square Ltd* [2013] UKUT 334 (LC), where *Daejan* was considered to have removed a significant risk in leasehold management. See also *R (Spaul) v Upper Tribunal* (Lands Chamber) [2013] EWHC 2016 (Admin), where it was suggested that dispensation might be refused if the financial prejudice outweighed the recoverable service charge.
66 LTA 1985 s30B.
67 LTA 1985 s30B(1).

landlord's behalf and allowing a reasonable period for the association to comment on the manner in which the managing agent has been discharging the obligations and the desirability of this continuing.[68]

3.47   If no such agent is employed when the notice is served, the landlord must – before employing any managing agent at any future stage – serve a notice setting out the name of the proposed managing agent, the obligations the landlord proposes to have the agent discharge, and allowing a period of at least one month for the RTA to make observations on the appointment.[69]

3.48   In either case, once the initial notice has been served, the landlord must – at least once every five years – serve on the RTA a notice specifying any changes which have occurred since the date of the last notice served on the landlord by the RTA and allow the association a reasonable period to comment on the manner in which the managing agent has discharged his or her obligations and the desirability of the landlord continuing to do so.[70]

3.49   The landlord must also serve on the RTA the name and proposed duties of any new managing agent, and allow a period of not less than one month for comments.[71]

3.50   The RTA may release the landlord from these obligations at any stage by serving a notice on the landlord to this effect.[72]

3.51   Any consultation obligations cease if the property becomes vested in a new landlord, although they may be reasserted in the manner set out above.[73]

3.52   There is no penalty (criminal or civil) for a landlord who fails to consult under LTA 1985 s30B, but a court could perhaps enforce the obligations with an injunction.[74]

68   LTA 1985 s30B(3).
69   LTA 1985 s30B(2).
70   LTA 1985 s30B(4)(a).
71   LTA 1985 s30B(4)(b).
72   LTA 1985 s30B(5).
73   LTA 1985 s30B(6).
74   Although for a contrary view, see by analogy *Di Marco v Morshead Mansions Ltd* [2014] EWCA Civ 96; [2013] L&TR 27.

3.53 **Flow charts**

Qualifying works: public notice required

STAGE 1 – Notice of intention	
The landlord must give notice in writing of their intention to carry out qualifying works to:[1] a) each tenant;[2] and b) where a RTA represents some or all of the tenants, to the RTA.[3]	The notice must: a) describe, in general terms, the works proposed to be carried out or specify the place and hours at which a description of the proposed works may be inspected;[4] b) state the landlord's reasons for considering it necessary to carry out the proposed works;[5] c) state that the reason why the landlord is not inviting recipients of the notice to nominate persons from whom the landlord should try to obtain an estimate for carrying out the works is that public notice of the works it to be given;[6] d) invite the making, in writing, of observations in relation to the proposed works and specify:[7] i) the address to which such observations may be sent;[8] ii) that they must be within the 'relevant period' (meaning a period of 30 days beginning with the date of the notice);[9] and iii) the date on which the relevant period ends.[10]

1 SC Consultation (England) Regs; SC Consultation (Wales) Regs – Sch 4 Part 1 para 1.
2 SC Consultation (England) Regs; SC Consultation (Wales) Regs – Sch 4 Part 1 para 1(1)(a).
3 SC Consultation (England) Regs; SC Consultation (Wales) Regs – Sch 4 Part 1 para 1(1)(b).
4 SC Consultation (England) Regs; SC Consultation (Wales) Regs – Sch 4 Part 1 para 1(2)(a). If the notice specifies a place and hours for inspection, the place and hours so specified must be reasonable and a description of the relevant matters must be available for inspection, free of charge, at that place and during those hours. If facilities to enable copies to be taken are not made available at the times at which the description may be inspected, the landlord shall provide to a tenant, on request and free of charge, a copy of the description: SC Consultation (England) Regs; SC Consultation (Wales) Regs – Sch 4 Part 1 para 2.
5 SC Consultation (England) Regs; SC Consultation (Wales) Regs – Sch 4 Part 1 para 1(2)(b).
6 SC Consultation (England) Regs; SC Consultation (Wales) Regs – Sch 4 Part 1 para 1(2)(c).
7 SC Consultation (England) Regs; SC Consultation (Wales) Regs – Sch 4 Part 1 para 1(2)(d).
8 SC Consultation (England) Regs; SC Consultation (Wales) Regs – Sch 4 Part 1 para 1(2)(e)(i).
9 SC Consultation (England) Regs; SC Consultation (Wales) Regs – reg 2(1); Sch 4 Part 1 para 1(2)(e)(ii).
10 SC Consultation (England) Regs; SC Consultation (Wales) Regs – Sch 4 Part 2 para 1(2)(e)(iii).

STAGE 2 – The 'relevant period'
A period of 30 days beginning with the date of the notice must be allowed to pass. The length of the period and the closing date must have been specified in the notice (see (d)(ii) and (d)(iii), above).

STAGE 3 – Duty to have regard
The landlord must 'have regard to' any observations made in response to the notice of intention during the relevant period.[11]

STAGE 4 – Preparation of landlord's contract statement ('the paragraph 4 statement')	
The landlord must prepare a statement in respect of the proposed contract under which the proposed works are to be carried out.[12]	The statement must set out: a) the name and address of the person with whom the landlord proposes to contract and particulars of any connection[13] between them, apart from the proposed contract;[14] b) where, as regards each tenant's unit of occupation, it is reasonably practicable for the landlord to estimate the amount of the relevant contribution to be incurred by the tenant attributable to the work to which the proposed contract relates, that estimated amount;[15] c) where it is not reasonably practicable to comply with (b), but it is reasonably practicable for the landlord to estimate, as regards the building or other premises to which the proposed contract relates, the total amount of his expenditure under the proposed contract, that estimated amount;[16] d) where is it not reasonably practicable to comply with either b) or c) but it is reasonably practicable for the landlord to ascertain the current unit cost or hourly or daily rate applicable to the woks to which the proposed contract relates, the cost or rate;[17] e) where is it not reasonably practicable to comply with (d), the reasons why he cannot comply and the

---

11 SC Consultation (England) Regs; SC Consultation (Wales) Regs – Sch 4 Part 1 para 3.
12 SC Consultation (England) Regs; SC Consultation (Wales) Regs – Sch 4 Part 1 para 4(1).
13 As to which, see SC Consultation (England) Regs; SC Consultation (Wales) Regs – Sch 4 Part 1 para 4(3).
14 SC Consultation (England) Regs; SC Consultation (Wales) Regs – Sch 4 Part 1 para 4(2).
15 SC Consultation (England) Regs; SC Consultation (Wales) Regs – Sch 4 Part 1 para 4(4).
16 SC Consultation (England) Regs; SC Consultation (Wales) Regs – Sch 4 Part 1 para 4(5).
17 SC Consultation (England) Regs; SC Consultation (Wales) Regs – Sch. 4, Pt 1, para 4(6).

	date by which he expects to be able to provide an estimated amount, cost or rate;[18] f) where the landlord has received observations (see Stage 2 and Stage 3, above), a summary of the observations and his response to them.[19]
STAGE 5 – Notice of proposed contract	
The landlord must give notice in writing of his or her intention to enter into the proposed contract:[20] a) to each tenant;[21] and b) where an RTA represents some or all of the tenants, to the RTA.[22]	The notice shall: a) comprise, or be accompanied by the paragraph 4 statement (see Stage 4) or specify the places and hours at which that statement may be inspected;[23] b) invite the making, in writing, of observations in relation to any matter mentioned in the paragraph 4 statement and specify:[24] i) the address to which such observations may be sent;[25] ii) that they must be within the 'relevant period' (meaning a period of 30 days beginning with the date of the notice);[26] and iii) the date on which the relevant period ends.[27]

18 SC Consultation (England) Regs; SC Consultation (Wales) Regs – Sch 4 Part 1 para 4(7). This must be within 21 days of receiving sufficient information to enable the landlord to estimate the amount, cost or rate. Notice must then be given to each tenant and, where an RTA represents some or all of the tenants, to the RTA: SC Consultation (England) Regs; SC Consultation (Wales) Regs – Sch 4 Part 1 para 7.
19 SC Consultation (England) Regs; SC Consultation (Wales) Regs – Sch 4 Part 1 para 4(8).
20 SC Consultation (England) Regs; SC Consultation (Wales) Regs – Sch 4 Part 1 para 5(1).
21 SC Consultation (England) Regs; SC Consultation (Wales) Regs – Sch 4 Part 1 para 5(1)(a).
22 SC Consultation (England) Regs; SC Consultation (Wales) Regs – Sch 4 Part 1 para 5(1)(b).
23 SC Consultation (England) Regs; SC Consultation (Wales) Regs – Sch 4 Part 1 para 5(2)(a). If the notice specifies a place and hours for inspection, the place and hours so specified must be reasonable and a description of the relevant matters must be available for inspection, free of charge, at that place and during those hours. If facilities to enable copies to be taken are not made available at the times at which the description may be inspected, the landlord shall provide to a tenant, on request and free of charge, a copy of the description – Sch 4 Part 1 para 2, which applies by virtue of Sch 4 Part 1 para 5(3).
24 SC Consultation (England) Regs; SC Consultation (Wales) Regs – Sch 4 Part 1 para 5(2)(b).
25 SC Consultation (England) Regs; SC Consultation (Wales) Regs – Sch 4 Part 1 para 5(2)(c)(i).
26 SC Consultation (England) Regs; SC Consultation (Wales) Regs – reg 2(1); Sch 4 Part 1 para 5(2)(c)(ii).
27 SC Consultation (England) Regs; SC Consultation (Wales) Regs – Sch 4 Part 1 para 5(2)(c)(iii).

STAGE 6 – The second 'relevant period'
A second period of 30 days beginning with the date of the notice must be allowed to pass. The length of the period and the closing date must have been specified in the notice (see b)ii) and b)iii), above).

STAGE 7 – Duty to have regard and to respond
The landlord must 'have regard to' any observations made in response to the notice of intention during the relevant period[28] and shall, within 21 days of their receipt, by notice in writing to the person by whom the observations were made, state his or her response to the observations.[29]

28 SC Consultation (England) Regs; SC Consultation (Wales) Regs – Sch 4 Part 1 para 6.
29 SC Consultation (England) Regs; SC Consultation (Wales) Regs – Sch 4 Part 1 para 7.

Qualifying works under qualifying long-term agreements

STAGE 1 – Notice of intention	

The landlord must give notice in writing of their intention to carry out qualifying works to:[30]
a) each tenant;[31] and
b) where an RTA represents some or all of the tenants, to the RTA.[32]
	The notice must:
	a) describe, in general terms, the works proposed to be carried out or specify the place and hours at which a description of the proposed works may be inspected;[33]
	b) state the landlord's reasons for considering it necessary to carry out the proposed works;[34]
	c) contain a statement of the total amount of expenditure estimated by the landlord as likely to be incurred by him on and in connection with the proposed works;[35]
	d) invite the making, in writing, of observations in relation to the proposed works and specify:[36]
	  i) the address to which such observations may be sent;[37]
	  ii) that they must be within the 'relevant period' (meaning a period of 30 days beginning with the date of the notice);[38] and
	  iii) the date on which the relevant period ends.[39]

30 SC Consultation (England) Regs; SC Consultation (Wales) Regs – Sch 3 para 1
31 SC Consultation (England) Regs; SC Consultation (Wales) Regs – Sch 3 para 1(1)(a).
32 SC Consultation (England) Regs; SC Consultation (Wales) Regs – Sch 3 para 1(1)(b).
33 SC Consultation (England) Regs; SC Consultation (Wales) Regs – Sch 3 para 1(2)(a). If the notice specifies a place and hours for inspection, the place and hours so specified must be reasonable and a description of the relevant matters must be available for inspection, free of charge, at that place and during those hours. If facilities to enable copies to be taken are not made available at the times at which the description may be inspected, the landlord shall provide to a tenant, on request and free of charge, a copy of the description – SC Consultation (England) Regs; SC Consultation (Wales) Regs – Sch 3 para 2.
34 SC Consultation (England) Regs; SC Consultation (Wales) Regs – Sch 3 para 1(2)(b).
35 SC Consultation (England) Regs; SC Consultation (Wales) Regs – Sch 3 para 1(2)(c).
36 SC Consultation (England) Regs; SC Consultation (Wales) Regs – Sch 3 para 1(2)(d).
37 SC Consultation (England) Regs; SC Consultation (Wales) Regs – Sch. 3 para. 1(2)(e)(i).
38 SC Consultation (England) Regs; SC Consultation (Wales) Regs – reg 2(1); Sch 3 para 1(2)(e)(ii).
39 SC Consultation (England) Regs; SC Consultation (Wales) Regs – Sch 3 para 1(2)(e)(iii).

STAGE 2 – The 'relevant period'
A period of 30 days beginning with the date of the notice must be allowed to pass. The length of the period and the closing date must have been specified in the notice (see d)ii) and d)iii), above).

STAGE 3 – Duty to have regard
The landlord must 'have regard to' any observations made in response to the notice of intention during the relevant period.[40]

STAGE 4 – Response to observations
Where the landlord receives observations to which he or she is required to have regard (see Stage 3, above), the landlord shall, within 21 days of their receipt, by notice in writing to the person by whom the observations were made, state his or her response to the observations.[41]

---

40   SC Consultation (England) Regs; SC Consultation (Wales) Regs – Sch 3 para 3.
41   SC Consultation (England) Regs; SC Consultation (Wales) Regs – Sch 3 para 4.

Qualifying works: public notice not required

STAGE 1 – Notice of intention	
The landlord must give notice in writing of their intention to carry out qualifying works to:[42] a) each tenant;[43] and b) where an RTA represents some or all of the tenants, to the RTA.[44]	The notice must: a) describe, in general terms, the works proposed to be carried out or specify the place and hours at which a description of the proposed works may be inspected;[45] b) state the landlord's reasons for considering it necessary to carry out the proposed works;[46] c) invite the making, in writing, of observations in relation to the proposed works and specify:[47] i) the address to which such observations may be sent;[48] ii) that they must be within the 'relevant period' (meaning a period of 30 days beginning with the date of the notice);[49] and iii) the date on which the relevant period ends.[50] d) invite each tenant and association (if any) to propose, within the relevant period, the name of a person from whom the landlord should try to obtain an estimate for the carrying out of the proposed works.[51]

42 SC Consultation (England) Regs; SC Consultation (Wales) Regs – Sch 4 Part 2 para 1.
43 SC Consultation (England) Regs; SC Consultation (Wales) Regs – Sch 4 Part 2 para 1(1)(a).
44 SC Consultation (England) Regs; SC Consultation (Wales) Regs – Sch 4 Part 2 para 1(1)(b).
45 SC Consultation (England) Regs; SC Consultation (Wales) Regs – Sch 4 Part 2 para 1(2)(a). If the notice specifies a place and hours for inspection, the place and hours so specified must be reasonable and a description of the relevant matters must be available for inspection, free of charge, at that place and during those hours. If facilities to enable copies to be taken are not made available at the times at which the description may be inspected, the landlord shall provide to a tenant, on request and free of charge, a copy of the description: SC Consultation (England) Regs; SC Consultation (Wales) Regs – Sch 4 Part 2 para 2.
46 SC Consultation (England) Regs; SC Consultation (Wales) Regs – Sch 4 Part 2 para 1(2)(b).
47 SC Consultation (England) Regs; SC Consultation (Wales) Regs – Sch 4 Part 2 para 1(2)(d).
48 SC Consultation (England) Regs; SC Consultation (Wales) Regs – Sch 4 Part 2 para 1(2)(e)(i).
49 SC Consultation (England) Regs; SC Consultation (Wales) Regs – reg 2(1); Sch 4 Part 1 para 1(2)(e)(ii).
50 SC Consultation (England) Regs; SC Consultation (Wales) Regs – Sch 4 Part 2 para 1(2)(e)(iii).
51 SC Consultation (England) Regs; SC Consultation (Wales) Regs – Sch 4 Part 2 para 1(3).

STAGE 2 – The 'relevant period'
A period of 30 days beginning with the date of the notice must be allowed to pass. The length of the period and the closing date must have been specified in the notice (see c)ii and c)iii), above).

STAGE 3 – Duty to have regard
The landlord must 'have regard' to any observations made in relation to the proposed agreement by any tenant or RTA made during the relevant period.[52]

STAGE 4 – Collection of estimates	

The landlord must try to obtain estimates from persons nominated by the tenants or the association.[53]	The estimates must be obtained from:
	a) if a single nomination was made by an RTA, the landlord shall try to obtain an estimate from the nominated person, regardless of whether or not any tenant made any nomination;[54]
	b) if a single nomination is made by only one tenant, the landlord shall try to obtain an estimate from the nominated person, regardless of whether or not a nomination was made by any RTA;[55]
	c) if more than one tenant made a nomination (regardless of whether or not a nomination was made by any RTA), the landlord shall try to obtain an estimate from:
	  i) the person who received the most nominations;[56] or
	  ii) if two or more persons receive the same number of nominations, from at least one of those people;[57] or
	  iii) in any other case, from any nominated person.[58]
	d) if more than one nomination was made by any tenant and more than one nomination is made by an RTA, the landlord shall try to obtain an estimate from at least one person nominated by a tenants and at least one other person nominated by the association.[59]

---

52 SC Consultation (England) Regs; SC Consultation (Wales) Regs – Sch 4 Part 2 para 3.
53 SC Consultation (England) Regs; SC Consultation (Wales) Regs – Sch 4 para 4.
54 SC Consultation (England) Regs; SC Consultation (Wales) Regs – Sch 4 para 4(1).
55 SC Consultation (England) Regs; SC Consultation (Wales) Regs – Sch 4 para 4(2).
56 SC Consultation (England) Regs; SC Consultation (Wales) Regs – Sch 4 para 4(3)(a).
57 SC Consultation (England) Regs; SC Consultation (Wales) Regs – Sch 4 para 4(3)(b).
58 SC Consultation (England) Regs; SC Consultation (Wales) Regs – Sch 4 para 4(3)(c).
59 SC Consultation (England) Regs; SC Consultation (Wales) Regs – Sch 4 para 4(4).

STAGE 5 – Second notice and the paragraph B statement	
The landlord must obtain[60] at least two[61] estimates for the carrying out of the proposed works[62] and must supply, free of charge,[63] to each tenant and any RTA,[64] a statement (the 'paragraph (b) statement'). At least one of the estimates must be from a person wholly unconnected[65] with the landlord[66] and, where the landlord has obtained an estimate from a nominated person, the estimate must be included in the 'paragraph (b) statement'.[67]	The 'paragraph (b) statement' must set out: a) as regards at least two estimates, the amount specified in the estimate as the estimated costs of the proposed works;[68] b) where the landlord has received observations (see Stage 3), a summary of the observations and the landlord's response to them.[69]

60 SC Consultation (England) Regs; SC Consultation (Wales) Regs – Sch 4 Part 2 para 4(5)(a).
61 SC Consultation (England) Regs; SC Consultation (Wales) Regs – Sch 4 Part 2 para 4(5)(b)(i).
62 SC Consultation (England) Regs; SC Consultation (Wales) Regs – Sch 4 Part 2 para 4(5).
63 SC Consultation (England) Regs; SC Consultation (Wales) Regs – Sch 4 Part 2 para 4(5)(b).
64 SC Consultation (England) Regs; SC Consultation (Wales) Regs – Sch 4 Part 2 para 4(9).
65 As to which see SC Consultation (England) Regs; SC Consultation (Wales) Regs – Sch 4 Part 2 para 4(7) (assumed connection) and reg 2(1) (close relative).
66 SC Consultation (England) Regs; SC Consultation (Wales) Regs – Sch 4 Part 2 para 4(6).
67 SC Consultation (England) Regs; SC Consultation (Wales) Regs – Sch 4 Part 2 para 4(8).
68 SC Consultation (England) Regs; SC Consultation (Wales) Regs – Sch 4 Part 2 para 4(5)(b)(i).
69 SC Consultation (England) Regs; SC Consultation (Wales) Regs – Sch 4 Part 2 para 4(5)(b)(ii).

	The estimates must also be made available for inspection at a specified place and time.[70] The landlord must also by notice in writing to each tenant and the association:[71] i) specify the place and hours where the estimates may be inspected;[72] ii) invite the making, in writing, of observations in relation to those estimates;[73] iii) specify the address to which such observations may be sent; that they must be delivered within he relevant period and specify the date on which the relevant period ends.[74]

STAGE 6 – The second 'relevant period'
A second period of 30 days beginning with the date of the notice must be allowed to pass. The length of the period and the closing date must have been specified in the notice.

STAGE 7 – Duty to have regard
The landlord must 'have regard to' any observations made in relation to the estimates relevant period.[75]

70 SC Consultation (England) Regs; SC Consultation (Wales) Regs – Sch 4 Part 2 para 4(5)(c) and Sch 4 Part 2 para 4(9)–(10). The place and hours so specified must be reasonable and a description of the relevant matters must be available for inspection, free of charge, at that place and during those hours. If facilities to enable copies to be taken are not made available at the times at which the description may be inspected, the landlord shall provide to any tenant, on request and free of charge, a copy of the description: SC Consultation (England) Regs; SC Consultation (Wales) Regs – Sch 4 Part 2 para 11.

71 SC Consultation (England) Regs; SC Consultation (Wales) Regs – Sch 4 Part 2 para 4(10).

72 SC Consultation (England) Regs; SC Consultation (Wales) Regs – Sch 4 Part 2 para 4(10)(c)(i). The place and hours so specified must be reasonable, and a description of the relevant matters must be available for inspection, free of charge, at that place and during those hours. If facilities to enable copies to be taken are not made available at the times at which the description may be inspected, the landlord shall provide to any tenant, on request and free of charge, a copy of the description: SC Consultation (England) Regs; SC Consultation (Wales) Regs – Sch 4 Part 2 para 11.

73 SC Consultation (England) Regs; SC Consultation (Wales) Regs – Sch 4 Part 2 para 4(10)(b).

74 SC Consultation (England) Regs; SC Consultation (Wales) Regs – Sch 4 Part 2 para 4(10)(c).

75 SC Consultation (England) Regs; SC Consultation (Wales) Regs – Sch 4 Part 2 para 5.

STAGE 8 – Duty on entering into the contract	
Unless the landlord enters into an agreement with a nominated person or a person who submitted the lowest estimate,[76] the landlord must, within 21 days of entering into an agreement relating to relevant matters, give written notice to each tenants and any RTA.[77]	The notice must: a) state the landlord's reasons for making the agreement or specify the place and hours where a statement of those reasons must be inspected;[78] b) where the landlord has received observations to which he or she is required to have regard (see Stage 8), summarise the observations and respond to them or specify the place and hours at which such a summary and response may be inspected.[79]

76 SC Consultation (England) Regs; SC Consultation (Wales) Regs – Sch 4 Part 2 para 6(2).
77 SC Consultation (England) Regs; SC Consultation (Wales) Regs – Sch 4 Part 2 para 6(1).
78 SC Consultation (England) Regs; SC Consultation (Wales) Regs – Sch 4 Part 2 para 6(1)(a). If the notice specifies a place and hours for inspection, the place and hours so specified must be reasonable and a description of the relevant matters must be available for inspection, free of charge, at that place and during those hours. If facilities to enable copies to be taken are not made available at the times at which the description may be inspected, the landlord shall provide to any tenant, on request and free of charge, a copy of the description – Sch 4 Part 2 para 2 which applies by virtue of Sch 4 Part 2 para 6(3).
79 SC Consultation (England) Regs; SC Consultation (Wales) Regs – Sch 4 Part 2 para 6(1)(b). If the notice specifies a place and hours for inspection, the place and hours so specified must be reasonable and a description of the relevant matters must be available for inspection, free of charge, at that place and during those hours. If facilities to enable copies to be taken are not made available at the times at which the description may be inspected, the landlord shall provide to any tenant, on request and free of charge, a copy of the description – Sch 4 Part 2 para 2 which applies by virtue of Sch 4 Part 2 para 6(3).

Qualifying long-term agreements: public notice not required

STAGE 1 – Notice of intention	
The landlord shall give notice in writing of their intention to enter into the agreement to:[80] a) each tenant;[81] and b) where an RTA represents some or all of the tenants, to the RTA.[82]	The notice must: a) describe, in general terms, the 'relevant matters' (that is, in relation to the proposed agreement, the goods or services to be provided or the works to be carried out (as the case may be) under the agreement)[83] or specify the place and hours at which a description of the relevant matters may be inspected;[84] b) state the landlord's reasons for considering it necessary to enter into the agreement;[85] c) where the relevant matters consists of or include qualifying works, state the landlord's reasons for considering it necessary to carry out those works;[86] d) invite the making, in writing, of observations in relation to the proposed agreement specifying:[87] i) the address to which such observations must be sent;[88] ii) that they must be delivered within the relevant period;[89] and

80 SC Consultation (England) Regs; SC Consultation (Wales) Regs – Sch 1 para 1.
81 SC Consultation (England) Regs; SC Consultation (Wales) Regs – Sch 1 para 1(1)(a).
82 SC Consultation (England) Regs; SC Consultation (Wales) Regs – Sch 1 para 1(1)(b).
83 SC Consultation (England) Regs; SC Consultation (Wales) Regs – reg 2(1).
84 SC Consultation (England) Regs; SC Consultation (Wales) Regs – Sch 1 para 1(2)(a). If the notice specifies a place and hours for inspection, the place and hours so specified must be reasonable and a description of the relevant matters must be available for inspection, free of charge, at that place and during those hours. If facilities to enable copies to be taken are not made available at the times at which the description may be inspected, the landlord shall provide to any tenant, on request and free of charge, a copy of the description – Sch 1 para 2.
85 SC Consultation (England) Regs; SC Consultation (Wales) Regs – Sch 1 para 1(2)(b).
86 SC Consultation (England) Regs; SC Consultation (Wales) Regs – Sch 1 para 1(2)(c).
87 SC Consultation (England) Regs; SC Consultation (Wales) Regs – Sch 1 para 1(2)(d).
88 SC Consultation (England) Regs; SC Consultation (Wales) Regs – Sch 1 para 1(2)(e)(i)
89 SC Consultation (England) Regs; SC Consultation (Wales) Regs – Sch 1 para 1(2)(e)(ii).

	iii) the date on which the relevant period ends.[90] e) invite each tenant and the association (if any) to propose, within the relevant period, the name of a person from whom the landlord should try to obtain an estimate in respect of the relevant matters.[91]
STAGE 2 – The 'relevant period'	
A period of 30 days beginning with the date of the notice must be allowed to pass. The length of the period and the closing date must have been specified in the notice (see d)ii) and d)iii), above).	
STAGE 3 – Duty to have regard	
The landlord must 'have regard' to any observations made in relation to the proposed agreement by any tenant or RTA made during the relevant period.[92]	
STAGE 4 – Collection of estimates	
The landlord must try to obtain estimates from persons nominated by the tenants or the association.[93]	The estimates must be obtained from: a) if a single nomination was made by an RTA, the landlord shall try to obtain an estimate from the nominated person, regardless of whether or not any tenant made any nomination;[94] b) if a single nomination is made by only one tenant, the landlord shall try to obtain an estimate from the nominated person, regardless of whether or not a nomination was made by any RTA;[95] c) if more than one tenant made a nomination (regardless of whether or not a nomination was made by any RTA), the landlord shall try to obtain an estimate from: i) the person who received the most nominations;[96] or ii) if two or more persons receive the same number of nominations, from at least one of those people;[97] or

90 SC Consultation (England) Regs; SC Consultation (Wales) Regs – Sch 1 para 1(2)(e)(iii).
91 SC Consultation (England) Regs; SC Consultation (Wales) Regs – Sch 1 para 1(3).
92 SC Consultation (England) Regs; SC Consultation (Wales) Regs – Sch 1 para 3.
93 SC Consultation (England) Regs; SC Consultation (Wales) Regs – Sch 1 para 4.
94 SC Consultation (England) Regs; SC Consultation (Wales) Regs – Sch 1 para 4(1).
95 SC Consultation (England) Regs; SC Consultation (Wales) Regs – Sch 1 para 4(2).
96 SC Consultation (England) Regs; SC Consultation (Wales) Regs – Sch 1 para 4(3)(a).
97 SC Consultation (England) Regs; SC Consultation (Wales) Regs – Sch 1 para 4(3)(b).

	iii) in any other case, from any nominated person.[98] d) if more than one nomination was made by any tenant and more than one nomination is made by an RTA, the landlord shall try to obtain an estimate from at least one person nominated by a tenants and at least one other person nominated by the association.[99]
STAGE 5 – Preparation of a proposal	
The landlord must prepare at least two proposals in respect of the relevant matters[100] (that is, in relation to the proposed agreement, the goods or services to be provided or the works to be carried out (as the case may be) under the agreement).[101] At least one of the proposals must propose that goods or service are provided, or works are carried out (as the case	Each proposal must contain: a) a statement of the relevant matters[102] (that is, in relation to the proposed agreement, the goods or services to be provided or the works to be carried out (as the case may be) under the agreement).[103] b) the name and address of each party to the proposed agreement other than the landlord and any connection[104] between the party and the landlord;[105] c) where, as regards each tenant's unit of occupation, it is reasonably practicable for the landlord to estimate the relevant contribution to be incurred by the tenant attributable to the relevant matters to which the proposed agreement relates, a statement of that contribution;[106] d) where, it is not reasonably practicable to comply with c), but it is reasonably practicable for the landlord to estimate, as regards the building or other premises to which the proposed agreement relates, the total amount of his expenditure under the proposed agreement, a statement of the amount of that estimated expenditure;[107]

98 SC Consultation (England) Regs; SC Consultation (Wales) Regs – Sch 1 para 4(3)(c).
99 SC Consultation (England) Regs; SC Consultation (Wales) Regs – Sch 1 para 4(4).
100 SC Consultation (England) Regs; SC Consultation (Wales) Regs – Sch 1 para 5(1).
101 SC Consultation (England) Regs; SC Consultation (Wales) Regs – reg 2(1).
102 SC Consultation (England) Regs; SC Consultation (Wales) Regs – Sch 1 para 5(4).
103 SC Consultation (England) Regs; SC Consultation (Wales) Regs – reg 2(1).
104 As to which, see SC Consultation (England) Regs; SC Consultation (Wales) Regs – Sch 1 para 5(6) (deemed connection) and reg 2(1) (close relative).
105 SC Consultation (England) Regs; SC Consultation (Wales) Regs – Sch 1 para 5(5).
106 SC Consultation (England) Regs; SC Consultation (Wales) Regs – Sch 1 para 5(7).
107 SC Consultation (England) Regs; SC Consultation (Wales) Regs – Sch 1 para 5(8).

may be) by a person wholly unconnected[108] with the landlord.[109] Where an estimate has been obtained from a nominated person, a proposal must be prepared based on that estimate.[110]	e) where it is not reasonably practicable for the landlord to comply with (c) or (d), but it is reasonably practicable for the landlord to ascertain the current unit cost or hourly or daily rate applicable to the relevant matters to which the proposed agreement relates, a statement of that cost or rate;[111]
	f) where the relevant matters comprise or include the proposed appointment by the landlord of an agent to discharge any of the landlord's obligations to the tenants which relate to the management by him or her of premises to which the agreement relates, each proposal shall contain a statement;[112]
	   i) that the person whose appointment is proposed is or is not a member of a professional body or trade association (together with the name of the professional body or association);[113] and
	   ii) that the person subscribes or does not subscribe to any code of practice or voluntary accreditation scheme relevant to the function of managing agents.[114]
	g) a statement as to the provisions (if any) for variation of any amount specified in, or to be determined under, the proposed agreement.[115]
	h) a statement as to the intended duration of the proposed agreement.[116]
	i) a summary of the observations received during the relevant period (see Stage 2 and Stage 3, above) and the response to them.[117]

108 As to which see SC Consultation (England) Regs; SC Consultation (Wales) Regs – Sch 1 para 5(6) (assumed connection) and reg 2(1) (close relative).

109 SC Consultation (England) Regs; SC Consultation (Wales) Regs – Sch 1 para 5(2).

110 SC Consultation (England) Regs; SC Consultation (Wales) Regs – Sch 1 para 5(3).

111 SC Consultation (England) Regs; SC Consultation (Wales) Regs – Sch 1 para 5(9).

112 SC Consultation (England) Regs; SC Consultation (Wales) Regs – Sch 1 para 5(10).

113 SC Consultation (England) Regs; SC Consultation (Wales) Regs – Sch 1 para 5(10)(b), (a)(i).

114 SC Consultation (England) Regs; SC Consultation (Wales) Regs – Sch 1 para 5(10)(a)(ii).

115 SC Consultation (England) Regs; SC Consultation (Wales) Regs – Sch 1 para 5(11).

116 SC Consultation (England) Regs; SC Consultation (Wales) Regs – Sch 1 para 5(12).

117 SC Consultation (England) Regs; SC Consultation (Wales) Regs – Sch 1 para 5(13).

STAGE 6 – Notice of proposal	
The landlord shall give notice in writing of their proposals prepared under Stage 5 (above) to:[118] a) each tenant;[119] and b) where an RTA represents some or all of the tenants, to the RTA.[120]	The notice must: a) be accompanied by a copy of each proposal (see Stage 5)[121] or specify the place and hours at which the proposals may be inspected;[122] b) invite the making, in writing, of observations in relation to the proposed agreement specifying:[123] i) the address to which such observations must be sent;[124] ii) that they must be delivered within the relevant period;[125] and iii) the date on which the relevant period ends.[126]

STAGE 7 – The second 'relevant period'
A second period of 30 days beginning with the date of the notice must be allowed to pass. The length of the period and the closing date must have been specified in the notice (see b)ii) and b)iii), above).

STAGE 8 – Duty to have regard
The landlord must 'have regard' to any observations made in relation to the proposed agreement by any tenant or RTA made during the relevant period.[127]

118 SC Consultation (England) Regs; SC Consultation (Wales) Regs – Sch 1 para 6(1).

119 SC Consultation (England) Regs; SC Consultation (Wales) Regs – Sch 1 para 6(1)(a).

120 SC Consultation (England) Regs; SC Consultation (Wales) Regs – Sch 1 para 6(1)(b).

121 SC Consultation (England) Regs; SC Consultation (Wales) Regs – Sch 1 para 6(2)(a).

122 SC Consultation (England) Regs; SC Consultation (Wales) Regs – Sch 1 para 6(2)(a). If the notice specifies a place and hours for inspection, the place and hours so specified must be reasonable and a description of the relevant matters must be available for inspection, free of charge, at that place and during those hours. If facilities to enable copies to be taken are not made available at the times at which the description may be inspected, the landlord shall provide to any tenant, on request and free of charge, a copy of the description – Sch 1 para 2 which applies by virtue of Sch 1 para 6(3).

123 SC Consultation (England) Regs; SC Consultation (Wales) Regs – Sch 1 para 6(2)(b).

124 SC Consultation (England) Regs; SC Consultation (Wales) Regs – Sch 1 para 6(2)(c)(i).

125 SC Consultation (England) Regs; SC Consultation (Wales) Regs – Sch 1 para 6(2)(c)(ii).

126 SC Consultation (England) Regs; SC Consultation (Wales) Regs – Sch 1 para 6(2)(c)(iii).

127 SC Consultation (England) Regs; SC Consultation (Wales) Regs – Sch 1 para 7.

STAGE 9 – Duty on entering into agreement	
Unless the landlord enters into an agreement with a nominated person or a person who submitted the lowest estimate[128] the landlord must, within 21 days of entering into an agreement relating to relevant matters, give written notice to each tenants and any RTA.[129]	The notice must: a) state the landlord's reasons for making the agreement or specify the place and hours where a statement of those reasons must be inspected;[130] b) where the landlord has received observations to which he or she is required to have regard (see Stage 8), summarise the observations and respond to them or specify the place and hours at which such a summary and response may be inspected.[131]

128 SC Consultation (England) Regs; SC Consultation (Wales) Regs – Sch 1 para 8(2).
129 SC Consultation (England) Regs; SC Consultation (Wales) Regs – Sch 1 para 8(1).
130 SC Consultation (England) Regs; SC Consultation (Wales) Regs – Sch 1 para 8(1)(a). If the notice specifies a place and hours for inspection, the place and hours so specified must be reasonable and a description of the relevant matters must be available for inspection, free of charge, at that place and during those hours. If facilities to enable copies to be taken are not made available at the times at which the description may be inspected, the landlord shall provide to any tenant, on request and free of charge, a copy of the description – Sch 1 para 2 which applies by virtue of Sch 1 para 8(3).
131 SC Consultation (England) Regs; SC Consultation (Wales) Regs – Sch 1 para 8(1)(b). If the notice specifies a place and hours for inspection, the place and hours so specified must be reasonable and a description of the relevant matters must be available for inspection, free of charge, at that place and during those hours. If facilities to enable copies to be taken are not made available at the times at which the description may be inspected, the landlord shall provide to any tenant, on request and free of charge, a copy of the description – Sch 1 para 2 which applies by virtue of Sch 1 para 8(3).

Qualifying long-term agreements: public notice required

STAGE 1 – Notice of intention	
The landlord must give notice in writing of their intention to enter into the agreement to:[132] a) each tenant;[133] and b) where an RTA represents some or all of the tenants, to the RTA.[134]	The notice must: a) describe, in general terms, the 'relevant matters' (that is, in relation to the proposed agreement, the goods or services to be provided or the works to be carried out (as the case may be) under the agreement)[135] or specify a place where a description of them can be inspected;[136] b) state the landlord's reasons for considering it necessary to enter into the agreement;[137] c) if the relevant matters consist of or include qualifying works, state the landlord's reasons for considering it necessary to carry out those works;[138] d) state that the reason why the landlord is not inviting recipients to nominate persons from whom he should try to obtain an estimate for the relevant matters is that public notice of the relevant matters is to be given;[139] e) invite the making in writing of observations in relation to the relevant matters specifying:[140] i) the address to which observations may be sent;[141]

132 SC Consultation (England) Regs; SC Consultation (Wales) Regs – Sch 1 para 1(1).
133 SC Consultation (England) Regs; SC Consultation (Wales) Regs – Sch 1 para 1(1)(a).
134 SC Consultation (England) Regs; SC Consultation (Wales) Regs – Sch 1 para 1(1)(b).
135 SC Consultation (England) Regs; SC Consultation (Wales) Regs – reg 2(1).
136 SC Consultation (England) Regs; SC Consultation (Wales) Regs – Sch 1 para 1(2)(a). If the notice specifies a place and hours for inspection, the place and hours so specified must be reasonable and a description of the relevant matters must be available for inspection, free of charge, at that place and during those hours. If facilities to enable copies to be taken are not made available at the times at which the description may be inspected, the landlord shall provide to a tenant, on request and free of charge, a copy of the description – Sch 2 para 2.
137 SC Consultation (England) Regs; SC Consultation (Wales) Regs – Sch 1 para 1(2)(b).
138 SC Consultation (England) Regs; SC Consultation (Wales) Regs – Sch 1 para 1(2)(c).
139 SC Consultation (England) Regs; SC Consultation (Wales) Regs – Sch 1 para 1(2)(d).
140 SC Consultation (England) Regs; SC Consultation (Wales) Regs – Sch 1 para 1(2)(e).
141 SC Consultation (England) Regs; SC Consultation (Wales) Regs – Sch 1 para 1(2)(f)(i).

	ii) that they must be within the 'relevant period' (meaning a period of 30 days beginning with the date of the notice);[142] and iii) the date on which the relevant period ends.[143]

STAGE 2 – The 'relevant period'

A period of 30 days beginning with the date of the notice must be allowed to pass. The length of the period and the closing date must have been specified in the notice (see e)ii) and e)iii), above).

STAGE 3 – Duty to have regard

The landlord must 'have regard to' any observations made in response to the notice of intention during the relevant period.[144]

STAGE 4 – Preparation of a proposal

The landlord must prepare a proposal in respect of the proposed agreement.[145]	The proposal must contain a statement setting out: a) the name and address of all parties (other than the landlord) to the proposed agreement and of any connection[146] (apart from the proposed agreement) between the landlord and any other party;[147] b) where, as regards each tenant's unit of occupation, it is reasonably practicable for the landlord to estimate the relevant contribution to be incurred by the tenant attributable to the relevant matters to which the proposed agreement relates, a statement of that contribution;[148] c) where it is not reasonably practicable to comply with b), but it is reasonably practicable for the landlord to estimate, as regards the building or other premises to which the proposed agreement relates, the total amount of the landlord's expenditure under the proposed agreement, a statement of the amount of that estimated expenditure;[149]

142 SC Consultation (England) Regs; SC Consultation (Wales) Regs – reg 2(1); Sch 1 para 1(2)(f)(ii).
143 SC Consultation (England) Regs; SC Consultation (Wales) Regs – Sch 1 para 1(2)(f)(iii).
144 SC Consultation (England) Regs; SC Consultation (Wales) Regs – Sch 1 para 3.
145 SC Consultation (England) Regs; SC Consultation (Wales) Regs – Sch 2 para 4(1).
146 As to which, see SC Consultation (England) Regs; SC Consultation (Wales) Regs – Sch 1 para 4(3).
147 SC Consultation (England) Regs; SC Consultation (Wales) Regs – Sch 2 para 4(2).
148 SC Consultation (England) Regs; SC Consultation (Wales) Regs – Sch 2 para 4(4).
149 SC Consultation (England) Regs; SC Consultation (Wales) Regs – Sch 2 para 4(5).

	d) where it is not reasonably practicable for the landlord to comply with b) or c), but it is reasonably practicable for the landlord to ascertain the current unit cost or hourly or daily rate applicable to the relevant matters to which the proposed agreement relates, a statement of that cost or rate;[150] e) where it is not reasonably practicable for the landlord to comply with (d), a statement of the reasons why he cannot comply and the date by which he expects to be able to provide an estimate, cost or rate;[151] f) where the relevant matters comprise or include the proposed appointment by the landlord of an agent to discharge any of the landlord's obligations to the tenants which relate to the management of premises to which the agreement relates, each proposal shall contain a statement:[152] i) that the person whose appointment is proposed is or is not a member of a professional body or trade association (together with the name of the professional body or association);[153] and ii) that the person subscribes or does not subscribe to any code of practice or voluntary accreditation scheme relevant to the function of managing agents;[154] g) a statement of the intended duration of the proposed agreement;[155] h) where the landlord has received observations (see Stage 2 and Stage 3, above), a statement summarising the observations and setting out the landlord's response to them.[156]

150 SC Consultation (England) Regs; SC Consultation (Wales) Regs – Sch 1 para 4(6).
151 SC Consultation (England) Regs; SC Consultation (Wales) Regs – Sch 1 para 4(7). This must be within 21 days of receiving sufficient information to enable him to estimate the amount, cost or rate. Notice must then be given to each tenant and, where an RTA represents some or all of the tenants, to the RTA – SC Consultation (England) Regs; SC Consultation (Wales) Regs – Sch 1 para 8.
152 SC Consultation (England) Regs; SC Consultation (Wales) Regs – Sch 1 para 4(8).
153 SC Consultation (England) Regs; SC Consultation (Wales) Regs – Sch 1 para 4(a)(i) and 4(b).
154 SC Consultation (England) Regs; SC Consultation (Wales) Regs – Sch 1 para 4(a)(ii).
155 SC Consultation (England) Regs; SC Consultation (Wales) Regs – Sch 1 para 4(9).
156 SC Consultation (England) Regs; SC Consultation (Wales) Regs – Sch 1 para 4(10).

STAGE 5 – Notice of proposal	
The landlord must give notice in writing of the proposal (see Stage 4, above) to:[157] a) each tenant;[158] and b) where an RTA represents some or all of the tenants, to the RTA.[159]	The notice must: a) be accompanied by a copy of the proposal (see Stage 4) or specify the place and hours at which the proposal may be inspected;[160] b) invite the making, in writing, of observations in relation to the proposal specifying:[161] i) the address to which observations may be sent;[162] ii) that they must be within the 'relevant period' (meaning a period of 30 days beginning with the date of the notice);[163] and iii) the date on which the relevant period ends.[164]

STAGE 6 – The second 'relevant period'
A second period of 30 days beginning with the date of the notice must be allowed to pass. The length of the period and the closing date must have been specified in the notice (see b)ii) and b)iii), above).

STAGE 7 – Duty to have regard and to respond
The landlord must 'have regard to' any observations made in response to the notice of intention during the relevant period[165] and shall, within 21 days of their receipt, by notice in writing to the person by whom the observations were made, state his or her response to the observations.[166]

157 SC Consultation (England) Regs; SC Consultation (Wales) Regs – Sch 1 para 5(1).
158 SC Consultation (England) Regs; SC Consultation (Wales) Regs – Sch 1 para 5(1)(a).
159 SC Consultation (England) Regs; SC Consultation (Wales) Regs – Sch 1 para 5(1)(b).
160 SC Consultation (England) Regs; SC Consultation (Wales) Regs – Sch 1 para 5(2)(a). If the notice specifies a place and hours for inspection, the place and hours so specified must be reasonable and a description of the relevant matters must be available for inspection, free of charge, at that place and during those hours. If facilities to enable copies to be taken are not made available at the times at which the description may be inspected, the landlord shall provide to a tenant, on request and free of charge, a copy of the description – Sch 2 para 2 which applies by virtue of Sch 1 para 5(3).
161 SC Consultation (England) Regs; SC Consultation (Wales) Regs – Sch 1 para 5(2)(b).
162 SC Consultation (England) Regs; SC Consultation (Wales) Regs – Sch 1 para 5(2)(c)(i).
163 SC Consultation (England) Regs; SC Consultation (Wales) Regs – reg 2(1); Sch 1 para 5(2)(c)(ii).
164 SC Consultation (England) Regs; SC Consultation (Wales) Regs – Sch 1 para 5(2)(c)(iii).
165 SC Consultation (England) Regs; SC Consultation (Wales) Regs – Sch 1 para 6.
166 SC Consultation (England) Regs; SC Consultation (Wales) Regs – Sch 2 para 7.

CHAPTER 4

Obtaining information

continued

Key points
- Landlords are obliged to provide certain information to tenants on request, eg name and address.
- Service charge demands and administration charge demands must also contain similar information. There is a prescribed summary of rights of tenants which must also accompany the demands.
- Ground rent demands must also be in a prescribed form.
- Tenants have the right to request information about the state of the service charge account and the monies in and out and can inspect the underlying documents.
- Specific rights also exist enabling tenants to inspect insurance documents.
- There are also rights to appoint external surveyors and accountants to examine the service charge accounts.

Advice for tenants
- Information is the key to all leasehold disputes, both in proceedings – for example, while challenging the service charges – or simply in order to make an informed decision about whether to attempt to exercise the right to manage.
- The vast majority of leases will confer very few – if any – rights to information about the landlord's activities. The statutory rights are therefore particularly important.
- While failure by a landlord to comply with a number of the obligations dealt with in this chapter is often a criminal offence, a private prosecution is not usually a realistic option. It is exceptionally unlikely that the police will intervene in such disputes.
- Serious consideration should be given to forming a recognised tenants' association (RTA) and exercising the right to a management audit or the appointment of a surveyor. The involvement of an external professional is often an effective way of persuading a recalcitrant landlord to provide information.

Rights to information about the landlord

4.1   There is a certain minimum amount of information that must be made available to all tenants. Failure to comply with these provisions without a reasonable excuse is a summary offence punishable by a fine.[1] While tenants are entitled to bring private prosecutions,[2] it is more common for the local housing authority to do so.[3] It is not possible to enforce these provisions by way of injunction in the civil courts.[4]

Disclosure of landlord's identity

4.2   All tenants have the right to know their landlord's identity.[5] A tenant may make a written request asking for the landlord's name and address, which may be made to anyone who demands, or the last person who received, any rent payable, or to anyone acting as agent for the landlord.[6]

4.3   That person must then supply a written statement of the landlord's name and address within 21 days from receipt of the request.[7]

4.4   If, after a successful request for the landlord's name and address, a tenant discovers that the landlord is a company, the tenant may make a request in writing for the name and address of every director and the secretary (if any) of the company.[8]

4.5   Such a request may be made to any person who demands rent or is acting as agent of the landlord.[9] That person must respond with the relevant names or addresses within 21 days.[10]

Change of landlord

4.6   If the landlord sells their interest in the property to a new landlord, the new landlord has a duty to give notice of this in writing to the

---

1   Landlord and Tenant Act (LTA) 1985 ss1(2), 2(4), 3(3) and 3A(3).
2   See *Taber v Macdonald* (1999) 31 HLR 73 for an example.
3   LTA 1985 s34.
4   *Di Marco v Morshead Mansions Ltd* [2014] EWCA Civ 96.
5   LTA 1985 s1.
6   LTA 1985 s1(1).
7   LTA 1985 s1(1).
8   LTA 1985 s2(1).
9   LTA 1985 s2(3).
10 LTA 1985 s2(2).

tenant within two months or on the next day that rent is payable, whichever is the later.[11]

4.7   Such a notice should indicate the new landlord's name and address.[12]

4.8   A former landlord will still be liable under any covenants with the tenant until they have given the tenant notice in writing of the new landlord's name and last-known address; or the new landlord has informed the tenant of their name and current address.[13]

Information to accompany demands for payment

4.9   Parliament has also made provision for certain information which must be provided with demands for payments.

Rent, service charges, administration charges: LTA 1987 s47

4.10   Any written demand for rent, service charges or administration charges must contain the name and address of the landlord.[14] This is not satisfied by giving the details of an agent,[15] nor by giving the details of a director of a corporate landlord.[16] In the case of an individual, the address must be the individual's home or other place where he or she carries on business and, in the case of a company, the address must be the registered office or place where it carries on business.[17]

4.11   If the landlord's address is outside England and Wales, the demand must also contain an address that is within England and Wales where notices – such as notices in proceedings – may be served.[18]

4.12   If such a demand does not contain the landlord's address and (where required) an address for service, the services charges and administration charges demanded are not due until that information

---

11 LTA 1985 s3(1).
12 LTA 1985 s3(1).
13 LTA 1985 s3(3A).
14 LTA 1987 s47(1)(a).
15 *Beitov Properties Ltd v Martin* [2012] UKUT 133 (LC); [2012] L&TR 23.
16 *Triplerose Ltd v Grantglen Ltd and Cane Developments Ltd* [2012] UKUT 204 (LC).
17 *Beitov Properties Ltd v Martin* [2012] UKUT 133 (LC); [2012] L&TR 23.
18 LTA 1987 s47(1)(b).

is supplied.[19] When the information is provided, the money will, however, be due.[20]

4.13   This provision does not apply if a manager or receiver has been appointed for the property by any court or tribunal.[21] It is also arguable that, given the definition of 'landlord' in the LTA 1987,[22] a management company under a tripartite lease is not required to comply with these provisions. In the view of the authors, while this is arguable, it is highly unattractive as there is plainly no logical basis for treating such companies in a different manner to 'true' landlords.

Rent, service charges, administration charges: LTA 1987 s48

4.14   A landlord must also provide the tenant with an address in England and Wales at which notices may be served on them by the tenant.[23] Failure to do so entitles the tenant to withhold payment of the rent, service charges or administration charges.[24] Once the information is provided, the money will, however, be due.[25]

4.15   This provision does not apply if a manager or receiver has been appointed for the property by any court or tribunal.[26] As above, it is arguable that this does not apply to management companies under tripartite leases.

Service charges and administration charges: LTA 1985 s21B; Commonhold and Leasehold Reform Act 2002 Sch 11

4.16   A demand for payment of service or administration charges must be accompanied by a summary of the rights and obligations of tenants of dwellings in relation to the charges.[27] If the demand is sent by post,

---

19   LTA 1987 s47(2).
20   *Staunton v Taylor* [2010] UKUT 270 (LC); *Graham Peter Wrigley v Landchance Property Management Ltd* [2013] UKUT 376 (LC).
21   LTA 1987 s47(3).
22   LTA 1987 s60, and defined as 'the person entitled to possession'.
23   LTA 1987 s48(1).
24   LTA 1987 s48(2).
25   *Rogan v Woodfield Building Services Ltd* (1995) 27 HLR 78 and *Lindsey Trading Properties Inc v Dallhold Estates (UK) Ltd* (1995) 70 P&CR 332.
26   LTA 1987 s48(3).
27   LTA 1985 s21B (service charges); Commonhold and Leasehold Reform Act (CLRA) 2002 Sch 11 para 4 (administration charges).

then the summary must be included in the same envelope (in practice, most demands have the information printed on the reverse).[28]

4.17 This requirement applies to any demand for service charge served on or after 1 October 2007 (in England) or 30 November 2007 (in Wales), and to any administration charges demanded on or after 30 September 2003 (in England) and 31 March 2004 (in Wales).[29] The crucial date is the date of the demand, not when the underlying costs were incurred.[30]

4.18 The form of summary is prescribed.[31] The summary must be printed or typewritten in a font no smaller than ten point.[32] A combined demand for service and administration charges must be accompanied by both summaries.

4.19 A tenant who has received a demand that does not contain such a summary may withhold payment.[33] It has been suggested that a tenant must state that he or she is exercising the right to withhold[34] but, in the view of the authors, this is not correct. The purpose of these provisions is to inform tenants of their rights, recognising that they are unlikely to be aware of what those rights are. A person who is unaware of his or her rights cannot be expected to assert them.

4.20 Any provisions of the lease relating to non-payment or late payment have no effect during the period that the tenant withholds service charges.[35] Once the information is provided, the sums will be payable.[36]

28 *Tingdene Holiday Parks Ltd v Cox and others* [2011] UKUT 310 (LC); [2011] 3 EGLR 30.

29 Commonhold and Leasehold Reform Act 2002 (Commencement No 2 and Savings) (England) Order 2003 SI No 1986 art 2(c) and Sch 2 para 8; Commonhold and Leasehold Reform Act 2002 (Commencement No 2 and Savings) (Wales) Order 2004 SI No 669 art 2(c) and Sch 2 para 8.

30 *Amourgam v Valepark Properties Ltd* [2011] UKUT 261 (LC).

31 By the Service Charges (Summary of Rights and Obligations, and Transitional Provision) (England) Regulations 2007 SI No 1257; Service Charges (Summary of Rights and Obligations, and Transitional Provisions) (Wales) Regulations 2007 SI No 3160; Administration Charges (Summary of Rights and Obligations) (England) Regulations 2007 SI No 1258; and Administration Charges (Summary of Rights and Obligations) (Wales) Regulations 2007 SI No 3162 respectively.

32 See note 31, reg 3 in all cases.

33 LTA 1985 s21B(3) (service charges); CLRA 2002 Sch 11 para 4(3) (administration charges).

34 *Ustimenko v Prescot Management Company Ltd* [2007] EWHC 1853 (QB).

35 LTA 1985 s21B(4) (service charges); CLRA 2002 Sch 11 para 4(4) (administration charges).

36 LTA 1985 s21B(4) (service charges); CLRA 2002 Sch 11 para 4(4) (administration charges).

4.21   There is no provision for a landlord to ask the tribunal to dispense with this requirement, if a tenant is validly withholding service charges the only recourse for the landlord is to serve another demand, this time with an accompanying summary.

4.22   Certain public sector tenancies which are not long leases[37] are excluded from these provisions.[38]

Ground rent: CLRA 2002 s166

4.23   By CLRA 2002 s166, a tenant 'is not liable' to pay ground rent unless the landlord has first given a notice in the prescribed form, which contains information about the dates for payment and possible consequences of non-payment (ie circumstances in which forfeiture for non-payment may occur).[39]

Rights to information about the service charge costs

4.24   It is often difficult to know, when faced with a service charge bill, on what basis it has been calculated. In particular, it is rarely clear what sums have been invoiced to the landlord and what sums have been paid out. Without this information, a tenant is in a poor position to challenge the service charges before a tribunal.[40]

Summary of costs

4.25   A tenant may request in writing that the landlord supply the tenant with a 'summary of relevant costs' for the previous 'accounting period'.[41] Alternatively, a request for a summary of costs may (with

---

37 As defined in LTA 1985 s26.
38 Reg 2 in all cases.
39 Landlord and Tenant (Notice of Rent) (England) Regulations 2004 SI No 3096; and Landlord and Tenant (Notice of Rent) (Wales) Regulations 2005 SI No 1355.
40 See 'Service charges: applicant's failure to comply with LVT's directions – power to dismiss', Akah-Douglas, (2007) 11 L&TRev 189 for a discussion of the problem.
41 LTA 1985 s21.

the consent of the tenant) be made by the secretary of a recognised tenants' association (RTA) that represents the tenant.[42]

4.26   An accounting period is 12 months long.[43] If the service charge accounts are made up in 12-month periods, then the previous accounting period will be the one that last ended before the request was made.[44] If the service charge accounts are made up in periods not of 12 months, then the relevant accounts will be for the 12-month period ending on the date of the request.[45] Note that 'accounting periods' for the purposes of a summary of costs need not be the same as those for consultation under qualifying long-term agreements (see chapter 3 of this book).

4.27   The request may be served on the landlord, an agent named in a rent book or similar document or any person who receives rent on behalf of the landlord.[46] That person must then forward the request to the landlord.[47] If some or all of the costs relate to costs incurred by a superior landlord, then provision is made for the landlord to obtain the information from the superior landlord.[48]

4.28   The landlord must – within the later of one month of the request or six months of the end of the accounting period[49] – provide a summary of costs which contains the following information:

a) whether any monies were received or are to be received as a grant under specified housing improvement statutes;[50]

b) whether the costs relate to external works as of a group repair scheme;[51]

c) costs in respect of which no demand for payment was received by the landlord within the accounting period;[52]

---

42 LTA 1985 s21(2). Note that, subject to increasingly rare exceptions, these provisions do not apply to rents registered under the Rent Act 1977 (s27).

43 LTA 1985 s21(1).

44 LTA 1985 s21(1)(a).

45 LTA 1985 s21(1)(b).

46 LTA 1985 s21(3).

47 LTA 1985 s21(3).

48 LTA 1985 s23.

49 LTA 1985 s21(4); note the possibility of an extension if information is required from a superior landlord: s23(1)(c).

50 LTA 1985 s21(5). It is considered that this is unlikely to be relevant to many cases.

51 LTA 1985 s21(5B). As above, this is unlikely to be relevant to many cases.

52 LTA 1985 s21(5)(a).

d) costs in respect of which a demand for payment was received by the landlord within the accounting period but which were not paid within that period;[53] and

e) costs in respect of which a demand for payment was received and paid by the landlord within the accounting period.[54]

4.29   The summary must then go on to specify the aggregate of any amounts received by the landlord down to the end of the accounting period on account of service charges and still standing to the credit of the tenants of those dwellings at the end of the period (ie surplus money that has not yet been spent on relevant costs).[55]

4.30   If there are more than four dwellings, then a qualified accountant must have certified that the summary is a fair summary complying with the requirements set out above and being sufficiently supported by accounts, receipts and other documents produced to them.[56]

4.31   A qualified accountant is someone who is eligible for appointment as a statutory auditor under Part 42 of the Companies Act 2006,[57] save that they must *not* be:

a) an officer, employee or partner of the landlord or, where the landlord is a company, of an associated company;[58]

b) a partner or employee of any such officer or employee;[59]

c) a managing agent of the landlord for any premises to which any of the costs covered by the summary in question relate or the statement of account relates;[60]

d) an employee or partner of any such agent.[61]

4.32   Where the landlord is a local authority, a new town corporation or a national park authority, then the qualified accountant may be an officer or employee of the landlord and may be a member of the Chartered Institute of Public Finance and Accountancy.[62]

---

53   LTA 1985 s21(5)(b).
54   LTA 1985 s21(5)(c).
55   LTA 1985 s21(5).
56   LTA 1985 s21(6).
57   LTA 1985 s28(2).
58   LTA 1985 s28(4)(b).
59   LTA 1985 s28(4)(c).
60   LTA 1985 s28(4)(d).
61   LTA 1985 s28(4)(e).
62   LTA 1985 s28(6).

Inspection of supporting documents

4.33 Once a summary of relevant costs has been received (even if it has not been demanded under LTA 1987 s21(1)) by a tenant or secretary of an RTA, the recipient may, within six months of receiving the summary, make a request in writing to the landlord to afford them facilities to inspect the accounts, receipts and other supporting documents and to take copies or extracts from them.[63] This applies with equal force both to immediate landlords and superior landlords.[64]

4.34 The facilities for inspection must be made available within one month of the request being made and must be made available for at least two months.[65] No charge may be made for the inspection of documents,[66] though a reasonable charge may be made for the taking of copies or extracts.[67] There is nothing to stop the landlord recovering the cost of making documents available for inspection as part of the service charge bill, provided that the lease would allow them to do so.[68]

Enforcement of rights

4.35 Failure to provide a summary of relevant costs, or access to supporting accounts is a summary offence, punishable by a fine on level 4 of the standard scale.[69] The offence cannot be committed by a local authority, a new town corporation or a national park authority.[70] It is not an abuse of process to prosecute a landlord who fails to provide some of the information in a summary of costs, although a trivial failure may lead the court to impose no penalty.[71] It is not an offence for a landlord to fail to provide a document they do not have.[72]

4.36 A landlord has a defence of reasonable excuse.[73] For example, if there were a binding arbitration clause, it might be reasonable for a

---

63 LTA 1985 s22(2).
64 LTA 1985 s23(2).
65 LTA 1985 s22(4).
66 LTA 1985 s22(5)(a).
67 LTA 1985 s22(5)(b).
68 LTA 1985 s22(6).
69 LTA 1985 s25.
70 LTA 1985 s26.
71 *R v Marylebone Magistrates' Court ex p Westminster City Council* (2000) 32 HLR 266 (QBD).
72 *Taber v Macdonald* (1999) 31 HLR 73.
73 LTA 1985 s25.

landlord to fail fully to comply with a request for supporting accounts where it would be open to the tenant to take any dispute with the landlord to arbitration.[74]

4.37   The rights in LTA 1985 ss21 and 22 may not be enforced by injunction.[75]

4.38   Assignment of the landlord's interest does not affect the exercise of rights under LTA 1985 ss21 and 22.[76]

Insurance

4.39   Tenants who pay service charges in respect of insurance costs possess certain specific rights in respect of information about that insurance, as set out in the Schedule to the LTA 1985. In particular:

a)   they may require the landlord to provide them with a written summary of the insurance in place at the time, including the insured amount, the name of the insurer and the risks insured;[77] and

b)   they may inspect (and copy) the insurance policy and any related accounts.[78]

4.40   Failure on the part of the landlord to comply (subject to a defence of reasonable excuse) with these duties is a criminal offence punishable by a fine.[79] The criminal sanction does not apply to tenants whose landlords are a local authority, a new town corporation or a national park authority.[80] Presumably these provisions cannot also be enforced by way of injunction.[81]

Rights to management information

4.41   The following two provisions are, in the experience of the authors, badly underused by tenants and deserve to be much more widely known and utilised: management audit and appointment of a surveyor.

---

74   *R v Marylebone Magistrates' Court ex p Westminster City Council* (2000) 32 HLR 266 (QBD).

75   *Di Marco v Morshead Mansions Ltd* [2014] EWCA Civ 96.

76   LTA 1985 s24.

77   LTA 1985 Schedule para 2; it is sufficient compliance for the landlord to provide a copy of the policy, para 2(6).

78   LTA 1985 Schedule para.3.

79   LTA 1985 Schedule para 6; see *Riniker v Mattey* [2013] EWHC 1851 (Admin).

80   LTA 1985 Schedule para 9.

81   See *Di Marco v Morshead Mansions Ltd* [2014] EWCA Civ 96.

Management audit

4.42 In general terms, tenants may appoint an auditor to conduct what is called a 'management audit'. [82] The purpose of any audit is to ascertain whether the landlord's obligations to the tenants, including their management obligations, are being discharged effectively and efficiently.[83]

4.43 A management audit must be requested by a minimum number of 'qualifying tenants' – the number depending on the number of dwellings in the 'qualifying premises'. Where there are only two dwellings, either or both tenants may request a management audit.[84] If there are more than two dwellings, at least two-thirds of the tenants must make a request.[85]

4.44 A 'qualifying tenant' is a tenant of a dwelling under a long lease that is not a business lease.[86] Each dwelling may have at most one qualifying tenant.[87] If a dwelling is sub-let on a long lease, the superior tenant is not a qualifying tenant.[88] If a dwelling is leased to more than one person jointly, they are treated as being jointly the qualifying tenant.[89]

4.45 The auditor, who must not be a tenant, must either be a qualified accountant[90] or a qualified surveyor.[91] A qualified surveyor is a fellow or professional associate of the Royal Institution of Chartered Surveyors (RICS) or the Incorporated Society of Valuers and Auctioneers (ISVA)[92] or a member or fellow of the Architects and Surveyors Institute (ASI).[93] An auditor may appoint any person to assist him or her with carrying out the audit.[94]

---

82 Leasehold Reform, Housing and Urban Development Act (LRHUDA) 1993 ss76–84.
83 LRHUDA 1993 s78(1).
84 LRHUDA 1993 s76(2)(a).
85 LRHUDA 1993 s76(2)(b).
86 LRHUDA 1993 s77(1).
87 LRHUDA 1993 s77(3).
88 LRHUDA 1993 s77(4)(a).
89 LRHUDA 1993 s77(4)(b).
90 See para 4.31 above.
91 LRHUDA 1993 s78(4).
92 LRHUDA 1993 s78(5).
93 Collective Enfranchisement and Tenants' Audit (Qualified Surveyors) Regulations 1994 SI No 1263.
94 LRHUDA 1993 s78(6).

4.46   The auditor is entitled to the following information and assistance:[95]

a) a summary of costs;[96]

b) reasonable facilities for inspecting, copying or taking extracts from the accounts, receipts and other documents supporting the summary;

c) reasonable facilities for inspecting, copying or taking extracts from any other document which is reasonably required by the auditor.

The auditor is also entitled to inspect the premises.[97]

4.47   In order to exercise the right to have a management audit, the auditor must give a notice to the landlord, which must be signed by all those tenants who are requesting the audit.[98] The notice must:[99]

a) state the name and address of each tenant;

b) state the name and address of the auditor;

c) identify the documents which the auditor requires to inspect, or copies of which the auditor requires; and

d) if the auditor is proposing to carry out an inspection of the common parts, state a date, which must be between one and two months from the date of giving notice, on which the auditor will be making the inspection.

Such a notice is duly given to a landlord if it is given to a person who receives rent behalf of the landlord and such a person must forward the notice immediately to the landlord.[100]

4.48   The landlord may respond by sending copies of requested documents, or affording facilities for their inspection or copying (as the case may be), or the landlord may give a notice objecting to the supply of documents, giving reasons for the objection.[101] The landlord may also either approve the date for the proposed inspection by the auditor, or propose an alternative date, which must not be later than two months from the date of the notice.[102]

4.49   Where within two months of a notice, the landlord or any other person has failed to comply with any of its requirements,[103] an

---

95 LRHUDA 1993 s79(2).

96 As provided for by LTA 1985 s21, see para 4.25 above.

97 LRHUDA 1993 s79(4).

98 LRHUDA 1993 s80(2).

99 LRHUDA 1993 s80(3).

100 LRHUDA 1993 s80(5).

101 LRHUDA 1993 s81(1).

102 LRHUDA 1993 s81(1)(c).

103 LRHUDA 1993 s81(6).

application may be made to a court for an order requiring compliance. Such an application must be made within four months of the date of the notice.[104]

Appointment of a surveyor

4.50 Housing Act (HA) 1996 s84 empowers an RTA to appoint a surveyor, who must be a qualified surveyor in the same sense as for a management audit.[105] The rights and powers of a surveyor are similar to that of an auditor appointed under the right to a management audit, and are set out in HA 1996 Sch 4.

4.51 The appointment of a surveyor is straightforward and may be done by giving the landlord (or any person who receives rent on the landlord's behalf)[106] notice in writing.[107]

4.52 The surveyor ceases to be appointed if either the association gives the landlord notice to that effect or the association ceases to exist (which presumably encompasses an RTA that ceases to be recognised, even if the association continues).[108]

Other ways of obtaining information

Freedom of Information Act 2000

4.53 Tenants of public authorities may be able to rely on the Freedom of Information Act 2000 to obtain information about the management of their property. This Act is beyond the scope of this work.

Procedural powers of the court

4.54 In the event of a trial in the court, it is very likely that there will be directions for disclosure.[109] The rules of civil disclosure are beyond the scope of this work. One point which is, however, worth noting, is the possibility of obtaining disclosure before proceedings start under Civil Procedure Rules (CPR) 31.16. The requirement that the parties are likely to be parties to subsequent litigation is not limited to

---

104 LRHUDA 1993 s81(7).
105 See para 4.45 above.
106 HA 1996 s84(5).
107 HA 1996 s84(3).
108 HA 1996 s84(4).
109 See generally, CPR Part 31.

litigation in the court and it may be that a judge could be persuaded to order disclosure under these provisions so as to facilitate litigation in the tribunal.

Tribunal procedural powers

4.55   In England, the tribunal has power to order disclosure of documents[110] and may issue a summons to require a person to produce a document.[111] In Wales, the tribunal may, by notice, require a person to produce any document which the tribunal may reasonably require.[112] Subject to a defence of reasonable excuse, non-compliance is an offence.[113]

Pending reforms

4.56   There are some pending reforms which are now unlikely to come into force and which have created considerable confusion.[114]

CLRA 2002 reforms

4.57   By CLRA 2002 s152, the summaries of costs in LTA 1985 s21 were to be replaced with the right to an annual 'statement of account'. This would require a landlord to provide a statement of account, whether or not it is requested by the tenant. It would have to be provided within six months of the end of the accounting period to which it related and, if a landlord were to fail to comply with this obligation, a tenant would be able to withhold paying a relevant part of the service charges until the landlord did comply.[115]

---

110 Tribunal Procedure (First-tier Tribunal) (Property Chamber) Rules 2013 SI No 1169 r18.
111 Tribunal Procedure (First-tier Tribunal) (Property Chamber) Rules 2013 r20.
112 Leasehold Valuation Tribunals (Procedure) (Wales) Regulations 2004 reg 22.
113 CLRA 2002 Sch 12 para 4.
114 See eg *Ustimenko v Prescot Management Co Ltd* [2007] EWHC 1853 (QBD), where Mr Ustimenko was unaware that these provisions were not in force; see also *Wrigley v Landchance Property Management Ltd* [2013] UKUT 376 (LC), in which it appears that neither the leasehold valuation tribunal (LVT) (as it was then) nor the Upper Tribunal were aware that these provisions were not in force.
115 See LTA 1985 s21A.

4.58   The government announced in 2005[116] that they would not be implementing the provisions as set out in CLRA 2002. A consultation paper was published in July 2007[117] proposing a revised set of accounting provisions.

Housing and Regeneration Act 2008 amendments

4.59   Housing and Regeneration Act 2008 Sch 12 contained the response to the consultation paper. It abolished CLRA 2002 s152 and replaced it with a power to make regulations about the information which leaseholders shall be entitled to receive from their freeholders. The power to withhold payment pending provision of the information was to be retained.

4.60   As at February 2013, the government had no plans to bring these provisions into force.[118]

4.61   If these provisions ever come into force, there will should be corresponding changes to increase the powers of any auditor appointed to conduct a management audit.

116 *Accounting for service charge monies: the way forward*, Government News Network, 29 July 2005, reference: 118995P.

117 *Commonhold and Leasehold Reform Act 2002 – a consultation paper on regular statements of account and designated client accounts* 07 HC 04774.

118 See Mark Prisk MP, HC Deb, 6 February 2013, col 255W, expressing the view that non-statutory guidance published by the Institute of Chartered Accountants for England and Wales (ICAEW) 2011 (*Guidance on accounting and reporting in relation to service charge accounts*) covered much the same ground.

CHAPTER 5

Insurance

Key points

- If the lease contains no, or inadequate provision for insuring the property, consider varying the lease.
- If the landlord organises the insurance themselves and recovers the cost of premiums from the tenant, the tenant will be paying for the insurance through their service charges.
- If the tenant organises the insurance but must use an insurer nominated or otherwise selected by their landlord, the tenant may challenge that choice of insurer.
- Tenants may argue that the insurance cover is unsatisfactory in any respect or the premiums are excessive.
- 'Unsatisfactory' insurance includes situations where the level of cover is inadequate or excessive, there is a material misdescription which might lead the insurers to declining liability or the cover is not provided by a reputable company.
- The phrase 'excessive premium' is not defined.
- Landlords often receive commissions from insurers. These are hard to challenge in themselves but can be used as evidence that the landlord is not negotiating at arms length in an open market.

Advice for tenants

- As with most leasehold disputes, access to relevant information is key. Tenants of flats have a number of rights to obtain information which they should make full use of in order to determine what sort of insurance problem they are dealing with.[1]
- Not all insurance disputes will be resolved in the same manner. A variation of the terms of the lease may be more effective than trying to challenge the landlord's chosen insurance company. In the event of any challenge to the quality of the insurance cover, it is vital to obtain 'like-for-like' quotes.
- There are specific and additional rights for tenants of leasehold houses.

1   See chapter 4.

Introduction

5.1   A common area of dispute between tenants and landlords is the provision of insurance cover. This may flow from entirely legitimate differences of view, often from the fact that tenants, having time-limited interests in the property, take a different view of some risks when compared with freeholders.

Disputes and remedies

5.2   There are three ways in which a dispute about insurance can arise, all of which have different remedies. The first is where the lease makes no, or no adequate, provision for insurance. The second is where tenants contribute to the costs of insurance via the service charge. The third is where the tenant (or, more commonly, a management company) is obliged to insure the property with a company nominated by the landlord.

No or inadequate insurance provision

5.3   Some leases make no provision for insurance or do not properly specify who is to insure particular parts of the building. In these circumstances, tenants run the risk of having to pay for serious damage without any insurance protection. This is a clear case for a variation of the leases, as discussed in chapter 7.

Insurance premiums as service charges

5.4   A common situation is for a lease to put the duty to insure on the landlord, who is then permitted to recover the cost of the insurance premiums from the tenants. In such a situation the costs recovered from the tenants are service charges.[2]

5.5   Such payments are subject to the same kinds of challenge as other service charges, a full discussion of which may be found in chapter 1. Three particular points should, however, be noted.

5.6   First, it is common for landlords to argue that, so long as the insurance is placed at arms' length, eg by a broker, then that is sufficient to show that the costs are reasonable within the meaning of

---

2 Landlord and Tenant Act (LTA) 1985 s18.

Landlord and Tenant Act (LTA) 1985 s19.[3] That is not correct. The obligation is to obtain a rate that is 'representative' of the market rate; the 'arms' length' nature of any broker does not, of itself, guarantee that a market rate has been obtained, although it may be useful evidence.[4]

5.7 Second, it is often the case that landlords are paid commissions for selecting particular insurers.[5] The insurance company then recovers the cost of the commission via higher premium payments, which will ultimately be borne by the tenants. A distinction should be drawn between commissions that are, in effect, payments to the landlord for providing a service on behalf of the insurance company, and simple profit-making.[6] The former may be kept by the landlord, but the latter should be credited to the leaseholders. The landlord should not recover more than the net amount of the insurance premium.[7]

5.8 Third, if the lease requires that insurance be taken out in the joint names of the landlord and the tenant, then failure to do so by the landlord may mean that the costs are irrecoverable as a service charge.[8]

Tenant required to insure

5.9 A further possibility is that the tenant is responsible for the insurance. In such situations, the lease almost always requires the use of a particular insurer or one nominated by the landlord.

5.10 Where a tenant of a dwelling[9] is required to insure it with an insurer nominated or approved by the landlord, either party may apply to the court or the tribunal for a determination as to whether:

a) the insurance which is available from the nominated or approved insurer is unsatisfactory in any respect;[10] and/or

---

3 Relying on *Berrycroft Management Co Ltd v Sinclair Gardens Investments (Kensington) Ltd* (1996) 75 P&CR 210 and/or *Havenridge Ltd v Boston Dryers* [1994] 2 EGLR 73; see, by way of example, *Avon Estates (London) Ltd v Sinclair Gardens Investments (Kensington) Ltd* [2013] UKUT 264 (LC).

4 *Avon Estates (London) Ltd v Sinclair Gardens Investments (Kensington) Ltd* [2013] UKUT 264 (LC).

5 *Williams v Southwark LBC* (2001) 33 HLR 224 as an example.

6 *Williams v Southwark LBC* (2001) 33 HLR 224.

7 *Peile v Executors of WAC Maidman* LVT/SC/010/98 (LVT).

8 *Green v 180 Archway Road Management Co Ltd* [2012] UKUT 245 (LC).

9 But not, it would seem, a management company under a tripartite lease.

10 LTA 1985 Schedule para 8(2)(a).

b) the premiums payable in respect of any such insurance are excessive.[11]

5.11 No application may be made in respect of any matter which has been agreed or admitted by the tenant; where there is an arbitration agreement to which the tenant is a party (not necessarily one contained in the lease) which requires the matter to be referred to arbitration; or which has been the subject of a determination by a court or arbitral tribunal.[12] Further, these provisions do not apply to tenants of certain public authorities.[13]

Unsatisfactory in any respect

5.12 'Unsatisfactory in any respect' is not defined in the legislation, but is clearly a widely drafted provision. The following are examples of the most usual complaints.

Level of cover is inadequate or excessive

5.13 This would include situations where the policy fails to deal with a likely risk, or is simply far too cautious. A failure to insure against flood damage if the property were near a river prone to flooding would clearly be an example of inadequate cover. Similarly, while terrorism insurance might be appropriate for properties in larger cities, it may well be seen as excessive in respect of a cottage in an isolated, rural area.[14]

5.14 Tenants should also ensure that the insurance policy provides for the property to be insured up to its re-build value as failure to do so must surely make the insurance 'unsatisfactory in any respect'.

The cover is defective in some other respect

5.15 Examples include a material misdescription of the property in the insurance policy or other error that might lead to the insurers declining liability.[15]

The cover is not provided by a reputable company

5.16 There is a long line of case-law to the effect that when a landlord has a covenant to insure the property, they must do so with an insurer

11 LTA 1985 Schedule para 8(2)(b).
12 LTA 1985 Schedule para 8(3).
13 LTA 1985 Schedule para 9.
14 *Scott and G&O Properties Ltd* LON/00AH/LSL/2004/0078 (LVT).
15 *Re Blocks C, E and G, Cherry Blossom Close, Chequers Way, London, N13* LVT/INS/027/003/00 (LVT).

of repute and good standing.[16] In practice, it should be considered adequate to insure with a firm of national repute.

Excessive premium payments

5.17   Interestingly, while LTA 1985 s19 has been interpreted in a manner which focuses primarily on the reasonableness of the landlord,[17] challenges to the landlord's nominated insurer on the grounds that a premium payment is excessive, focus on the payment from the point of view of the tenant.[18]

Remedies

5.18   If a leasehold valuation tribunal (LVT) finds the insurance arrangements to be unsatisfactory, it may make an order requiring the landlord to nominate an insurer specified in the order, or requiring the landlord to nominate another insurer who will be capable of meeting the requirements listed in the order.[19] Tenants are advised to bring evidence of the insurers they wish to see nominated and their reasons for so wishing.

5.19   Any agreement by the tenant (other than an arbitration agreement) which purports to provide for an alternative method of resolution or determination of insurance issues is void in so far as it would trespass on the rights of either party to make an application under paragraph 8 of the Schedule to the LTA 1985.[20]

Leasehold houses

5.20   Since 28 February 2005 (in England)[21] and 31 May 2005 (in Wales)[22] where a tenant has a long lease[23] of a house[24] and is required by the

---

16   *Tredegar v Harwood* [1929] AC 72; *Bandar Properties v JS Darwen* [1968] 2 All ER 305; 19 P&CR 785; *Havenridge Ltd v Boston Dyers Ltd* [1994] 2 EGLR 73; [1994] 49 EG 111.
17   See para 1.41 above.
18   *Harker v Forcelux Ltd* M/INS/3 (LVT).
19   LTA 1985 Schedule para 8(4).
20   LTA 1985 Schedule para 8(6).
21   Commonhold and Leasehold Reform Act 2002 (Commencement No 5 and Savings and Transitional Provisions) Order 2004 SI No 3056.
22   Commonhold and Leasehold Reform Act 2002 (Commencement No 3 and Saving and Transitional Provision) (Wales) Order 2005 SI No 1353.
23   Commonhold and Leasehold Reform Act (CLRA) 2002 ss76 and 77.
24   As defined in Leasehold Reform Act 1967 Part 1.

lease to insure the house with an insurer nominated or approved by the landlord, the tenant is not required to effect the insurance with the landlord's insurer if the tenant instead ensures that the house is insured under a policy of insurance with an authorised insurer.[25]

5.21   If a tenant chooses to take such a step, there are a number of guarantees which must be contained in the policy of insurance:[26]

a) the policy must protect both the interests of the landlord and the tenant;[27]
b) the policy must cover all the risks which the lease requires to be covered;[28]
c) the amount of cover must not be less than that which the lease requires to be provided by insurance.[29]

5.22   In addition, there is a strict procedure to be followed by any tenant thinking of taking this route.

5.23   The tenant must give the landlord a notice of cover in prescribed form.[30] The notice of cover must be served on the landlord within 14 days of the date on which it took effect or was renewed.[31] In the case of a new landlord, the tenant may be requested to provide a copy of the notice of cover within one month and 14 days of the new landlord acquiring the interest of the previous landlord.[32]

5.24   If the notice of cover is to be posted to the landlord, it must be sent to the address specified by the landlord, either as the address for service of notices or, if that is unknown, the address used for demands for rent. Alternatively, the landlord may nominate an entirely different address in England or Wales.[33] It is strongly recommended that any such notice of cover be sent by recorded delivery.

---

25 CLRA 2002 s164.
26 CLRA 2002 s164(2).
27 CLRA 2002 s164(2)(a).
28 CLRA 2002 s164(2)(b).
29 CLRA 2002 s164(2)(c).
30 Leasehold Houses (Notice of Insurance Cover) (England) Regulations 2004 SI No 3097; or Leasehold Houses (Notice of Insurance Cover) (Wales) Regulations 2005 SI No 1354.
31 CLRA 2002 s164(3).
32 CLRA 2002 s164(4).
33 CLRA 2002 s164(8) and (9).

Other rights

5.25   The following additional rights also exist.

Right to notify insurer of a claim

5.26   Any tenant who pays a service charge in respect of insurance provision is also entitled to report any damage that may be subject of a claim under the insurance policy to the insurers.[34] If the insurance policy imposes a time limit, then this limit will also apply to the right to notify.[35] This does not confer on a tenant the right to make a claim under the policy, or to compel a landlord to do so or to spend any insurance monies received on reinstatement of the property.

Rights to require insurance money to be used to rebuild the property

5.27   There have been reports of situations where a landlord refuses to apply money obtained as a result of a claim under an insurance policy. Such situations are comparatively rare, since a lease with an insurance provision should also contain a covenant to apply the sums received by way of insurance to the rebuilding or repairing of the property. Insurance legislation often exists to overcome this problem, for example, Fire Prevention (Metropolis) Act 1774 provides that certain tenants may claim on their landlord's policy in respect of a fire.[36]

5.28   If a lease does not contain a covenant in the terms suggested above, then it should be varied. This should be done by agreement with the landlord, but failing that an application to the tribunal to vary the lease may be necessary.[37]

5.29   If the policy of insurance is taken out in the names of both the tenant and landlord, they will be entitled to share any insurance payments in the same proportion as their respective interests in the premises. This may provide an alternative means to ensuring tenants are able to put insurance money back into the property.[38]

---

34   LTA 1985 Schedule para 7.
35   LTA 1985 Schedule para 7(2).
36   See also *Mumford Hotels v Wheeler and another* [1964] 1 Ch 117.
37   See chapter 7.
38   *Beacon Carpets v Kirby* [1985] QB 755; [1984] 3 WLR 489; [1984] 2 All ER 726.

5.30   A third possible remedy in this situation is to sue the landlord for breach of covenant. Where a tenant pays a proportion of the premium of an insurance policy in favour of the landlord, the latter is obliged to exercise the rights conferred by the policy to protect the tenant's interest.[39]

---

39   *Vural v Securities* (1990) 60 P&CR 258.

CHAPTER 6

Administration charges

Key points

- An administration charge is one charged by a landlord in association with the cost of granting approvals; considering applications; providing information; failures by tenants to make a payment; or, breaches of covenant.
- Some administration charges are classified as 'variable'. If a sum is specified in the lease or calculated by reference to a formula then it is not 'variable'.
- The tribunal has the power to vary leases where 'fixed' charges are unreasonable. The variation is binding for the future on all parties and any successors to the lease. This remedy cannot be used to challenge sums which have already become payable.
- A tenant may apply to the tribunal for a determination of the payability of an administration.
- 'Variable' administration charges are payable only to the extent the amount is reasonable.
- A tenant has the right to withhold any administration charges until the landlord provides a summary of the rights and obligations of the tenant in relation to those charges.

Advice for tenants

- There are various charges which arise out of the landlord–tenant relationship which may not be service charges. Prior to the Commonhold and Leasehold Reform Act 2002, these charges were largely unregulated. But that Act introduced a new class of 'administration charges' subject to the jurisdiction of the tribunal.
- There are two kinds of administration charges and the remedies available depend on which kind. Variable administration charges must be reasonable. Charges that are not 'variable' need not be reasonable, but the tribunal may vary the lease provisions to remove or ameliorate any unfairness. This is such a difference that it is important to know exactly what kind of administration charge you are dealing with.
- There is a growing trend among landlords to argue that legal costs are administration charges and as a result not service charges and, hence, subject to weaker statutory regulation. Tenants and their advisers must be alert to this argument.

Introduction

6.1 Landlords frequently impose charges on leaseholders that are not service charges, for example, fees for considering applications for consent to sub-let. During the late 1990s, the government expressed concern that some unscrupulous landlords were using these fees both to extort large sums of money from leaseholders and as a basis for threatening forfeiture of the lease.[1] The Commonhold and Leasehold Reform Act (CLRA) 2002 was intended to address these matters by introducing a new regime for the control of 'administration charges'[2] and does so in section 158 and Schedule 11.

What are administration charges?

6.2 The primary definition[3] of 'administration charge' is[4] an amount payable[5] by a tenant[6] of a dwelling[7] as part of (or in addition to) the rent, which is payable directly or indirectly:[8]

a) for or in connection with the grant of approvals under his lease, or applications for such approvals;[9]

---

1 *Leasehold reform: the way forward*, Department of the Environment, Transport and the Regions, 1999.

2 See HC Deb 13 March 2002, vol 381, col 953 et seq.

3 Note that there is power to amend this definition by secondary legislation: CLRA 2002 Sch 11 para 1(4). No such orders have yet been made.

4 Subject to the exclusions in CLRA 2002 Sch 11 para 1(2) concerning registered rents under Rent Act 1977 Part 4.

5 Although the CLRA 2002 does not say that the charge must be payable under the terms of the lease or, possibly, some other contractual relationship, that is plainly a pre-requisite, ie this does not create a free-standing right to charge, see HL Deb 29 January 2001, col 621, col 458 and *Christoforou v Standard Apartments Ltd* [2013] UKUT 586 (LC).

6 As defined in CLRA 2002 Sch 11 para 6.

7 As defined in CLRA 2002 Sch 11 para 6.

8 CLRA 2002 Sch 11 para 1.

9 Such as a charge for considering an application for consent to sub-let: *Holding & Management (Solitaire) Ltd v Norton* [2012] UKUT 1 (LC); *Re Bradmoss Ltd* [2012] UKUT 3 (LC); *Crosspite Ltd v Sachdev* [2012] UKUT 321 (LC); *Freehold Managers (Nominees) Ltd v Piatti* [2012] UKUT 241(LC). Note that the lease need not require that a fee be payable for considering an application to consent, it is sufficient that there is a requirement to obtain the consent of the landlord, who is entitled to make his or her consent conditional upon payment of his or her costs: *Norton; Bradmoss; Crosspite; Freehold Managers.*

b) for or in connection with the provision of information or documents by or on behalf of the landlord or other party to the lease[10] otherwise than as landlord or tenant;[11]

c) in respect of a failure by the tenant to make payment by the due date to the landlord or a person who is party to the lease otherwise than as landlord or tenant;[12]

d) in connection with a breach (or alleged breach) of a covenant or condition.[13]

6.3   Note that these charges are not limited to those levied by landlords and can, in principle, therefore include disputes between leaseholders.[14]

6.4   A charge for a deed of variation is not an administration charge as it is not a charge for the provision of information or documents (and hence falls outside of the CLRA 2002).[15]

6.5   The CLRA 2002 then goes on to identify a sub-set of administration charges, which it labels 'variable administration charges'.[16] These are defined as administration charges which are payable by a tenant and which are neither specified in the lease nor calculated in accordance with a formula specified in the lease.[17] Although the CLRA 2002 does not say so, it seems to have been assumed that it is the *amount* which must not be specified.[18]

---

10   Such as a leaseholder-owned/controlled management company.

11   Such as sales packs and solicitors' inquiries on conveyancing.

12   Presumably this covers interest and late payment fees.

13   Which includes the costs of proceedings to recover a service charge (*Christoforou v Standard Apartments* Ltd [2013] UKUT 586 (LC)) and may well include legal costs and the costs of a Law of Property Act 1925 s146 notice: *Re Forcelux Ltd* LRX/33/2003 and *Havelli v Glass* LRX/22/2005. In *The Moorings (Bournemouth) Ltd v McNeill* [2013] UKUT 243 (LC), penalty charges under a parking scheme were held to be administration charges.

14   *Schmid v (1) Stansfield (2) Bertacco* LON/00AU/LAC/2013/0020.

15   *Mehson Property Co Ltd v Pellegrino* [2009] UKUT 119 (LC).

16   CLRA 2002 Sch 11 para 1(2).

17   CLRA 2002 Sch 11 para 1(2).

18   After all, if there was no *liability* specified then there could be no obligation to pay, see fn 4 and *Holding & Management (Solitaire) Ltd v Norton*. But note that, in *Botterill v Hampstead Garden Suburbs Trust Ltd* LRX/135/2007 (a case on Estate Management Schemes under CLRA 2002 s159, worded in the same manner as CLRA 2002 Sch 11), the Lands Tribunal held that a formula which was $x/y = z$ was a formula which was specified. *Botterill* does not appear to have been cited in any of the other cases mentioned in this paragraph. In the first and second editions of this work, we explain why we believe *Botterill* to be wrongly decided, a view which seems to be shared by the current Deputy President of the Upper Tribunal (Lands Chamber): *Scriven v Calthorpe Estates Ltd* [2013] UKUT 469 (LC).

Rights in respect of all administration charges

6.6 Regardless of whether the administration charge is variable or not, any demand for the payment of the charge must be accompanied by a summary of rights and obligations.[19] The form and content of the summary are prescribed.[20] A tenant may withhold payment of an administration charge which is not accompanied by the prescribed summary (duplicate copies in Welsh and English are required in Wales).[21] Provisions in the lease relating to, for example, interest on late payment, do not apply so long as the prescribed summary has not been provided.[22] Demands for administration charges which are payable under the terms of the lease must also comply with Landlord and Tenant Act (LTA) 1987 ss47 and 48.

6.7 An application may also be made to the tribunal[23] to determine whether an administration charge is payable and, if so, by and to whom it is payable, the amount which is payable, the date at or by which it is payable and the manner in which it is payable.[24] There is no requirement that a landlord has made a formal demand for payment so long as the landlord has indicated that some amount is due.[25] As with the analogous provisions in respect of service charges, there appears to be no restriction on who can bring such an application.[26]

6.8 An application may be made regardless of whether payment has been made or not, although a tenant who disputes the charge is well-advised to ensure that any payment made is clearly made 'under protest'.[27]

---

19 CLRA 2002 Sch 11 para 4(1).
20 CLRA 2002 Sch 11 para 4(2); Administration Charges (Summary of Rights and Obligations) (England) Regulations 2007 SI No 1258; Administration Charges (Summary of Rights and Obligations) (Wales) Regulations 2007 SI No 3162.
21 CLRA 2002 Sch 11 para 4(3).
22 CLRA 2002 Sch 11 para 4(4). See further, the discussion on LTA 1985 s21B at para 4.16, which contains similar provisions.
23 Although the county court has concurrent jurisdiction to determine such matters: CLRA 2002 Sch 11 para 5(2). In practice, it is likely that the county court would simply transfer the case to the tribunal: see generally *Cussens v Realreed Ltd* [2013] EWHC 1229 (QB).
24 CLRA 2002 Sch 11 para 5.
25 *Drewett v Bold* LRX/90/2005.
26 See *Oakfern Properties Ltd v Ruddy* [2006] EWCA Civ 1389; [2007] Ch 335; [2007] 3 WLR 524.
27 CLRA 2002 Sch 11 para 5(2).

6.9   An application may not be made in respect of a matter which:[28]

a) has been agreed or admitted;[29]
b) has been or is to be referred to arbitration pursuant to a post-dispute arbitration agreement to which the tenant is a party;
c) has been the subject of a determination by court; or
d) has been the subject of a determination by an arbitral tribunal pursuant to a post-dispute arbitration agreement.

6.10   Further, it has been held that the tribunal cannot determine how much will eventually be due, ie it can rule on existing demands, but not on total liability.[30] The difficulty for this ruling is that it appears to make the jurisdiction of the tribunal over administration charges for approvals useless. Until an approval is granted, the tenant has no liability to pay and hence (on the authority of *Drewett v Bold*[31]) no way to challenge any proposed fee for the approval. After the approval is signed, the tenant will have, as part of the approval, agreed the sum paid. That agreement takes away the jurisdiction of the tribunal. Clarity is needed here, either by a challenged to the *Drewett v Bold* decision or by amendment to the CLRA 2002.

6.11   The CLRA 2002 also contains anti-avoidance mechanisms to prevent parties from contracting out of these provisions.[32]

Rights in respect of variable administration charges

6.12   A variable administration charge is payable only to the extent that is reasonable.[33] It is for the landlord to demonstrate that the costs are reasonable.[34] This appears to be a broader jurisdiction than under LTA 1985 s19, as it is not limited to whether costs are 'reasonably incurred'. Nonetheless, it is anticipated that much of the case-law on LTA 1985 s19 will be of relevance.[35] In order to ventilate such a dispute, the tenant (or landlord) could apply to the tribunal under CLRA

---

28 CLRA 2002 Sch 11 para 5(4).
29 Payment does not, of itself, amount to an admission: CLRA 2002 Sch 11 para 5(2), (5), but may, when taken with other evidence, be sufficient: *Shersby v Grenehurst Park Residents Co Ltd* [2009] UKUT 241 (LC).
30 *Drewett v Bold* LRX/90/2005.
31 *Drewett v Bold* LRX/90/2005.
32 CLRA 2002 Sch 11 para 6.
33 CLRA 2002 Sch 11 para 2.
34 *Crosspite Ltd v Sachdev* [2012] UKUT 321 (LC).
35 See para 1.41.

2002 Sch 11 para 5 (as discussed above) or issue proceedings in the county court for a declaration.[36]

Rights in respect of non-variable administration charges

6.13 Given the definition of 'variable' administration charges, it stands to reason that there must be some administration charges which are non-variable, ie they are specified in the lease or are calculated in accordance with a formula specified in the lease. In respect of such charges, a leaseholder may apply to the tribunal for an order varying the lease.[37] Such an application may be made in advance of a dispute actually arising.[38]

6.14 The grounds for such an application are that the specified charge is unreasonable or the formula used to calculate the charge is unreasonable.[39] If the grounds are made out then the tribunal may[40] make an order varying the lease in such manner as it thinks fit.[41] This may be in the manner proposed by the applicant[42] or some other form.[43] Alternatively, the tribunal may direct the parties to vary the lease in a specified manner.[44] It appears that the tribunal would effect this variation by directing that a memorandum be endorsed and accompany the lease.[45] Any variation will bind both the parties and successors in title.[46]

6.15 Unlike the situation for variations of a lease under the LTA 1987, an order for varying the lease may not be retrospective and there is no power for the tribunal to order the payment of compensation to any person.

---

36 Although it is likely that the county court would simply transfer the case to the Tribunal: see generally *Cussens v Realreed Ltd* [2013] EWHC 1229 (QB).
37 CLRA 2002 Sch 11 para 3.
38 *Drewett v Bold* LRX/90/2005.
39 CLRA 2002 Sch 11 para 3(1).
40 Ie it has a discretion.
41 CLRA 2002 Sch 11 para 3(3).
42 CLRA 2002 Sch 11 para 3(3)(a).
43 CLRA 2002 Sch 11 para 3(3)(b).
44 CLRA 2002 Sch 11 para 3(4).
45 CLRA 2002 Sch 11 para 3(5).
46 CLRA 2002 Sch 11 para 3(6).

6.16   As yet, there are no authoritative decisions on how this power should be exercised. It seems likely that the existing jurisprudence on lease variations under the LTA 1987 will be relevant.[47]

Areas of potential difficulty

6.17   There is a developing issue in respect of legal costs and whether they are service charges or administration charges.[48] This is important because, in general terms, leaseholders have greater rights in respect of the former.[49]

6.18   Prior to the CLRA 2002, where a landlord had a right to recover legal costs under the terms of the lease it was commonly thought that they were a service charge within the meaning of LTA 1985 s18.[50] Indeed, LTA 1985 s20C[51] is expressly predicated on those costs being a service charge.

6.19   Many landlords now argue that legal costs are an administration charge in that they are levied 'in connection with a breach (or alleged breach) of a covenant or condition in his lease'.[52] There are some tribunal decisions to this effect.[53] In other cases, it has been held that legal costs are both a service charge and an administration charge.[54]

6.20   This is an important issue. Surely it was not the intention of parliament to reduce the protection available to leaseholders in respect of legal costs. To the contrary, the evidence suggests that the introduction of the new category of administration charges in the CLRA 2002 was intended to increase the protection of leaseholders against previously unregulated charges. The question of whether legal costs are administration charges or service charges is of fundamental

---

47 As to which, see chapter 7.

48 See eg HL Debates, 6 March 2013, vol 743, col 1548.

49 There is, for example, no equivalent to LTA 1985 s20 or s20B in respect of administration charges.

50 See eg *Iperion Investments Corp v Broadwalk House Residents Ltd* (1994) 27 HLR 196, CA; *Re Forcelux Ltd* LRX/33/2003.

51 Power of tribunal or court to prevent landlord enforcing a contractual right to costs.

52 CLRA 2002 Sch 11 para 1(1)(d).

53 See, by way of example, *Christoforou v Standard Apartments Ltd* [2013] UKUT 586 (LC) and *Davies v Drayton Park Management Ltd* LON/00AU/ LSC/2008/0164.

54 See *Shersby v Grenehurst Park Residents Co Ltd* CHI/43UF/LVA/2010/0001; although this cannot be right for the reasons given by the Lands Tribunal in *Re Forcelux Ltd* LRX/33/2003.

importance, as there are very different statutory regimes governing each set of charges. What role – if any – is there for LTA 1985 s20C, if legal costs are an administration charge?

Lease variations

Key points

- Any party to a lease may apply to vary a lease. Right to manage companies are treated as a party, but managing agents are not.
- An application may be made if the lease of a flat fails to make satisfactory provision for repair or maintenance of the building; repair or maintenance of the installations; insurance; provision or maintenance of services; recovery of expenditure; or, computation of service charges.
- It is possible to apply to have a number of leases, such as all those relating to a block of flats, to be varied at once. A qualified majority of tenants would be needed in these situations.
- The tribunal may order compensation to be paid to any person suffering loss or disadvantage as a result of the variation. It must refuse to vary a lease where this would result in substantial prejudice to any person.
- The varied lease is binding on third parties and any successors in title.
- It is the duty of the applicant to inform the respondent and anyone else they know or have reason to believe may be affected by the variation. Failure to do so may result in the variation being set aside or the payment of damages to those affected
- Proposed variations should be drafted by a legally qualified person in order to reduce the prospect of delay, re-drafting and amendment.

Advice to tenants

- Often, the most effective way of resolving seemingly intractable disputes is to vary the lease. While the landlord and tenant are always entitled to come to an agreement to this effect, in certain circumstances the tribunal has a power to impose variations on one or more leases. For example, where the lease makes unsatisfactory provision for the apportionment of service charges, or to ensure uniformity across a group of leases. Tenants may be able to use the threat of applying to the tribunal for a variation of the lease as a bargaining chip to persuade a landlord to negotiate a variation.

- It is likely that right to manage (RTM) companies will want to consider lease variations once they have acquired the right to manage.
- Professional advice will almost always be necessary, if only to produce a draft of the proposed variation. The tribunal is unlikely to accept a variation that it fears will cause further difficulties in later years. In addition, the Land Registry may specify requirements for the form of any order varying the lease.

Introduction

7.1   Many leases of flats are defective. For example, the lease may not specify who is to pay for work that needs to be done, or it may allocate service charges in a way that does not add up to 100 per cent of the total cost. These kinds of situation may arise because the lease was poorly drafted or because of changes in the building or estate since the grant of the lease. This chapter explains one remedy open to the parties to such a lease: an application to the tribunal for the variation of a lease or leases.

7.2   This can be done in one of two ways: there is a power to vary a single lease where that lease fails to make satisfactory provision in respect of one or more prescribed matters; and there is also a procedure whereby a qualified majority can apply to vary all the leases in respect of a property.

7.3   These provisions apply only to leases of flats. No analogous power exists for leases of houses. There is only a more limited power to vary insurance provisions in leases of leasehold houses.

Failure to make satisfactory provision: Landlord and Tenant Act 1987 s35

7.4   Any party to a long lease[1] may apply to the tribunal for its variation if the lease fails to make satisfactory provision with respect to one or more specified matters.[2] In general terms, they are:

---

1   As defined in Landlord and Tenant Act (LTA) 1987 s60; additionally, note that business tenancies are excluded, as are any leases which demise three or more flats in the same building: LTA 1987 s35(6).

2   LTA 1987 s35(1).

- repair or maintenance of the building;
- insurance;
- repair or maintenance of installations;
- provision or maintenance of services;
- recovery of expenditure;
- the computation of service charges; and
- other grounds as prescribed by regulations.[3]

Satisfactory provision

7.5   Whether a lease fails to make satisfactory provision is a question for the tribunal to judge in all the circumstances of the case.[4] Those circumstances include the nature of the landlord – eg where the landlord is a lessee-owned company, a lease that fails to make provision for the recovery of management fees may be unsatisfactory, although the same may not be true of a large commercial landlord.[5]

7.6   A lease does not fail to make satisfactory provision simply because it could have been better or more explicitly drafted.[6] Nor is it necessarily unsatisfactory if the problem can be remedied by implying a term.[7] Further, there is no rule that a lease is unsatisfactory simply because not all leaseholders are required to contribute to certain costs, particularly if that is the result of the different contractual bargains.[8]

7.7   In considering whether a lease fails to make satisfactory provision, it must be remembered that the court or tribunal can, as a matter of construction, correct obvious errors even without the need for formal variation or rectification.[9] An error which can be corrected by this approach is not one which would require an application to the tribunal.

Repair or maintenance

7.8   This applies not only to the repair or maintenance of the flat itself and the building in which it is contained, but of any other land or

3   LTA 1987 s35(2).
4   *Gianfrancesco v Haughton* LRX/10/200.
5   *Cleary v Lakeside Developments Ltd* [2011] UKUT 264 (LC).
6   *Gianfrancesco v Haughton* LRX/10/2007.
7   *Gianfrancesco v Haughton* LRX/10/2007.
8   *Cleary v Lakeside Developments Ltd* [2011] UKUT 264 (LC).
9   *East v Pantiles (Plant Hire) Ltd* [1982] 2 EGLR 111, CA; *KPMG LLP v Network Rail Infrastructure Ltd* [2007] EWCA Civ 363; *Campbell v Daejan Properties Ltd* [2012] EWCA Civ 1503.

building which is let to the tenant or over which the tenant also has rights under the lease.[10]

7.9 Thus if the lease fails to provide for repair or maintenance to external garages, recreation areas or communal laundries, an application to vary the lease could be made so as to make the landlord responsible for their upkeep, subject to the recovery of costs through the service charge bill. Further, the absence of a reserve fund which, in turn, hampers major repair or maintenance work could fall within this category.[11]

Insurance

7.10 In the same way, 'insurance' means insurance cover in respect of the flat itself and the building in which it is contained, but also of any other land or building which is let to the tenant or over which the tenant also has rights under the lease.[12]

7.11 The power of the tribunal to vary provisions of a lease concerning insurance is restricted in three specific ways.[13] The tribunal cannot vary a term of the lease which gives the landlord the right to nominate an insurer;[14] nor may the tribunal insert a term that requires the landlord to nominate a list of insurers from which the tenant may select;[15] nor may the lease be varied so that it requires insurance with a particular insurer.[16]

Repair or maintenance of any installations

7.12 This applies to those installations that are reasonably necessary to ensure that occupiers of the flat enjoy a reasonable standard of accommodation.[17]

7.13 This ground includes (but is not limited to) factors relating to the common parts of the building containing the flat, as well as the safety

---

10 LTA 1987 s35(2)(a).
11 The Royal Institution of Chartered Surveyors (RICS) *Service Charge Residential Management Code* (2nd edn) expressly recommends varying a lease to create a reserve fund if one does not already exist: para 9.12.
12 LTA 1987 s35(2)(b).
13 LTA 1987 s38(7); this is in addition to the other restrictions in section 38, see paras 7.36–7.40 below.
14 LTA 1987 s38(7)(a).
15 LTA 1987 s38(7)(b).
16 LTA 1987 s38(7)(c).
17 LTA 1987 s35(2)(c).

and security of the flat, its occupiers and the common parts of that building.[18]

7.14   It is less clear how far 'necessary' extends. Lighting of the common parts and lifts giving access to upper floors in high-rise flats would seem uncontroversial, while provision of cable television is almost certainly not required for the enjoyment of a reasonable standard of accommodation.

Provision or maintenance of services

7.15   The same considerations as above apply to provision or maintenance of services,[19] so that cleaning of the common parts would certainly be included while the delivery of newspapers would not.

The recovery of expenditure for the benefit of another party

7.16   A lease may make unsatisfactory provision for the recovery of expenditure by one party (usually the landlord) from another party or parties (usually the tenants).[20]

7.17   This includes (but is not limited to) a situation where the lease does not provide for the tenant to pay interest or other sums on arrears of service charges.[21]

The computation of a service charge

7.18   A lease fails to make satisfactory provision in respect of service charges if the total service charge recovery is more or less than 100 per cent.[22]

7.19   No variation can be made under this ground to the proportions payable (no matter how unfair they might be) if the lease provides for 100 per cent recovery.[23] Recovery of more than 100 per cent is clearly a basis for a variation.[24]

---

18 LTA 1987 s35(3).
19 LTA 1987 s35(2)(d) and (3).
20 LTA 1987 s35(2)(e).
21 LTA 1987 s35(3A).
22 LTA 1987 s35(2), (3), s35(4); see also *Lardy v Gytenbeek* [2010] UKUT 347 (LC).
23 *Morgan v Fletcher* [2009] UKUT 186 (LC); [2010] 1 P&CR 17.
24 See the discussion in *Campbell v Daejan Properties Ltd* [2012] EWCA Civ 1503; [2013] HLR 6.

Other grounds

7.20 The secretary of state may, by regulation, add other grounds for variation as he or she sees fit.[25] To date, this power has not been exercised.

Applications in response to an LTA 1987 s35 application

7.21 Once an application to vary a lease (the original lease) has been made under LTA 1987 s35,[26] any other party to the lease may apply to the tribunal seeking to vary other leases if an order is made varying the original lease.[27] Such applications are likely to be restricted to landlords since it is unusual for a tenant to be a party to multiple leases from the same landlord.

7.22 The other leases to be varied must share the same landlord as under the original lease, though they need not be leases for flats in the same building.[28]

7.23 The grounds for the application must be the same as the original application, ie all leases to be varied must have the same defect as the original lease.[29] Thus, if a respondent landlord wished to make various additional variations then a fresh application would be needed.

7.24 In addition, it must be in the interests of the person making the additional application (or the other parties to the leases) for all the leases to be varied to the same effect.[30]

Applications with qualified majority support: LTA 1987 s37

7.25 In cases where one lease is defective, it will be very common for most or all the other leases of flats also to be defective. In such a case, an application for variation of some or all of the relevant leases may be

25 LTA 1987 s35(2)(g).
26 As per paras 7.4–7.20 above.
27 LTA 1987 s36.
28 LTA 1987 s36(2), ie such an application could cover multiple blocks on an estate.
29 LTA 1987 s36(3)(a).
30 LTA 1987 s36(3).

made if, as defined below, a sufficient proportion of the parties to the lease agree.[31]

7.26   Such an application may be made by the landlord or any of the tenants under the lease.[32] An application may only be made in respect of two or more leases.[33] All the leases must be made with the same landlord though they need not all be in the same building nor need the leases be in identical terms.[34]

7.27   An application under LTA 1987 s37 is capable of being more flexible than one under sections 35 and 36 because it does not need to be made under one of the grounds that restrict those sections as discussed above,[35] although the restrictions on the kind of variation a tribunal can make to the insurance provisions of a lease will still apply. There is nothing to prevent applications being made under both sections 35 and 37 at the same time and expressed in the alternative.[36]

7.28   An application may only be made if it is supported by a minimum number of parties to the various leases involved.[37] Where there are fewer than nine dwellings, then all, or all but one, of the parties must agree to the proposed variation.[38] Where there are nine or more dwellings, at least 75 per cent of the parties must consent and no more than ten per cent may oppose the application.[39]

7.29   The percentage of those in favour or opposed is as at the date when the application is made to the tribunal. Any consent received or opposition expressed after that date will not be taken into account by the tribunal in deciding whether the percentage threshold was passed.[40]

7.30   Whether a person was opposed to the application when it was issued is an issue that should be determined objectively by the tribunal.[41] It is for the applicant to establish that the required percentage are in favour, but there is no prescribed procedure which an applicant must follow in order to do so.[42]

31 LTA 1987 s37.
32 LTA 1987 s37(4).
33 LTA 1987 s37(1).
34 LTA 1987 s37(2).
35 Under LTA 1987 s35, see paras 7.4–7.20.
36 *Shellpoint Trustees Ltd v Barnett* [2012] UKUT 375 (LC).
37 LTA 1987 s37(5).
38 LTA 1987 s37(5)(a).
39 LTA 1987 s37(5)(b).
40 *Dixon v Wellington Close Management Ltd* [2012] UKUT 95 (LC).
41 *Dixon v Wellington Close Management Ltd* [2012] UKUT 95 (LC).
42 *Dixon v Wellington Close Management Ltd* [2012] UKUT 95 (LC).

7.31   Where someone is a party to more than one lease, they count as more than one party (one for each lease).[43] Joint tenants of a lease count as one party.[44]

7.32   An application may only be made if the object to be achieved by the variation cannot be satisfactorily achieved unless all the leases are varied to the same effect.[45] It follows that the applicant should identify the object or objects sought to be achieved by the variations and lead evidence that will enable the tribunal to make a finding on that point.[46]

7.33   Having identified the object or objects, the tribunal must consider whether they can be achieved without varying all the leases.[47] This is a mixed question of fact and law.[48] The tribunal must decide whether the proposed variation would achieve the identified object and, if so, whether the leases need to be varied to achieve the same.[49] The tribunal must not lose sight of the fact that the jurisdiction is narrow and is not intended to allow a rewriting of the lease merely because that is the will of the majority.[50]

Making a final order

7.34   Regardless of whether the application is made under LTA 1987 s35,[51] s36[52] or s37,[53] if the tribunal is satisfied that the grounds for an application for the variation of a lease have been made out then they may[54] make an order varying the lease, or order the parties to vary the lease themselves.[55] The variation may take effect retrospectively.[56]

---

43 LTA 1987 s37(6).
44 LTA 1987 s37(6).
45 LTA 1987 s37(3).
46 *Shellpoint Trustees Ltd v Barnett* [2012] UKUT 375 (LC).
47 *Shellpoint Trustees Ltd v Barnett* [2012] UKUT 375 (LC).
48 *Shellpoint Trustees Ltd v Barnett* [2012] UKUT 375 (LC).
49 *Shellpoint Trustees Ltd v Barnett* [2012] UKUT 375 (LC).
50 *Shellpoint Trustees Ltd v Barnett* [2012] UKUT 375 (LC).
51 Above, paras 7.4–7.20.
52 Above, paras 7.21–7.24.
53 Above, paras 7.25–7.33.
54 Ie even if the grounds are made out, there is still a discretion to decline to make a variation: *Shellpoint Trustees Ltd v Barnett* [2012] UKUT 375 (LC).
55 LTA 1987 s38(1)–(3), depending on whether the application was made under section 35, 36 or 37.
56 *Brickfield Properties Ltd v Botten* [2013] UKUT 133 (LC).

7.35   If the tribunal makes an order varying the lease, it may make an order providing for one or more parties to the lease to pay compensation to any other party to the lease or any other person.[57] The compensation may be ordered for any loss or disadvantage the payee is likely to suffer as a result of the variation. There are no Lands Tribunal or Upper Tribunal cases on how such compensation should be calculated, or the factors to be considered. It is likely that expert valuation evidence would be required.

7.36   There are certain circumstances in which the tribunal is prohibited from making a variation.[58]

7.37   The first is where the variation would be likely to substantially prejudice the respondent or any other person, and that prejudice cannot be adequately compensated with a payment of money.[59] For example, where the sort of prejudice suffered is not capable of financial compensation.[60]

7.38   When considering the issue of prejudice, it must be remembered that the variation will interfere with the contractual bargain between the parties.[61] For example, a proposed variation which would have permitted the landlord to recover (via the service charge) the costs of enforcing all covenants was regarded as 'quite exceptional' and 'substantially prejudicial' as it would shift the financial risk and liability from landlord to tenant, contrary to the original lease terms.[62]

7.39   In addition, the tribunal must not make an order if it would not be reasonable to do so.[63] Whether it is reasonable to make a variation must be considered as at the date of the hearing before the tribunal.[64] An ongoing enfranchisement claim has been held to be a good reason why it would not be reasonable to grant a variation.[65]

7.40   Further, the power of the tribunal to vary provisions of a lease concerning insurance is restricted in three specific ways:[66] the tribunal may not vary a term of the lease that gives the landlord the right

---

57   LTA 1987 s38(10).
58   LTA 1987 s38. See generally *Thirlaway v Masculet* [2012] UKUT 302 (LC).
59   LTA 1987 s38(6)(a).
60   *Shellpoint Trustees Ltd v Barnett* [2012] UKUT 375 (LC).
61   *Shellpoint Trustees Ltd v Barnett* [2012] UKUT 375 (LC).
62   *Shellpoint Trustees Ltd v Barnett* [2012] UKUT 375 (LC).
63   LTA 1987 s38(6)(b).
64   *Mahwood v Sinclair Gardens Investments (Kensington) Ltd* LRX/59/2007.
65   *Mahwood v Sinclair Gardens Investments (Kensington) Ltd* LRX/59/2007.
66   LTA 1987 s38(7); this is in addition to the other restrictions in section 38, see paras 7.36–7.40.

to nominate an insurer;[67] nor may the tribunal insert a term that requires the landlord to nominate a list of insurers from which the tenant may select;[68] nor may the lease be varied so that it requires insurance with a particular insurer.[69]

7.41 The Upper Tribunal has previously been prepared to assume that the power to make an order varying the lease is wide enough to embrace a variation that requires one party to pay the costs of the variation.[70]

Form of variation and order

7.42 In the case of an application under LTA 1987 s35 or s36, the tribunal is not obliged to accept the variation proposed by the applicant but can make any variation they think fit.[71] Strangely, it seems that no such similar power exists for applications under section 37, such that the tribunal must either accept or reject the variation as drafted.[72]

7.43 The tribunal may, by order, directly vary the lease, or it may direct the parties to carry out the variation.[73] The tribunal may also order that a memorandum of variation should be endorsed on specified documents.[74]

7.44 A variation order may be registered with the Land Registry in the same manner as a deed of variation.[75]

Effect of order

7.45 An order for the variation of a lease is binding on third parties and is not restricted to those who were parties to the lease at the time of the application.[76] In particular, it is binding on any surety who guaranteed the performance (whether by a tenant or landlord) of any

---

67 LTA 1987 s38(7)(a).
68 LTA 1987 s38(7)(b).
69 LTA 1987 s38(7)(c).
70 *Baystone Investments Ltd v Persons* [2010] UKUT 70 (LC).
71 LTA 1987 s38(4).
72 LTA 1987 s38(5), note the absence of the phrase 'or such other variation as the tribunal thinks fit' and compare with section 38(4).
73 LTA 1987 s38(8).
74 LTA 1987 s38(9).
75 Land Registry Practice Guide 27, para 7.4.
76 LTA 1987 s39(1).

obligation under the lease despite the fact that the obligation may be changed by the variation.[77]

7.46   Anyone who should have been notified of the application to the tribunal by the applicant, but who was not notified, may apply to the tribunal for the cancellation or modification of the variation.[78] The tribunal may either accede to their request or order the payment of compensation.[79] If the tribunal cancels or modifies the variation, it may back-date that cancellation or modification so that it takes effect on the date the original variation was ordered, or it may order it to take effect on any later date that it sees fit.[80]

Houses

7.47   The provisions discussed above apply only to leases of flats. No analogous provisions exist for leasehold houses. There is, however, a right for any party to a long lease of a dwelling other than a flat[81] to apply to the tribunal for an order varying their lease on the grounds that the lease fails to make satisfactory provision with respect to any matter relating to the insurance of the house, including (but not limited to) the costs of the insurance.[82] The provisions of LTA 1987 ss36 and 38 apply, with suitable amendments.[83]

7.48   No application may be made in respect of a business tenancy, or if the demised property consists of three or more dwellings.[84] Nor may an application be made by any tenant who holds three or more

---

77 LTA 1987 s39(2).

78 LTA 1987 s39(3). A potential problem arises here. In England, the Tribunal Procedure (First-tier Tribunal) (Property Chamber) Rules 2013 SI No 1169 seems to assume that the tribunal will serve all documents, even on third parties (rule 29). But the Act requires the applicant to serve the relevant parties. Presumably, therefore, the applicant should continue to do so, notwithstanding the change in the procedural rules. Under the old regulations (Leasehold Valuation Tribunals (Procedure) (England) Regulations 2003 SI No 2099) and still in Wales (Leasehold Valuation Tribunals (Procedure) (Wales) Regulations 2004 SI No 681), it is explicitly provided that the applicant must serve third parties.

79 LTA 1987 s39(4).

80 LTA 1987 s39(5).

81 Which excludes a flat: *John Lyons Charity v Haysport Properties Ltd* [1995] EGCS 171.

82 LTA 1987 s40.

83 LTA 1987 s40(2), (3).

84 LTA 1987 s40(4).

leases of dwellings from the same landlord.[85] Where the tenant is a company, this includes leases held by associated companies.[86]

Other remedies

Correcting errors as a matter of construction

7.49 Some errors are so obvious that a court or tribunal will interpret a lease as it was intended, implicitly 'correcting' the error.[87] In such circumstances, there may be no need for a formal application for a variation under the LTA 1987.

7.50 If certainty is desired, but all that is needed is for a court formally to declare that a lease has a particular meaning, a court may (but a tribunal may not) issue a 'declaration' to that effect.

Rectification

7.51 The 'normal' remedy where a contract fails accurately to reflect the intentions of the parties is to bring an action for rectification.[88] This must be done in the court.

Law of Property Act 1925

7.52 Finally, it may be possible to use the Law of Property (LPA) Act 1925 to modify or remove a restrictive covenant in a lease. The Upper Tribunal (Lands Chamber) has power to modify or discharge a restrictive covenant in certain leases.[89] The nature of such an application is beyond the scope of this work.[90]

---

85 LTA 1987 s40(4A)

86 LTA 1987 s40(4B).

87 *East v Pantiles (Plant Hire) Ltd* [1982] 2 EGLR 111, CA; *KPMG LLP v Network Rail Infrastructure Ltd* [2007] EWCA Civ 363; *Campbell v Daejan Properties Ltd* [2012] EWCA Civ 1503; [2013] HLR 6.

88 *Fowler v Fowler* (1859) 4 DeG&J 250.

89 Those within LPA 1925 s84(12).

90 See generally, Megarry & Wade, *The law of real property*, 8th edn, Sweet & Maxwell, 2012, ch 32; Francis, *Restrictive covenants and freehold land*, 4th edn, Jordans, 2013.

CHAPTER 8

Appointment of a manager

Key points

- A common complaint of tenants is that their property has been badly managed. Many service charge disputes have poor property management as their cause. The tribunal has a power to appoint a manager where problems arise.
- There are a number of limits on the right to apply to the tribunal. The most important is that 'resident landlords' who live in the property and manage it themselves are usually exempt from having applications made against them.
- The tribunal regards the appointment of a manager against the wishes of the landlord to be a draconian step and will usually require these preliminary stages to be completed. In exceptional circumstances, the tribunal will be willing to waive compliance.
- A tenant must show that it would be just and convenient in all the circumstances for a manager to be appointed.
- The tenant must also show that the respondent is in breach of a management obligation under the lease; unreasonable service charge demands have been made, are proposed or are likely to be made; unreasonable variable administration charge demands have been made, are proposed or are likely to be made; there have been breaches of the relevant codes of practice or other circumstances exist which make it just and convenient for the order to be made.
- There is no requirement that a professional manager be appointed but tribunal prefers this to be the case.
- The manager is the servant of the tribunal and will manage the property in the best interests of the property, rather than as agent for landlord or tenants. That may result in increased service charge demands, as long-delayed works are carried out.
- The tribunal can give the manager a wide range of powers and is not simply limited to requiring him to administer the obligations in the lease.

Advice for tenants

- Where management of the leasehold property has gone wrong, it may be possible to persuade the tribunal to appoint someone else to take over the management. This is a very flexible power that can be used to address a wide variety of problems. However, a tribunal-appointed manager is a neutral party. The manager will not do the bidding of either the tenants or the landlord, but will manage the property in the best interests of the building itself. It is not unknown for service charge costs to increase significantly once a manager is appointed as works that have been delayed are now carried out. Tenants who wish to have a more 'hands on' role should consider using the 'right to manage' process.
- As far as possible, all tenants, not just those bringing the application, should support the appointment of a manager. Tribunals regard the decision to 'strip the landlord of his right to maintain his own building' as 'Draconian' and not to be invoked lightly.[1] If there are tenants who are not parties to the application, they should be asked to provide letters of support for the proposed manager suggested by the applicants.

Introduction

8.1   Property management is a complex matter. Some landlords choose to manage their properties themselves and, in doing so, fail (whether deliberately or not) to perform properly their obligations under the lease. Some landlords choose to appoint a company or individual that holds itself out as a professional manager, but this is no guarantee of quality. In situations where tenants are dissatisfied with the management of the property, the Landlord and Tenant Act (LTA) 1987 may give the tribunal power to appoint a manager.

8.2   The power to appoint a manager 'for cause' – that is, where there has been specific default on the part of the existing manager – is to be contrasted with the 'right to manage' (RTM) provisions which is as of right: the conduct of the existing management is irrelevant.[2]

8.3   The process to be followed by tenants wishing to have the tribunal appoint a manager begins by giving a notice to the landlord,

---

1   *Re 26 and 28 Birdhurst Rise, South Croydon* LON/00AH/NAM/2003/006.
2   See chapter 9.

setting out the nature of the problem, which the landlord must have an opportunity to remedy. If that does not solve the problem, then an application may be made to the tribunal for the appointment of a manager. Provision is also made for dispensing with service of the notice in appropriate cases.

8.4   The grounds on which a tribunal may appoint a manager are set out in the Landlord and Tenant Act 1987. If one or more of the statutory grounds is made out, the tribunal is empowered to appoint a manager on such terms as it thinks fit. The manager is not limited to carrying out the functions of the landlord under the lease and they may be given power over property that was not part of the premises being managed before the appointment.

Venue for applying to appoint a manager

8.5   The High Court has always had power to appoint a receiver or manager over property whenever it was just and convenient to do so.[3] It has, however, been held that if it is possible to apply to the tribunal, then that option should be taken, rather than applying to the High Court.[4]

Conditions for appointment

8.6   When considering whether or not to appoint a manager, the tribunal must go through a four-stage process:[5]

a) it must be satisfied that the applicants are entitled to apply to have a manager appointed and that the property is one in respect of which a manager may be appointed;

b) it must consider whether the statutory criteria for the appointment of a manager are met and whether or not to exercise its discretionary power to appoint a manager in those circumstances;

c) it must identify the scope of the property over which the manager is to be appointed;

d) it must determine what functions to confer upon the manager.

---

3 See now, Senior Courts Act 1981 s37.

4 LTA 1987 s21(6); *Stylli and others v Haberton Properties Ltd* [2002] EWHC 394 (Ch); *Di Marco v Morshead Mansions Ltd* [2013] EWHC 1068 (Ch) (not affected by the appeal [2014] EWCA Civ 96).

5 *Cawsand Fort Management Company Ltd v Stafford and others* [2007] EWCA Civ 118.

These are addressed in turn.

Entitlement to apply

8.7   This involves consideration of two questions: Is the application being made by a qualifying tenant in respect of a qualifying property? And, has the relevant notice been served or dispensed with?

Qualifying conditions

8.8   Any tenant of a flat contained in the premises may apply for the appointment of a manager.[6] Where there are joint tenants, any one or more of those tenants may make the application.[7] Tenants of two or more flats may make joint applications[8] and applications may be made in respect of two or more premises.[9]

8.9   This general rule is subject to certain exceptions.[10] No application may be made where the landlord is an exempt landlord[11] or against the Welsh Ministers in their new towns residuary capacity.[12] Subject to limited re-inclusion provisions, properties with a resident landlord are also excluded.[13] Tenants under business tenancies are not entitled to apply.[14] No application can be made in respect of any premises included within the functional land of a charity.[15] Crown properties are, however, included.[16]

Statutory notice

8.10   The process starts with the service of a preliminary notice by the tenant (LTA 1987 s22). The notice must be served on the landlord[17] and any other person who owes management obligations to the tenant

---

6   LTA 1987 s21(1).
7   LTA 1987 s21(5).
8   LTA 1987 s21(4)(a).
9   LTA 1987 s21(4)(b).
10   Set out in LTA 1987 s21(3).
11   In general terms, public authorities: ss58, 60.
12   LTA 1987 s21(3).
13   See ss58, 60; but see also LTA 1987 s21(3A), which overrides the resident landlord condition in certain circumstances.
14   LTA 1987 s21(7).
15   LTA 1987 s21(3)(b); s60.
16   Commonhold and Leasehold Reform Act (CLRA) 2002 s172(1)(b).
17   See LTA 1987 s22(1)(i); the landlord must then serve his mortgage company: LTA 1987 s22(4).

under the terms of the lease (eg a management company under a tripartite lease).[18] It may be sent by post.[19]

8.11   The notice must:[20]

a) specify the tenant's name; the address of the flat; and an address in England or Wales at which notices may be served on the tenant;

b) state that the tenant intends to apply to the tribunal for the appointment of a manager but that no application will be made if the matters are remedied within a reasonable period (see d) below), insofar as they are capable of remedy;

c) specify the grounds (under LTA 1987 s24, see below) on which the Tribunal would be asked to make an order and the matters (ie allegations and facts) which will be relied upon by the tenant for the purpose of proving the grounds; and

d) where the matters are capable of remedy, specify a reasonable period within which steps should be taken to so remedy them.[21]

8.12   If it is not practicable to serve a notice on any person, the tribunal may dispense with service.[22] Tenants should not rely on the tribunal granting dispensation as a matter of course and will be expected to produce evidence of the impracticability of serving the notice. Evidence that the Post Office were unable to deliver the documents should be sufficient. If dispensation is granted, the tribunal may direct that other notices are served or other steps (such as placing an advert in a local newspaper) are taken.

Conditions for appointment and exercise of discretion

8.13   If the preliminary notice specified a date for remedy, then, once the date has passed, the tenant may apply to the tribunal for the appointment of a manager.[23] If no date was specified (because the breaches were not capable of remedy) then the application can be made at any time.[24] If the tribunal dispensed with service of the notice, then the

18 See LTA 1987 s22(1)(ii).

19 See LTA 1987 s54(1).

20 See LTA 1987 s22(2). The Secretary of State may, in addition, prescribe further information to be included, but has not yet done so.

21 Failure to give a reasonable period of time does not necessarily invalidate the application: LTA 1987 s24(7). See also *Howard v Midrome Ltd* [1991] 1 EGLR 58, for a particularly generous approach to the contents of a LTA 1987 s24 notice.

22 See LTA 1987 s22(3).

23 LTA 1987 s23(1)(a)(i).

24 LTA 1987 s23(1)(a)(ii).

dispensation order should have made provision for when an application could be made.[25]

8.14　In any event, the tribunal is entitled to proceed with the application if it thinks fit, even if the notice fails to comply with any of the requirements set out above or (in the view of the tribunal) the period specified in the notice is not a reasonable period.[26]

8.15　The tribunal may only make an order if certain conditions are satisfied:[27]

a) it is just and convenient in all the circumstances to make an order and:
   i) a relevant person[28] is in breach of a management obligation owed by him or her to the tenant under the lease (or would be in breach but for the fact that it was not reasonably practicable to give notice of the breach, eg an absentee landlord); or
   ii) unreasonable service charges have been demanded or are proposed or likely to be so demanded; or
   iii) unreasonable variable administration charges have been demanded or are proposed or likely to be so demanded; or
   iv) a relevant person has failed to comply with the provisions of a prescribed code of practice[29]; or
b) other circumstances make it just and convenient to make an order.

Breach of an obligation

8.16　Where the tribunal is satisfied that a relevant person is in breach of an obligation owed to the tenant under the terms of their lease which relates to the management of the premises or, if the breach would only arise if the relevant person had notice of the defect, but it has not been reasonably practicable for the tenant to give the appropriate notice, then this ground is made out.[30] While there is no definition of

---

25　LTA 1987 s23(1)(b); if no direction was made, then it seems that the application could be made immediately.

26　LTA 1987 s24(7).

27　See LTA 1987 s24(2).

28　A person on whom the LTA 1987 s22 notice was or could have been served: LTA 1987 s24(2ZA).

29　Approved under Leasehold Reform, Housing and Urban Development Act 1993 s87.

30　LTA 1987 s24(2)(a)(i).

'management' for these purposes, it includes matters relating to the repair, maintenance, improvement or insurance of the premises.[31]

8.17   The tribunal has previously held that the question of whether or not there is a breach of an obligation must be assessed at the date of the application being issued, rather than the date of the hearing.[32] It is not obvious that this is correct. There is nothing in the wording of LTA 1987 s24 to indicate that the assessment should not be conducted by the tribunal on the evidence as it currently stands. If the matter is not to be assessed as at the date of the hearing, why should it be assessed at the date of the application and not the service of the preliminary notice?

Demanding unreasonable service charges

8.18   Where the tribunal is satisfied that unreasonable service charges have been demanded, proposed or are likely to be demanded, a ground is made out.[33]

8.19   Three particular circumstances are set out in the act in which a service charge shall be taken as unreasonable, namely:[34]

a) if the amount is unreasonable having regard to the items for which it is payable;

b) if the items for which it is payable are of an unnecessarily high standard; or

c) if the items for which it is payable are of an insufficient standard with the result that additional service charges are or may be incurred.

8.20   This list is of course not exhaustive and there may be other reasons why a service charge is unreasonable. While there is a degree of overlap with the statutory limitations on service charges under LTA 1985 ss19 and 27,[35] it is not necessary to have secured a determination under these provisions before this ground can be made out (although, in practice, such a determination would provide highly compelling evidence).

---

31 LTA 1987 s24(11).
32 *Petrou v Metropolitan Properties Company Ltd* LVT/AOM/014/013/98 (LVT).
33 LTA 1987 s24(2)(ab).
34 LTA 1987 s24(2A).
35 See chapter 1.

Demanding unreasonable administration charges

8.21 Where the tribunal is satisfied that unreasonable variable administration charges[36] have been demanded, proposed or are likely to be demanded, this ground is made out.[37]

8.22 There is no guidance as to what would constitute an unreasonable administration charge for these purposes. Presumably the tribunal should adopt a similar approach to that adopted for service charges (see above).

Failure to comply with the relevant code of practice

8.23 The secretary of state (and in Wales, the Welsh Assembly) has the power to approve codes of practice for property management.[38] The approved codes of practice are:

a) in England:[39]
   i) Royal Institution of Chartered Surveyors (RICS) Service Charge Residential Management Code;[40]
   ii) Association of Retirement Housing Managers (AHRM) Code of Practice for Private Retirement Housing;[41] and
   iii) RICS Rent Only Residential Management Code.[42]

b) in Wales:
   i) AHRM Code of Practice for Private Retirement Housing (Wales);[43] and
   ii) RICS Rent Only Residential Management Code.[44]

8.24 While in the past it was unlikely for an application for the appointment of a manager to succeed solely on the basis that there had been a

36 CLRA 2002 Sch 11 para 1; see chapter 6.
37 LTA 1987 s24(2)(aba).
38 Leasehold Reform, Housing and Urban Development Act 1993 s87.
39 At the time of publication, new versions of both codes had recently concluded public consultation schemes and were awaiting approval by the secretary of state.
40 Approval of Code of Management Practice (Residential Management) (Service Charges) (England) Order 2009 SI No 512.
41 Approval of Code of Management Practice (Private Retirement Housing) (England) Order 2005 SI No 3307.
42 Approval of Codes of Management Practice (Residential Property) (England) Order 2004 SI No 1802.
43 Approval of Code of Practice (Private Retirement Housing) (Wales) Order 2007 SI No 578.
44 Approval of Codes of Management Practice (Residential Property) (Wales) Order 2006 SI No 178.

breach of a code of practice, the surveyor members of tribunal appear to be taking any failure increasingly seriously. Advisers should study the relevant codes carefully, and clearly set out any alleged failure.

Just and convenient

8.25   Most applications that fail do so because they fail to meet the 'just and convenient' test. Whether it is just and convenient to appoint a manager will vary from case to case and no absolute rules can exist. However, in general terms, the tribunal is likely to be influenced by the following factors:

a) the seriousness of any alleged deficiencies in the management;
b) the effect of those deficiencies on the tenants;
c) the duration of the deficiencies;
d) the response of the landlord to the preliminary notice;
e) the level of support for the application amongst the leaseholders;
f) the conduct of the parties in the proceedings before the tribunal;
g) the respective interests of the parties – long leaseholders with many years to run are likely to have a more significant financial interest in the property than the freeholder;
h) the suitability of the proposed manager;
i) the availability of other remedies;
j) whether the landlord supports the application.

8.26   Although not set out in the LTA 1987, it is worth noting that, as a matter of practice:

a) the tribunal will usually appoint an individual, rather than a firm;
b) the individual should attend the hearing and:
   i)   provide a CV or other evidence of his experience;
   ii) demonstrate familiarity with service charge law and practice;
   iii) have adequate professional indemnity insurance;
   iv) produce a report and draft budget showing management plans for the coming year;
c) the tribunal is less likely to appoint a non-professional managing agent.

Interim or final appointment?

8.27 The tribunal may appoint the manager on either an interim or final basis.[45] Interim appointments tend to be appropriate where there is some particularly urgent matter which requires immediate attention.[46]

Scope of property to be managed

8.28 While there must be a causal link or nexus between the functions to be conferred and the premises in question, the manager is not limited to only dealing with the building(s) containing the demised flats, but can, for example, be authorised to carry out works over adjoining lands over which the lessees enjoy easements.[47] The property covered by the order can be more or less extensive than that sought in the application.[48]

Functions to be conferred

8.29 The tribunal may appoint a manager to carry out such functions in connection with the management of the premises; such functions of a receiver; or, both as it thinks fit.[49] 'Management' is to be given a wide interpretation.[50] It is defined (LTA 1987 s24(11)) as *including* 'the repair, maintenance, improvement or insurance' of the premises. The management order may also include such 'incidentals or ancillary matters' as the tribunal thinks fit.[51]

---

45 LTA 1987 s24(1).

46 *Hart and others v Emelkirk Ltd* [1983] 1 WLR 1289; *Daiches v Bluelake Investments Ltd* (1985) 17 HLR 543; eg *Bell St Partnership v CEMI Ltd* LON/00BK/ LAM/2012/0013.

47 *Cawsand Fort Management Co Ltd v Stafford* [2007] EWCA Civ 1187; [2008] 1 WLR 371; see also *Schilling v Canary Riverside* LRX/41/2007, for an example of the 'causal link' in practice. It would follow that a manager can be appointed over commercial parts in a mixed-use building, or over rent-charge functions in respect of freehold properties on a mixed freehold/leasehold estate.

48 LTA 1987 s24(4).

49 LTA 1987 s24(1); note that it cannot appoint a receiver, merely someone with the functions of a receiver: *PC Residents (Finchley Road) Ltd v Abiola and others* [2013] UKUT 165 (LC).

50 *Maunder Taylor v Blaquiere* [2002] EWCA Civ 1633; [2003] 1 WLR 379.

51 LTA 1987 s24(4).

8.30   In particular, the management order may provide for:[52]

a) rights and liabilities under contracts to be transferred to the manager;

b) the manager to bring claims in contract or tort, whether accruing before or after the manager's appointment (eg to allow the manager to sue for arrears of service charges that pre-date his or her appointment, if the tribunal so orders);

c) the manager's fees to be paid by any relevant person or the tenants;

d) the manager's functions to be exercised for a specific period of time or without limit.

8.31   The purpose of any order is to create a coherent scheme of management and not merely ensure that the efficient management of the landlord's obligations.[53] The tribunal is not limited merely to requiring the manager to apply the terms of the lease.[54] Indeed, it may be preferable to create a bespoke management order that confers different powers from those under the lease (eg to provide for payment of service charges on account).

8.32   The tribunal may confer rights and impose obligations under the terms of the management order, thus, where an order provides for the payment of the manager's fees by the leaseholders, it is immaterial that the lease would not allow such fees to be charged.[55]

8.33   An order appointing a manager is capable of being registered at the land registry.[56] It is good practice for the tribunal to direct that this be done, so as to ensure that there can be no doubt about the order binding successors in title.

8.34   If an order is made, the tribunal may attach any conditions that it thinks fit to the order. In particular, it may suspend the operation of the order on terms.[57]

---

52   See LTA 1987 s24(5).

53   *Blaquiere,* approved in *Cawsand Fort Management Co Ltd v Stafford* [2007] EWCA Civ 1187.

54   *Maunder Taylor v Blaquiere* [2002] EWCA Civ 1633; [2003] 1 WLR 379.

55   *Maunder Taylor v Joshi* LRX/107/2005.

56   LTA 1987 s24(8).

57   LTA 1987 s24(6).

Role and position of the manager

8.35 A manager appointed by the tribunal is not appointed to favour the tenants, nor to carry out the functions of the landlord under the lease. The manager is appointed to oversee a scheme of management and acts independently of the parties, as a servant of the tribunal.[58]

8.36 This has a number of important consequences.

a) The tenants cannot hold previous failings of the landlord against the manager and, for example, cannot raise a set-off in respect of breaches of covenant by the landlord against service charge demands made by the manager.[59]

b) Because the role of the tribunal is to create an effective scheme of management, rather than simply require the manager to discharge the landlord's obligations under the lease, the manager may be given power over property owned by the landlord, but which is not part of any of the flats demised to the tenants.[60]

c) Because the powers of the manager are derived from the order appointing him or her, the order can be worded so as to allow the manager to recover service charges or fees which are not included in the lease and – in effect – to remedy any defects in the drafting.[61]

Remuneration of the manager

8.37 The tribunal has power to provide for remuneration to be paid either by the landlord or by the tenant or to be shared. [62] The starting point should be that the landlord will pay the costs of the manager (including disbursements and the costs of attending any tribunal hearings) which are not recoverable from the tenants under their leases.[63] The terms of the appointment of the manager should make clear who is to pay the manager and what the manager's fees are to be.[64]

---

58 *Maunder Taylor v Blaquiere* [2002] EWCA Civ 1633; [2003] 1 WLR 379; [2003] 1 EGLR 52.

59 *Maunder Taylor v Blaquiere* [2002] EWCA Civ 1633; [2003] 1 WLR 379; [2003] 1 EGLR 52.

60 *Cawsand Fort Management Company Ltd v Stafford and others* [2007] EWCA Civ 1187; [2007] 48 EG 145.

61 *Maunder Taylor v Joshi* LRX/107/2005 (Lands Tribunal).

62 LTA 1987 s24(5)(c).

63 *Re: Morshead Mansions* LRX/49/2002 (Lands Tribunal).

64 *Maunder Taylor v Joshi* LRX/107/2005 (Lands Tribunal).

8.38   If the order appointing the manager merely refers to 'reasonable' fees then, in the event of a dispute, any party may apply to the tribunal for a direction as to what level of fees may be recovered.[65]

8.39   The manager is entitled to apply to the tribunal for directions in respect of any matter contained in his management order.[66] Ordinarily a direction should take the form of an order, requiring the manager to do (or not to do) some specific act and should not be worded as a declaration.[67] A direction cannot be used to vary the terms of the original appointment,[68] although the tribunal does have the power to clarify the meaning of an order, which may serve the same purpose. The tribunal retains jurisdiction to issue directions to the manager about matters arising during this management period, even if the management order has expired.[69]

Variation or discharge

8.40   Any interested party may apply to vary or discharge a management order,[70] but no such order may be made unless the tribunal is satisfied that the variation or discharge would not result in the recurrence of the problems which led to the appointment of the manager and it is just and convenient in all the circumstances to vary or discharge the order.[71]

8.41   If the order has been registered with the Land Registry, the tribunal is empowered to direct that the order be cancelled. [72]

8.42   The manager is entitled to apply to vary or discharge any order and may wish to do so in order to resign.[73]

8.43   An order will not be discharged merely because of some subsequent development that means that the premises are no longer

---

65   *Maunder Taylor v Joshi* LRX/107/2005 (Lands Tribunal).
66   See LTA 1987 s24(4).
67   *Re: Morshead Mansions* LRX/49/200.
68   *Re: Morshead Mansions* LRX/49/200.
69   *Re Romney Court:* LON/00AN/209/011; directions given in respect of litigation which was ongoing after the expiry of the management order.
70   See LTA 1987 s24(9).
71   See LTA 1987 s24(9A). The power to vary or discharge does not require the tribunal to reconsider all the grounds in LTA 1987 s24(2): *Orchard Court Residents' Association v St Anthony's Homes* [2003] EWCA Civ 1049; [2003] 2 EGLR 28.
72   LTA 1985 s24(9).
73   *Re: Morshead Mansions* LRX/49/2002; *Denning v Beamsafe Ltd and others* BIR/00CS/LVM/2006/001 (LVT).

premises in respect of which an application for the appointment of a manager could be made because there is now a resident or exempt landlord, or the premises are now within the functional land of a charity.[74]

8.44 The power to vary includes a power to extend an existing order; there are no express criteria for extending the duration of an existing order and it is not necessary for the tribunal again to make findings of fact about the default of the landlord or the landlord's managing agents.[75] Any extension of the original order must, however, be made before the order expires.[76] It has been suggested by the Court of Appeal that it is preferable to apply to vary an order that is said to be too extensive in scope, rather than appealing it.[77]

Pending reforms

8.45 The CLRA 2002[78] contains provisions which would allow the tribunal to appoint a manager[79] where the landlord has failed to comply with the requirements to hold service charge funds in a designated trust account.[80] As is explained in chapter 2, the provisions relating to trust accounts are unlikely to come into force, with the result that this extension of the power to appoint a manager is also unlikely to come into force.

Where there is an RTM company

8.46 If an RTM company[81] is exercising the right to manage, and an application is made for the appointment of a manager, the procedure outlined above applies with some variations:[82]

74 LTA 1985 s24(10).
75 *Orchard Court Residents Association v St Anthony Homes Ltd* [2003] EWCA Civ 1049; [2003] 2 EGLR 28.
76 *Eaglesham Properties Ltd v Jeffrey* [2013] UKUT 157 (LC).
77 *Cawsand Fort Management Company v Stafford* [2007] EWCA Civ 1187; it is not clear that this is right. It would, surely, be an abuse of process to apply to vary an order made after a contested hearing at which the arguments which underpin the variation application were rejected by the tribunal.
78 LTA 1987 Sch 10 para 14.
79 LTA 1987 s24(2)(abb).
80 LTA 1987 ss42–42A.
81 See chapter 9.
82 CLRA 2002 Sch 7 para 8.

a) references to the landlord are to the RTM company;
b) the landlord is deemed to be a tenant of a flat;
c) the exception for exempt or resident landlords does not apply;
d) the breach of an obligation by the RTM company is a ground for the appointment of a manager;
e) it is just and convenient to appoint a manager if the RTM company no longer wishes to exercise the right to manage;
f) the management order may make provision about contracts to which the RTM company is a party and the prosecution of claims in respect of causes of action, whether tortious or contractual, accruing before or after the right to manage ceases to be exercisable.

Right to manage

continued

Key points

- The Commonhold and Leasehold Reform Act 2002 (CLRA 2002) created a 'no fault' right to manage. Leaseholders can now establish a Right to Manage company (RTM). This is not a simple procedure and legal professionals should be consulted.
- The first step is to establish an RTM company, which all 'qualifying tenants' are entitled to join.
- All qualifying tenants must be invited to join the company and at least half must be members. After this a notice of the company's intention to take control of the management of the property must be served on the landlord and tenants.
- At this stage anyone objecting may serve a counter, alleging for example that the RTM company was not validly formed. The tribunal may then be required to adjudicate between the parties.
- If the disputes are resolved in the RTM company's favour, it will acquire the right to manage the property.
- The right to manage does not apply to all properties and cannot be established against all landlords. Most local authority landlords, for example, are exempt.
- Those who establish the company are usually liable for the costs associated with the process, including the landlords costs.
- In addition, an RTM company would place tenants in the position of having to collect service charges from each other. This may mean that friendships are strained. There may be a tension between the duties of the RTM company and its directors, and the desires of friends and other tenants.

Advice to tenants

- In most cases, a majority of leaseholders have a right to take over the management of their building using a Right to Manage (RTM) company. The establishment of an RTM company is not something to be undertaken lightly and before attempting to do so, tenants should understand what they will be taking on as well as being very clear about what they want to achieve.

continued

- There are two distinct advantages of using an RTM company over having a manager appointed 'for cause' by the tribunal.[1] First, it allows tenants much greater control of their property. Second, there is no need to prove fault by the landlord, making it a much more certain and potentially easier process. Even where a landlord has not managed the property badly, tenants may prefer to make the management decisions themselves rather than leaving them to a landlord, who may have little stake in the property.
- There are, however, potential problems involved in creating an RTM company, which should carefully be considered. For example, depending on the size and complexity of the property, the process may be costly and most of that cost will be borne by the promoters of the company. The RTM company will also take over many of the duties and responsibilities of the landlord.
- The most difficult aspect of running an RTM company is that in order to pay for management the company will have to collect service charges from tenants. This could place directors in conflict with their friends and neighbours if disputes about service charge demands arise. There will inevitably be a tension between the duties of the RTM company to ensure adequate and prompt repairs and maintenance, and the desires of the tenants to keep costs down.
- There is also a difficulty with continuity of management, especially where there are a relatively small number of members of the RTM company. The moment a tenant sells their flat, they cease to be a member of the company. This means that even if the RTM starts with an enthusiastic group prepared to run it well, that group will change over the years and the RTM may run into difficulties.
- Independent professional advice will almost always be necessary. It is almost inevitable that the RTM company will need to employ lawyers and accountants in order to meet its legal obligations.
- The RTM company represents a considerable investment in terms of time and energy on the part of the tenants, and the benefits may not be entirely obvious. If the tenants' objectives can be achieved without establishing an RTM company, it may well preferable to do so.

---

1 See chapter 8.

Introduction

9.1 By chapter 1 of Part 2 of the Commonhold and Leasehold Reform Act (CLRA) 2002, qualifying long leaseholders of flats are entitled to establish and join a 'Right to Manage' company ('RTM company') through which they may take over management of their building. In general terms, so long as the building qualifies and the correct notices are served, the leaseholders are entitled to acquire the RTM without more (ie there is no need to show any default on the part of the landlord/ manager). It has proved quite a popular right, with just over 4,300 active companies with 'RTM' in their name registered at Companies House.

About the RTM company

9.2 An RTM company is a private company limited by guarantee whose articles of association state that its object, or one of its objects, is the acquisition of the right to manage the premises.[2]

9.3 A company is not an RTM company if:

a) it is a commonhold association;[3]
b) there is another RTM company in relation to the premises or part of the premises;[4] or
c) the freehold of the property is transferred to the RTM company.[5]

9.4 All qualifying tenants are entitled to be members of the RTM company and, from the date on which it acquires the right to manage, so may any landlords.[6] The form and content of the articles of association are prescribed,[7] and any provision of the articles that is inconsistent with the prescribed form is of no effect.[8] One practical effect

---

2 CLRA 2002 s73(2). So long as these conditions are met, then the company will be an RTM company, even if there are other defects, such as an apparent failure to adopt the prescribed articles of association: *Fairhold Mercury Ltd v HQ (Block 1) Action Management Co Ltd* [2013] UKUT 487 (LC).

3 CLRA 2002 s73(3).

4 CLRA 2002 s73(4).

5 CLRA 2002 s73(5).

6 CLRA 2002 s74.

7 CLRA 2002 s74(2); RTM Companies (Model Articles) (England) Regulations 2009 SI No 2767; RTM Companies (Model Articles) (Wales) Regulations 2011 SI No 2680.

8 CLRA 2002 s74(5), with the result that the company is deemed to have the prescribed articles even if, in fact, it has adopted some other form of articles: *Fairhold Mercury Ltd v HQ (Block 1) Action Management Co Ltd* [2013] UKUT 487 (LC).

of this is that the company must have a name ending in 'RTM Company Ltd'.[9]

9.5   One RTM company can, in principle, acquire the management functions over more than one block of flats, so long as each block meets the qualifying conditions.[10]

Qualification criteria

9.6   It is not all buildings and leases which come within the scope of the right to manage. In each case, there are detailed qualifying conditions.

Qualifying buildings

9.7   The right to manage may only be claimed in respect of premises that consist of:

a) a self-contained building or part of a building, with or without appurtenant property;

b) containing two or more flats held by qualifying tenants;

c) where the total number of flats held by such tenants is not less than two-thirds of the total number of flats contained in the premises.[11]

Self-contained building

9.8   A self-contained building is one that is 'structurally detached'.[12] This does not require that the building be physically separate and unconnected to any other building.[13] Rather, it is a question of fact and degree whether any particular attachment is structural in nature.[14]

---

9   RTM Companies (Model Articles) (England) Regulations 2009 SI No 2767; RTM Companies (Model Articles) (Wales) Regulations 2011 SI No 2680.

10 *Ninety Broomfield Road RTM Co Ltd v Triplerose and other cases* [2013] UKUT 606.

11 CLRA 2002 s72(1).

12 CLRA 2002 s72(2).

13 Contrary to the suggestion in the first two editions of this work, relying on *Parsons v Gage* [1974] 1 WLR 435.

14 *No 1 Deansgate (Residential) Ltd v No 1 Deansgate RTM Co Ltd* [2013] UKUT 580 (LC); *Albion Residential Ltd v Albion Riverside Residents RTM Co Ltd* [2014] UKUT 6 (LC).

Self-contained part of a building

9.9 A part of a building is self-contained if:

a) it constitutes a vertical division of the building;[15]

b) the structure of the building is such that it could be redeveloped independently of the rest of the building;[16] and,

c) relevant services (services provided by means of pipes, cables or other fixed installations[17]) provided for the occupiers of the allegedly self-contained part are either:[18]

   i) provided independently of the relevant services provided for occupiers of the rest of the building;[19] or

   ii) could be so provided without involving works which are likely to result in significant interruption in the provision of any relevant services for occupiers of the rest of the building.[20]

9.10 The requirement that the part of the building must constitute a vertical division is unqualified, and any deviation from the vertical (save for truly 'de minimis') will exclude the part of the building from the scope of the right to manage.[21] There is no discretion as to whether or not a building qualifies, nor is it appropriate to consider whether or not the area which falls outside of the line is material.[22]

9.11 Whether or not a part of a building is capable of being redeveloped independently of the rest of the building it likely to be a question of fact (with expert evidence likely to be necessary) in each case. Likewise, the question of whether or not services are provided independently would usually be a question of fact.

9.12 However, where services are not currently provided independently, one must consider whether they are capable of being so provided without it being likely that there would be a significant interruption in the provision of services for occupiers of the rest of the building.

---

15 CLRA 2002 s72(3)(a).

16 CLRA 2002 s72(3)(b).

17 CLRA 2002 s72(5).

18 CLRA 2002 s72(3)(c).

19 CLRA 2002 s72(4)(a).

20 CLRA 2002 s72(4)(b).

21 *Re: Holding and Management (Solitaire) Ltd* LRX/138/2006; [2008] L&TR 16; [2008] 1 EGLR 107, where a building which, when severed vertically, would have two per cent of an underground car-park outside of the vertical division, was held not to qualify.

22 *Re: Holding and Management (Solitaire) Ltd* LRX/138/2006; [2008] L&TR 16; [2008] 1 EGLR 107.

9.13   What amounts to a 'significant interruption' for these purposes is unclear. A county court judge,[23] in a case concerning similar provisions in the Leasehold Reform, Housing and Urban Development Act 1993, has held that there are five steps to take:

1) identify the services that are not independently provided to occupiers of the part of the building in respect of which the RTM is claimed;

2) consider whether those services can be provided to the part in respect of which the RTM is claimed independently of the provision of the same service(s) to the remainder of the building;

3) ascertain whether the works required to separate the respective parts of the services supplying the part in respect of which the RTM is claimed and the remainder of the building, so that such services would thereafter be supplied to each such parts independently of the other;

4) assess the interruption to the latter services (ie, those not subject to the claim to exercise the RTM) which carrying out those works would entail;

5) decide whether or not that interruption was 'significant'.

9.14   The first is a question of fact; the second, third and fourth are matters of fact requiring expert evidence; and the fifth is a matter of construction of the Act, considering the fact and degree of the interruption. It is for those who are claiming the right to manage to prove that the works to separate the services could be done without resulting in a significant interruption.[24]

9.15   Significance should be judged against the fact that the RTM process is supposed to be a quick and efficient method of transferring the management of a property. The longer the duration of the interruption, the more likely it is to be regarded as 'significant', although one should also have regard to the seriousness of the interruption.[25]

9.16   The interruption should be judged with reference to the availability of the service, if required. The significance does not depend on any subjective inconvenience caused to an actual occupier. For example, works to a central heating system are not to be regarded as less significant if conducted during the summer.[26]

23 *Oakwood Court (Holland Park) Ltd v Daejan Properties Ltd* [2007] 1 EGLR 121, HHJ Hazel Marshall QC.

24 *Oakwood Court (Holland Park) Ltd v Daejan Properties Ltd* [2007] 1 EGLR 121.

25 *Oakwood Court (Holland Park) Ltd v Daejan Properties Ltd* [2007] 1 EGLR 121.

26 *Oakwood Court (Holland Park) Ltd v Daejan Properties Ltd* [2007] 1 EGLR 121.

Excluded properties

9.17 Even if the above tests are met, it does not follow that the property will qualify for the right to manage as CLRA 2002 excludes various categories of property.[27]

Buildings with substantial non-resident parts

9.18 Buildings with substantial non-residential parts[28] are those where the internal floor area of any non-residential part or parts exceeds 25 per cent of the internal floor area of the premises. For these purposes:

a) a part of premises is non-residential if it is neither occupied nor intended to be occupied for residential purposes not comprised in any common parts of the premises;[29]

b) any part of the premises (such as a garage, parking space or storage area) which is used or intended to be used in conjunction with a particular dwelling in the premises is taken to be occupied or intended to be occupied for residual purposes;[30] and

c) the floor or floors are taken to extend without interruption throughout the whole of the interior of the building or part, save that common parts are disregarded.[31]

9.19 Whether part or parts of a property are occupied or intended to be occupied for residential purposes is a question of fact to be decided in each case,[32] although an unlawful use of part or parts of the property for residential purposes may be excluded.[33]

Buildings with self-contained parts in different ownership

9.20 Building with self-contained parts in different ownership[34] are those that are capable of being divided into self-contained parts, each of which have different freehold owners.

---

27 CLRA 2002 s72(6); Sch 6.
28 CLRA 2002 Sch 6 para 1(1).
29 CLRA 2002 Sch 6 para 1(2).
30 CLRA 2002 Sch 6 para 1(3).
31 CLRA 2002 Sch 6 para 1(4).
32 *Connaught Court RTM Co Ltd v Abouzaki Holdings Ltd* LRX/115/2007; [2008] 3 EGLR 175.
33 *Gaingold Ltd v WHRA RTM Company Ltd* LRX/19/2005; [2006] 1 EGLR 81.
34 CLRA 2002 Sch 6 para 2.

Resident landlords

9.21   Premises with resident landlords and no more than four units[35] are also excluded from the right to manage, provided that:

a) the premises in question are not (nor form part of) a purpose-built block of flats;

b) one of the flats is occupied by the freeholder or an adult member of the freeholder's family as that person's only or principal home for the last 12 months or, in the case of recently purchased property, there was previously a resident landlord and the new freeholder (or an adult member of his or her family) occupied the flat as their only or principal home within 28 days of purchasing the flat.

Local housing authority as landlord

9.22   Premises where the local housing authority[36] is the immediate landlord of any qualifying tenant are also excluded.[37]

Premises where the RTM has previously been exercised

9.23   Premises where the RTM has previously been exercised[38] are also excluded. This means those premises where there is currently an RTM company that could exercise the right to manage.[39] In addition, any premises where there has been an RTM company which could have exercised the RTM in the previous four years are excluded,[40] unless the previous RTM company ceased to exercise the RTM only as a result of acquiring the freehold[41] or a tribunal gives permission for a new RTM company to acquire the management.[42]

9.24   This provision is a potential source of difficulty. It refers to the right to manage 'being exercisable' by an RTM company. This, presumably, is there to prevent 'duelling' RTM companies being established by rival groups of leaseholders. However, the paragraph refers to the right being 'exercisable' – not that it has been or is being exercised. Suppose that there is an RTM company in existence, but not

---

35   CLRA 2002 Sch 6 para 3.
36   As defined in Housing Act (HA) 1985 s1 – most commonly, a district council, unitary authority or London Borough Council.
37   CLRA 2002 Sch 6 para 4.
38   CLRA 2002 Sch 6 para 5.
39   CLRA 2002 Sch 6 para 5(1)(a).
40   CLRA 2002 Sch 6 para 5(1)(b).
41   CLRA 2002 Sch 6 para 5(2).
42   CLRA 2002 Sch 6 para 5(3).

actually taking steps to acquire the RTM. Would this prevent a 'new' RTM company from being established and seeking to acquire the management?

9.25 This is not a novel or far-fetched point. There are a number of individuals and companies who are establishing RTM companies for developments with which they have no links. They are then (in effect) blocking the RTM process and offer to sell their existing RTM company to the leaseholders. This is clearly undesirable and an abuse of the RTM legislation. But what can be done? This issue (ie 'blocking' RTM companies) is due to be considered by the Upper Tribunal in 2014.[43]

Qualifying tenants

9.26 A 'qualifying tenant' is a person who is a tenant of a flat under a long lease.[44]

9.27 A flat is a separate set of premises (whether or not on the same floor) which:[45]

a) forms part of a building;
b) is constructed or adapted for use for the purposes of a dwelling (which, in turn, requires it to be occupied or intended to be occupied as a separate dwelling);[46] and
c) either the whole or a material part of which lies above or below some other part of the building.

9.28 Whether any property meets this test is a question of fact.[47]

9.29 A long lease is a lease:[48]

a) granted for a term exceeding 21 years;
b) granted for a term fixed by law with a covenant or obligation for perpetual renewal;
c) which took effect under Law of Property Act 1925 s149(6) (leases terminable after a death, marriage or formation of a civil partnership);[49]

---

43 *Re Danescroft RTM Co Ltd* LRX/89/2013.
44 CLRA 2002 s75(2).
45 CLRA 2002 s112(1).
46 CLRA 2002 s112(1).
47 *Re: Stanhope Castle RTM Ltd* [2010] UKUT 1 (LC); [2010] L&TR 16.
48 CLRA 2002 s76; see also section 77 for further technical exclusions and qualifications.
49 A so-called *Mexfield* tenancy, see *Berrisford v Mexfield Housing Co-operative Ltd* [2011] UKSC 52.

d) granted in pursuance of the right to buy under HA 1985 Part 5;

e) a shared ownership lease, regardless of whether the tenant has 'staircased' to 100 per cent or not;[50] or

f) granted pursuant to the right to acquire in HA 1996 s17.

9.30 If the lease is one to which Landlord and Tenant Act (LTA) 1954 Part 2 (business leases) applies[51] or the lease was granted in breach of the terms of a superior lease, where that breach has not been waived,[52] then it is excluded from the RTM process.

9.31 No flat has more than one qualifying tenant.[53] In the case of flats that are held under two or more long leases, a tenant whose lease is superior to that of another tenant is not a qualifying tenant.[54] Joint tenants are regarded as jointly being the qualifying tenant.[55]

9.32 Trustees who are qualifying tenants may join an RTM company unless the trust instrument expressly prohibits it.[56]

9.33 Importantly, there is no requirement that the 'qualifying tenant' actually be resident in the property, nor that they own only one flat within the property.

Procedure

9.34 The first step is to establish the company with the correct articles of association. Once formed, it can start the process of acquiring the right to manage.

Notice inviting participation

9.35 The RTM company must give notice to each qualifying tenant who is not already a member (or has not agreed to become a member) of the company.[57] The notice must:

---

50 Although the CLRA 2002 provides that the tenant must have 'staircased' to 100 per cent, it has been held that a shared ownership lease where the tenant holds less than 100 per cent still qualifies as a long lease under CLRA 2002 s76(2)(a): *Corscombe Close Block 8 RTM Company Ltd v Roseleb Ltd* [2013] UKUT 81 (LC).

51 CLRA 2002 s75(3).

52 CLRA 2002 s75(4).

53 CLRA 2002 s75(5).

54 CLRA 2002 s75(6).

55 CLRA 2002 s75(7).

56 CLRA 2002 s109.

57 CLRA 2002 s78(1).

a) state that the RTM company intends to acquire the right to manage the premises;[58]
b) state the names of the members of the RTM company;[59]
c) invite the recipients of the notice to become members of the company;[60] and
d) contain such other information as may be prescribed.[61]

9.36 In England, the secretary of state has specified that the following additional information must be included:[62]

a) the RTM company's registered number, the address of its registered office and the names of its directors and, if applicable, secretary;
b) the names of the landlord and any third party;
c) a statement that, subject to the exclusions mentioned in sub-paragraph e), if the right to manage is acquired by the RTM company, the company will be responsible for–
    i) the discharge of the landlord's duties under the lease; and
    ii) the exercise of the landlord's powers under the lease,
    with respect to services, repairs, maintenance, improvements, insurance and management;
d) a statement that, subject to the exclusion mentioned in sub-paragraph e)ii), if the right to manage is acquired by the RTM company, the company may enforce untransferred tenant covenants;
e) a statement that, if the right to manage is acquired by the RTM company, the company will not be responsible for the discharge of the landlord's duties or the exercise of the landlord's powers under the lease–
    i) with respect to a matter concerning only a part of the premises consisting of a flat or other unit not subject to a lease held by a qualifying tenant; or
    ii) relating to re-entry or forfeiture;

---

58 CLRA 2002 s78(2)(a).
59 CLRA 2002 s78(2)(b).
60 CLRA 2002 s78(2)(c).
61 CLRA 2002 s78(2)(d) and (3); currently contained in the Right to Manage (Prescribed Particulars and Forms) (England) Regulations 2010 SI No 825 and Right to Manage (Prescribed Particulars and Forms) (Wales) Regulations 2011 SI No 2684.
62 Right to Manage (Prescribed Particulars and Forms) (England) Regulations 2010 SI No 825 Sch 1.

f) a statement that, if the right to manage is acquired by the RTM company, the company will have functions under the statutory provisions referred to in CLRA 2002 Sch 7;

g) a statement that the RTM company intends or, as the case may be, does not intend, to appoint a managing agent; and–

   i) if it does so intend, a statement–

      aa) of the name and address of the proposed managing agent (if known); and

      bb) if it be the case, that the person is the landlord's managing agent; or

   ii) if it does not so intend, the qualifications or experience (if any) of the existing members of the RTM company in relation to the management of residential property;

h) a statement that, where the RTM company gives a claim notice, a person who is or has been a member of the company may be liable for costs incurred by the landlord and others in consequence of the notice;

i) a statement that, if the recipient of the notice (of invitation to participate) does not fully understand its purpose or implications, that person is advised to seek professional help; and

j) the information provided in the notes to the form set out in the regulations.

9.37   The position is similar in Wales.[63] Both the English and Welsh regulations contain prescribed forms setting out the prescribed information.

9.38   This notice must either be accompanied by a copy of the articles of association of the RTM company or include a statement specifying a place in England or Wales, where they may be inspected, the times at which they may be inspected, a place from which they may be ordered and a reasonable fee for a provision of a copy.[64]

9.39   Despite these onerous requirements, a notice of invitation to participate is not invalidated by any inaccuracy in the particulars required.[65] There is, however, a difference between an inaccuracy and a complete omission; the former can be saved under this provision, whereas the latter cannot.[66]

---

63 Right to Manage (Prescribed Particulars and Forms) (Wales) Regulations 2011 SI No 2684 Sch 1.

64 CLRA 2002 s78(4), (5).

65 CLRA 2002 s78(7). See generally *Assethold Ltd v 14 Stansfield Road RTM Company Ltd* [2012] UKUT 262 (LC).

66 *Assethold Ltd v 14 Stansfield Road RTM Company Limited* [2012] UKUT 262 (LC); *Assethold v 15 Yonge Park RTM Company Ltd* [2011] UKUT 379 (LC); *Assethold Limited v 13–24 Romside Place RTM Company Ltd* [2013] UKUT 0603 (LC).

9.40   Further, there is a freestanding power to waive any defect where the tribunal considers that there has not been any prejudice to the landlord.[67] It is for the RTM company to demonstrate that there is no prejudice.[68]

9.41   All those qualifying leaseholders who respond to the notice and request membership must be enrolled as members of the RTM company and their membership noted in the official records.[69]

9.42   Although the legislation does not require the RTM company to produce any form of plan or budget, it may be wise to do so as it will both focus the minds of those involved in the RTM process and provide clear direction for the RTM company. It may also forestall any objections from leaseholders or even the landlord about the costs and standards envisaged by the RTM.

Notice of claim to acquire right

9.43   At least 14 days after giving a valid[70] notice of invitation to participate, the RTM company may claim the right to manage.[71] It does not appear that there is any maximum period after which a claim notice cannot be served, such that, in principle, it is possible to delay service of the claim notice indefinitely after service of the notice of invitation to participate.[72]

---

67   *Sinclair Gardens (Investments) Ltd v Oak Investments RTM Company Ltd* LRX/52/2004; [2005] RVR 426, where the Lands Tribunal held that the failure to serve a notice of invitation to participate on a qualifying tenant was immaterial where the tenant had been fully aware of the proceedings and his admission was inadvertent. See also *Avon Freeholds Ltd v Regents Court RTM Co Ltd* [2013] UKUT 213 (LC) to the same effect, ie that this is a 'directory' requirement and, in the case of breach, the tribunal must ask itself whether there was substantial compliance and whether parliament intended invalidity to result from the failings.

68   *Assethold Ltd v 7 Sunny Gardens Road RTM Company Ltd* [2013] UKUT 509 (LC).

69   Although not made clear in the CLRA 2002, if this is not done, then there will be a problem when dealing with section 80(3), below.

70   See *Assethold Ltd v 13–24 Romside Place RTM Company Ltd* [2013] UKUT 0603 (LC).

71   CLRA 2002 s79(1)–(2).

72   So long as there is no change in circumstances which would render the notice of invitation to participate invalid: *Gateway Property Holdings Ltd v 6–10 Montrose Gardens RTM Co Ltd* [2011] UKUT 349.

9.44   The RTM company may only give such a notice if sufficient numbers of qualifying tenants have joined the company.[73] In the case of a building with only two qualifying tenants, both must be members; otherwise, not less than half of the number of qualifying tenants must have joined.[74]

9.45   A notice must be given to the following classes of person:

a) any landlord under a lease of the whole or part of the premises;[75]
b) any other party to a lease who is neither a landlord nor a tenant;[76]
c) any manager appointed under LTA 1987 Part 2;[77]
d) all qualifying tenants;[78] and
e) if a manager has been appointed under LTA 1987 Part 2, to the court or tribunal which appointed the manager.[79]

9.46   There is no requirement that a notice must be given in a way that would constitute service for the purpose of the Civil Procedure Rules (CPR); notice simply has to be given (or, to put it another way, simply has to be received by the intended recipient).[80] A notice may be given by sending it by post, although allowances must be made for the time that the notice will spend in the postal system, when calculating eg the date for service of a counter notice.[81]

9.47   There is no need to serve a claim notice on a person who cannot be found or whose identity cannot be ascertained. In this case an application should be made to the tribunal who will determine what, if any, further steps should be taken by the RTM company. [82]

9.48   The notice of claim must be in writing and must:[83]

---

73 In *Southall Court (Residents Ltd) and others v Buy Your Freehold Ltd and others* LRX/124/2007, it had been held that this requires them to be members of the company for the purposes of the Companies Act 1985 (as it was then) ie to have agreed to become members and had their name entered on the register of members; the absence of a register of members meant that there were no members of the company and the claim notice was invalid.

74 CLRA 2002 s79(4)–(5).

75 CLRA 2002 s79(6)(a).

76 CLRA 2002 s79(6)(b).

77 CLRA 2002 s79(6)(c).

78 CLRA 2002 s79(8).

79 CLRA 2002 s79(9).

80 *Plintal SA and another v 36–48A Edgewood Drive Rtm Company Ltd and another* LRX/16/2007.

81 *Moskovitz and others v 75 Worple Road Rtm Company Ltd* [2010] UKUT 393 (LC).

82 CLRA 2002 s85.

83 CLRA 2002 s80.

a) specify the premises and contain a statement of the grounds on which it is claimed that they are premises to which the right to manage applies;[84]

b) state the full name of each person who is the qualifying tenant of a flat contained in the premises, and a member of the RTM company, and the address of his or her flat;[85]

c) contain, in relation to each such person, such particulars of his or her lease as are sufficient to identify it, including:[86]

    i)   the date on which it was entered into;

    ii) the term for which it as granted; and

    iii) the date of commencement of the term;

d) state the name and registered office of the RTM company;[87]

e) specify a date, not earlier than one month after the service of the notice, by which each person who was given the notice may respond to it by giving a counter-notice;[88]

f) specify a date, at least three months after that, on which the RTM company intends to acquire the right to manage the premises.[89]

9.49 In England, the secretary of state has specified that the following additional information must be included:[90]

a) a statement that a person who–

    i) does not dispute the RTM's company's entitlement to acquire the right to manage; and

    ii) is the manager party under a management contract subsisting immediately before the date specified in the claim notice must give a notice in relation to the contract to the person who is the contractor party in relation to the contract and to the RTM company;

b) a statement that, from the acquisition date, landlords under leases of the whole or any part of the premises to which the claim notice relates are entitled to be members of the RTM company;

---

84 CLRA 2002 s80(2); the claim notice need not specify whether or not the claim extends to appurtenant property since it will be included if the claim succeeds: *Gala Unity Ltd v Ariadne Court RTM Company Ltd* [2011] UKUT 425 (LC); *Pineview Ltd v 83 Crampton Street RTM Co Ltd* [2013] UKUT 598 (LC).

85 CLRA 2002 s80(3).

86 CLRA 2002 s80(4).

87 CLRA 2002 s80(5).

88 CLRA 2002 s80(6).

89 CLRA 2002 s80(7).

90 Right to Manage (Prescribed Particulars and Forms) (England) Regulations 2010 SI No 825 Sch 2.

    c) a statement that the notice is not invalidated by any inaccuracy in any of the particulars, but that a person who is of the opinion that any of the particulars contained in the claim notice are inaccurate may–

      i) identify the particulars in question to the RTM company by which the notice was given; and

      ii) indicate the respects in which they are considered to be inaccurate;

    d) a statement that a person who receives the notice but does not fully understand its purpose, is advised to seek professional help; and

    e) the information provided in the notes to the form set out in Schedule 2 to the regulations.

9.50   There is no material difference in the Welsh regulations.[91] Both regulations contain prescribed forms, which must be used. The prescribed form provides that it must be signed 'by authority of the company'. This does not mean that the notice must be signed by a member or director of the company; in particular there is no reason why a firm of solicitors cannot sign this statement[92] or some other person who is properly authorised.[93]

9.51   An RTM company has a power to request any person to provide information which is in their possession or control and which the company reasonably requires for the purpose of preparing a claim notice.[94]

9.52   As with a notice inviting participation, a claim notice is not invalidated by any inaccuracy in any of the particulars, although there is a distinction between an inaccuracy and an omission.[95]

9.53   Once a claim notice has been served, no further notice may be served so long as it continues in force unless it has been withdrawn

---

91 Right to Manage (Prescribed Particulars and Forms) (Wales) Regulations 2011 SI No 2684 Sch 2.

92 *Pineview Ltd v 83 Crampton Street RTM Co Ltd* [2013] UKUT 598 (LC).

93 *Assethold Ltd v 14 Stansfield Road RTM Company Ltd* [2012] UKUT 262 (LC).

94 CLRA 2002 s82.

95 CLRA 2002 s81(1); there are conflicting decisions on the scope of this provision. In *Moskovitz and others v 75 Worple Road RTM Company Ltd* [2010] UKUT 393 (LC), it was held that the particulars are those required under CLRA 2002 s80(4) and (8) (ie the details of the lease and the matters prescribed by regulations). In *Assethold Ltd v 15 Yonge Park RTM Co Ltd* [2011] UKUT 379 (LC), by contrast, it was held that 'the particulars' were any of the matters required by CLRA 2002 s80. This latter approach has prevailed: *Assethold Ltd v 14 Stansfield Road RTM Company Ltd* [2012] UKUT 262 (LC).

or otherwise ceased to have effect.[96] A claim notice that is invalid does not need to be withdrawn and there is no impediment to the service of a second notice.[97] Even if the notice appears to be invalid, it will still be treated as valid for the purposes of establishing CLRA 2002 s80 liability for costs.[98]

9.54   After a claim notice is served, those authorised by the RTM, the landlord, any other party to a lease or a manager must, upon giving ten days written notice to any person occupying or entitled to occupy any part of the premises, be given access to that premises if it is reasonable to do so in connection with any matter arising out of the claim to the right to manage.[99] It is not clear why this power arises only *after* the claim notice is served. It would make more sense if it arose earlier, so that the RTM company could, for example, arrange to measure any non-residential parts in order to satisfy itself that the premises were ones to which the CLRA 2002 applied.

9.55   As was noted above,[100] one RTM company can. in principle, acquire the management functions over more than one block of flats, so long as each block meets the qulifying conditions.[101] In such a case, the RTM company may either serve notice for all the blocks or one notice for each block; the crucial question is whether it is sufficiently clear what is being claimed.[102]

Counter-notice

9.56   Any person given a claim notice by an RTM company may give a counter-notice.[103] This must be done no later than the date specified in the claim notice.[104]

---

96 CLRA 2002 s81(3)–(4).
97 *Avon Freeholds Ltd v Regents Court RTM Co Ltd* [2013] UKUT 213 (LC).
98 *Plintal SA and another v 36–48A Edgewood Drive RTM Company Ltd and another* LRX/16/2007; for a contrary view, see in the context of a claim for collective enfranchisement, *Sinclair Gardens Investments (Kensington) Ltd v Poets Chase Freehold Company Ltd* [2007] EWHC 1776 (Ch); [2008] 1 WLR 768.
99 CLRA 2002 s83. It is unclear what the purpose of this right is. Surely it would make more sense to give the RTM company a power to inspect before the claim notice is served, so as to satisfy itself that the building is one to which the RTM applies.
100 Para 9.4.
101 *Ninety Broomfield Road RTM Co Ltd v Triplerose and other cases* [2013] UKUT 606.
102 Ibid.
103 CLRA 2002 s84(1).
104 See para 9.48, above.

9.57   The notice must contain a statement either admitting that the RTM company was on the relevant date entitled to acquire the right to manage the premises specified in the claim notice, or alleging that the RTM company was on that date not entitled.[105] If the latter course is taken, the counter-notice must specify the reason why it is said that the RTM company was not entitled to acquire the management, but these reasons are not 'once and for all' and a party may raise additional arguments in any subsequent hearing.[106]

9.58   In England, the Secretary of State has specified that the following additional information must be included:[107]

a) a statement that, where the RTM company has been given one or more counter-notices containing denying that it is entitled to exercise the RTM, the company may apply to the Tribunal for a determination that, on the date on which notice of the claim was given, the company was entitled to acquire the right to manage the premises specified in the claim notice;

b) a statement that, where the RTM company has been given one or more counter-notices denying that it is entitled to exercise the RTM, the company does not acquire the right to manage the premises specified in the claim notice unless –

   i) on an application to the tribunal, it is finally determined that the company was entitled to acquire the right to manage the premises; or

   ii) the person by whom the counter-notice was given agrees, or the persons by whom the counter-notices were given agree, in writing that the company was so entitled; and

c) the information provided in the notes to the form set out in Schedule 3 to the regulations.

9.59   There is no material difference in the Welsh regulations.[108] Both regulations contain prescribed forms, which must be used.

---

105 CLRA 2002 s84(2); see also *Burnman v Mount Cook Land Ltd* [2002] Ch 256, CA, a case under the Leasehold Reform, Housing and Urban Development Act 1993.

106 *Fairhold (Yorkshire) Ltd v Trinity Wharf (SE16) RTM Co Ltd* [2013] UKUT 503 (LC); *Albion Residential Ltd v Albion Riverside Residents RTM Co Ltd* [2014] UKUT 6 (LC).

107 Right to Manage (Prescribed Particulars and Forms) (England) Regulations 2010 SI No 825 Sch 3.

108 Right to Manage (Prescribed Particulars and Forms) (Wales) Regulations 2011 SI No 2684 Sch 3.

Role of the tribunal

9.60   If one or more counter-notices are received which dispute the right of the RTM company to acquire the management of the property, an application may be made by the company to the tribunal for a determination of this question.[109] The onus is on the RTM company to take this step as the right to manage cannot be exercised until this matter is determined or the person(s) who produced the counter notice gives notice in writing of the withdrawal of their objections.

9.61   Any such application must be made no later than two months after the day on which the last counter-notice was given.[110] The RTM company cannot acquire the RTM unless the tribunal determines that it is entitled to do so, or the person who gave the counter-notice accepts – in writing – that the RTM company is entitled to acquire the RTM.[111]

9.62   If an appeal is launched from the decision of the tribunal, the RTM process is held in abeyance until the determination or abandonment of the appeal.[112]

Withdrawal of a claim

9.63   An RTM company may withdraw from the process at any time by service of a 'notice of withdrawal' on each person who is:[113]

a) a landlord under a lease;
b) a party to such a lease;
c) a manager appointed under the LTA 1987;
d) a qualifying tenant.

9.64   Additionally, an application is deemed to be withdrawn if, having received a counter notice, the RTM company does not apply for a determination of the issue by the tribunal within two months.[114]

9.65   If the RTM company makes the necessary application but then withdraws the application, the RTM process is deemed to have ceased.[115]

109 CLRA 2002 s84(3).
110 CLRA 2002 s84(4).
111 CLRA 2002 s84(5).
112 CLRA 2002 s82(7).
113 CLRA 2002 s86.
114 CLRA 2002 s87(1)(a).
115 CLRA 2002 s87(1)(b).

9.66   The claim notice is also deemed to be withdrawn if a winding-up order is made or a resolution for winding-up is passed; a receiver or a manager of the RTM company is appointed; if the assets of the RTM company are compromised; a voluntary arrangement (within the meaning of Insolvency Act 1986 Part 1) is made; or the RTM company is struck off the register of companies.[116]

Costs of the RTM process

9.67   The RTM company is liable for the reasonable costs of the landlord, manager and other parties to the lease in respect of actions taken by them once a claim notice has been served.[117]

9.68   The costs of professional services (such as lawyers or accountants) are regarded as reasonable only to the extent that the person claiming them might reasonably have been expected to have incurred them and if that person would be personally liable for those costs.[118]

9.69   The RTM company is also liable for costs incurred by any such person in proceedings before the tribunal if the tribunal dismisses the application for a determination that it is entitled to acquire the right to manage.[119]

9.70   In the event of a dispute about any costs claimed, the issue shall be decided by the tribunal.[120]

9.71   If the RTM process is withdrawn, the general rule is that the RTM company is liable for the reasonable costs (as above) which have been incurred up to the date of withdrawal. Each person who is or has been a member of the RTM company is liable jointly and severally with the RTM company for those costs.[121]

---

116 CLRA 2002 s87(4).
117 CLRA 2002 s88(1). There is no reason in principle why this cannot include in-house legal costs *Fairhold Mercury Ltd v Merryfield RTM Co Ltd* [2012] UKUT 311 (LC).
118 CLRA 2002 s88(2).
119 CLRA 2002 s88(3).
120 CLRA 2002 s88(4).
121 CLRA 2002 s89.

What does the RTM company acquire and when?

Date of acquisition

9.72　If there was no dispute as to the notice of claim, the RTM company acquires the right to manage on the date specified in the notice of claim.[122]

9.73　If there was a dispute which the tribunal determined in favour of the RTM company, the acquisition date is three months after the determination becomes final.[123]

9.74　If the landlord could not be found and the RTM company made an application under CLRA 2002 s85, the acquisition date is as set out in the order made by the tribunal.[124]

What is acquired?

9.75　The RTM company acquires a range of functions and powers which were previously exercised by the landlord or tripartite management company.

Management functions

9.76　On the acquisition date, the RTM company effectively steps into the shoes of the landlord or manager in relation to management functions under the leases (ie functions with respect to services, repairs, maintenance, improvements, insurance and management).[125] In effect, references in the lease (and under a range of statutes – see CLRA 2002 Sch 7) to, for example, the landlord or management company, become references to the RTM company.

9.77　The only functions which are expressly excluded from those exercised by the RTM company are those relating to re-entry and forfeiture, as are functions relating to matters concerning only a part of the property or other unit not held by a qualifying tenant.[126]

9.78　No landlord, other party to the lease or manager appointed under LTA 1987 Part 2 may carry out any function which the RTM company is required or empowered to do, without the agreement of the RTM

122　CLRA 2002 s90(2).
123　CLRA 2002 s90(4).
124　CLRA 2002 s90(6).
125　CLRA 2002 s96(1)–(5). Note that leaseholders cannot be required to pay service charges to the RTM company for matters that occurred prior to the acquisition date: CLRA 2002 s97(5).
126　CLRA 2002 s96(6).

company,[127] although this does not prevent a person from insuring the whole or part of the premises at his or her own expense.[128]

Approvals

9.79   Many leases provide for landlords to approve certain structural or other changes to the flats before tenants can act. Once the RTM is acquired, such consent can now validly be given by the RTM company.[129]

9.80   However, in any circumstance where consent is so needed, the RTM company must give at least 14 days' notice of its proposed decision to the landlord. This 14-day period rises to 30 days in the case of assignment, under-letting, charging, parting with possession, the making of structural alternations or improvements or alterations of use.[130]

9.81   If, during the 14- or 30-day notice period, the landlord objects, the RTM company may only grant its approval to the proposals if:[131]

a) the person who objected later consents in writing; or
b) the tribunal determines that such consent should be given.

9.82   An application to the tribunal for a determination of this question may be made by the RTM company, the tenant, any sub-tenant or the landlord.[132] The legislation is silent as to what criteria the tribunal will use to make its decision, although, given that this application can only arise if a landlord refuses to consent to the proposals, it seems likely that the test will be 'whether the landlord has acted reasonably in all the circumstances in refusing his consent'.

9.83   Presumably, in the case of structural alterations, proposals that would lower the value of the freehold will be rejected, as no reasonable landlord could be asked to consent to such activities. It also seems clear that tenants under leases with only a short time left to run will find it more difficult to show that structural alterations are reasonable than those with leases having a longer period to run.

127 CLRA 2002 s97(2).
128 CLRA 2002 s97(3).
129 CLRA 2002 s98(2).
130 CLRA 2002 s98(4).
131 CLRA 2002 s99(1).
132 CLRA 2002 s99(5).

Right to information

9.84 Where the right to manage is to be acquired by the RTM company, it may serve notice require the following categories of person to provide such information as is reasonably required in connection with the exercise of the right to manage:[133]

a) a landlord under a lease of the whole or part of the premises;
b) any party to a lease other than as a landlord or tenant; and
c) any manager appointed under LTA 1987 Part 2, in respect of some or all of the premises.

9.85 The notice may not require anything to be done before the acquisition date, but, subject to that, the recipient must comply within 28 days of the date on which the notice is given.[134] This presumably is intended to cover, eg details of electricity suppliers and such-like.

Service charges

9.86 Not only is the RTM company entitled to collect the service charges going forward, but it is also entitled to receive all 'uncommitted' and accrued service charges.

9.87 Where a landlord, other party to the lease or manager appointed under LTA 1987 Part 2, has collected service charges in advance, but not yet spent them all, they are under an obligation to hand the sums over to the RTM company.[135] This does not require a notice from the RTM company – the legislation places the duty firmly on the landlord, although it would be wise for the RTM company to remind the landlord of this.

9.88 The sums must be paid on the acquisition date, or as soon after as is reasonably practicable.[136] The total sum to be paid is calculated by taking any monies paid by the leaseholders as service charges plus any interest or investment income generated by such money less the landlord's outgoings on the provision of services up to the acquisition date.[137]

9.89 The intention is that the outgoing manager is obliged to hand over to the RTM company whatever monies are held in the bank account or accounts relating to the property.[138] This does not include

133 CLRA 2002 s93.
134 CLRA 2002 s93(3)–(4).
135 CLRA 2002 s94(1).
136 CLRA 2002 s94(4).
137 CLRA 2002 s94(2).
138 *OM Ltd v New River Head RTM Company Ltd* [2010] UKUT 394 (LC).

an obligation to pay over monies that *should* be in the bank account, but are not.[139]

9.90   In the event that the landlord and RTM company cannot agree a figure, either party may apply to the tribunal to determine the amount to be paid.[140] The tribunal has no power to award interest on any disputed sums.[141]

The position of the landlord after the right to manage is acquired

9.91   The landlord is not removed entirely from the management of the property once the RTM has been acquired.

Enforcement of covenants

9.92   Any obligation owed by the RTM company to a leaseholder under the lease is also owed to the landlord,[142] such that it will be able to enforce covenants against the RTM company as if the landlord was a leaseholders. Note also that the RTM company must keep under review any breaches of covenant by the tenant and report the same to the landlord.[143]

Contribution to service charges

9.93   Where the property contains one or more flats or other units which was not held by a qualifying tenant (an 'excluded unit') and the rest of the flats in the building pay service charges which are calculated as a proportion of the total expenditure (ie variable service charges within the meaning of LTA 1985 s18), and the total recoverable from those flats is less than 100 per cent of the service charge expenditure,

---

139 *OM Ltd v New River Head RTM Company Ltd* [2010] UKUT 394 (LC); where, on the facts of the case, monies which had been found to be unreasonable under LTA 1985 s19 were not capable of being ordered to be repaid from the manager to the RTM company; rather, tenants had to pursue their own individual remedies in respect of such sums.

140 CLRA 2002 s94(3).

141 *OM Ltd v New River Head RTM Company Ltd* [2010] UKUT 394 (LC).

142 CLRA 2002 s97(1), ie the landlord can enforce covenants against the RTM company which the landlord previously had to discharge as against the leaseholders.

143 CLRA 2002 s101.

then the holder of the excluded unit[144] must contribute towards the shortfall in a proportion to be calculated with reference to the internal floor area of the excluded unit.[145] The landlord is entitled to apply to a tribunal to challenge the service charges in the same way that a tenant could prior to the right to manage.[146]

Existing contracts

9.94 Where the RTM company applies to acquires the right to manage[147] and there is a pre-existing contract between the current manager and another person, in respect of a matter which will become a function of the RTM company once it acquires the right to manage, the current manager must give notice to the contractor and the RTM company.[148] The form of notice is different in each case and is prescribed.[149]

Miscellaneous other matters

No contracting out

9.95 An agreement relating to a lease is void if it:

a) purports to exclude or modify the rights of any person to be or do anything as a member of an RTM company;

b) provides for the termination or surrender of the lease if the tenant becomes or does anything as a member of the RTM company (or if the RTM company does anything); or

c) provides for the imposition of a penalty or disability in those circumstances.[150]

---

144 Effectively, the person with the most immediate right to possession; the landlord under the lease of the unit; in the case of sub-leases, the landlord under the most inferior lease; or, the freeholder.

145 CLRA 2002 s103.

146 CLRA 2002 s103; Sch 7.

147 Other than in cases of absentee landlords: see CLRA 2002 s85.

148 CLRA 2002 ss91–92.

149 Right to Manage (Prescribed Particulars and Forms) (England) Regulations 2010 SI No 825; Right to Manage (Prescribed Particulars and Forms) (Wales) Regulations 2004 SI No 678.

150 CLRA 2002 s106.

Enforcement of obligations

9.96   The county court has power to make an order requiring a person who has failed to comply with a requirement imposed on him by, under, or by virtue of the right to manage provisions, to make good his default within a specified time.[151] No application may be made for such an order unless notice has been given to the person in question, requiring that person to make good the default, and more than 14 days have passed since the notice was given.[152]

Known issues and problems with the right to manage

Failure to serve a counter notice

9.97   There appears to be a lacuna in the legislation if the landlord fails to serve a counter-notice, but the premises are clearly not ones to which the RTM applies. In the absence of a counter-notice, the right to manage is acquired without more. The jurisdiction of the tribunal is contingent upon a counter-notice having been served. Further, it has been suggested that the High Court has no jurisdiction to resolve the matter by way of eg a declaration.[153]

Solvency of the RTM company

9.98   In the experience of the authors, many RTM companies charge their running costs (eg Companies House charges; company secretarial costs) through the service charge. This is unlikely to be lawful. The RTM company can only charge service charges in accordance with the lease; very few leases will allow for the recovery of such costs.[154] Thus, these costs must be borne by the RTM company members themselves.

9.99   Closely related to this issue, is how does the RTM company get the money from defaulting leaseholders? The freeholder, of course, can just issue a debt claim in the county court, obtain judgment (often in default) and then notify the mortgage company (if there is one) who

---

151   CLRA 2002 s107(1).

152   CLRA 2002 s107(2).

153   *Alleyn Court RTM Company Ltd v Micha'al Abou-Hamdan* [2012] UKUT 74 (LC).

154   *Wilson v Lesley Place (RTM) Co Ltd* [2010] UKUT 342 (LC).

will pay. Even if the case is transferred to the tribunal for a contested hearing, the mortgage company will ultimately pay. An RTM company does not usually have that option. The reason, of course, that the mortgage company pays the freeholder is because the freeholder can forfeit the lease. The RTM company[155] cannot do so.[156]

Application of the right to manage on estates

9.100   The way in which the case-law has developed has given rise to a potential problem in relation to the management of estates. If the estate comprise a mixture of freehold (or leasehold) houses and a block (or blocks) of flats, then the houses will always be outside the scope of the right to manage. If the flats form a right to manage company, they will only acquire responsibility for the management of the estate insofar as it affects the leasehold flat owners; the landlord will retain responsibility for the services to the houses.[157] This means that:

a) the RTM company and the landlord will have to come to an agreement as to who performs the estate functions, with one party agreeing to pay the other a contribution (since, if no agreement is reached and both perform the same function, eg cleaning the communal car-park, then there will be litigation as to whether both costs are reasonable); and

b) the RTM companies risk insolvency. Suppose that there is an estate consisting of 80 flats and 20 houses. The RTM company acquires the management of the flats. Under the terms of the leases, it now has an obligation to cut the grass in the common estate parts. The garden costs £100 pa to manage. The RTM company can only recover 80 per cent of that via the service charge. How will it recover the shortfall if the landlord refuses to provide the funds? It will be difficult for the RTM company to sue the landlord, as it is unlikely to owe any obligation to pay the RTM company. Further, surely when the RTM company places a contract for the £100, it is facing insolvency as it knows it can't recover 100 per cent of the costs as a service charge. Do the RTM company members make up the difference themselves?

9.101   A similar problem arises where there are multiple RTM companies on one estate; they will all be required to perform the same 'estate'

---

155 Or lessee-owned/controlled management company.
156 See CLRA 2002 s96.
157 *Gala Unity Ltd v Ariadne Road RTM Co Ltd* [2012] EWCA Civ 1372.

functions, but will each only be able to recover a small proportion of the costs from the leaseholders in each block. Unless they reach agreement, they face the same problems as outlined above.[158]

---

158 *Ninety Broomfield Road RTM Co Ltd v Triplerose and other cases* [2013] UKUT 606.

Landlords' legal costs

Key points

- Although the tribunal has limited costs powers, many leases provide for landlords to recover legal costs from tenants, either as a service charge or an administration charge.
- If as a service charge, tenant can ask the tribunal (or court) to prevent the landlord from recovering costs (in full or in part). If as an administration charge, the rights of tenants are more restricted.

Advice for tenants

- While the tribunal has relatively limited costs powers, leases often give landlords the contractual right to recover legal costs from leaseholders.
- There are different statutory protections for leaseholders depending on whether the costs are service charges or administration charges.
- Tenants are usually in a much weaker position than their landlords and so tenants need to ensure that they fully appreciate the costs risks they face before getting involved in any litigation.

Introduction

10.1   Both the First-tier Tribunal (Property Chamber) (FTT(PC)) and the leasehold valuation tribunal (LVT) have certain powers to award costs against parties to proceedings.[1] Those powers (and, in particular, the restrictions on when they can be exercised) should not be confused with the situation where the lease itself gives the landlord (or third party management company) a power to recover legal and other professional costs, including costs incurred before the tribunal, as the two matters are conceptually different.[2]

---

1   Discussed in chapter 15 (LVT) and chapter 16 (FTT), respectively.
2   *Christoforou and others v Standard Apartments Ltd* [2013] UKUT 586 (LC); *Canary Riverside Pte Ltd v Schilling* LRX/65/2005; *Staghold Ltd v Takeda* [2005] 3 EGLR 45.

10.2   If there is a contractual entitlement to costs, the question becomes whether those costs are service charges or administration charges, as there are different protections for each type of charge.[3] Readers are referred to the relevant chapters of this work for more details.[4]

Contractual entitlement to costs as a service charge

10.3   Whether a particular lease provides for the recovery of legal costs is a question to be decided in each case.[5] Clear words are usually required before a clause will be considered to allow the recovery of legal costs.[6] It may be that, in an appropriate case, a term will be implied permitting the recovery of such costs.[7]

Landlord and Tenant Act 1985 s20C

10.4   If the lease permits the recovery of costs as a service charge,[8] the tribunal[9] may order that some or all of the costs incurred, or to be incurred, by the landlord in connection with the proceedings, are not to be included in the service charges payable by the tenant or any other person or persons specified in the application.[10] The tribunal may make such order as it considers 'just and equitable'.[11]

10.5   There is no presumption that an order should (or should not) be made,[12] and what is 'just and equitable' is a matter for the tribunal in each case.[13] Further, the tribunal is not required to approach the

---

3   See the discussion in chapter 11.

4   Service charges: chapter 1; administration charges: chapter 6.

5   *Morgan v Stainer* (1993) 25 HLR 467. In particular, a clause which allows for the recovery of costs where the landlord is the applicant may not be of assistance when seeking to recover costs in proceedings where the landlord is the respondent.

6   *Sella House v Mears* [1989] 1 EGLR 65; (1989) 21 HLR 147; *St Mary's Mansions v Limegate Investments Co Ltd* [2003] 1 EGLR 41; [2003] HLR 24; *Iperion Investments v Broadwalk House Residents Ltd* [1995] 2 EGLR 47; (1994) 27 HLR 196; *Plantation Wharf Management Co Ltd v Jackson* [2011] UKUT 488 (LC); *Greening v Castelnau Mansions Ltd* [2011] UKUT 326 (LC).

7   *Embassy Court Residents' Association v Lipman* (1984) 271 EG 545, CA.

8   But not an administration charge.

9   LVT, FTT(PC), Upper Tribunal (Lands Chamber) (UT(LC)) or court: Landlord and Tenant Act (LTA) 1985 s20C(1).

10   LTA 1985 s20C.

11   LTA 1985 s20C(3).

12   *Tenants of Langford Court v Doren* LRX/37/2000.

13   *Avon Estates (London) Ltd v Sinclair Gardens Investments (Kensington) Ltd* [2013] UKUT 264 (LC).

matter in the same way as a court assessing costs under Civil Procedure Rules (CPR) Part 44 and should deal with matters in a broad-brush and robust manner.[14]

10.6 It follows that one must be cautious about stating any general rules, but the following factors have been considered significant by the Lands Tribunal, Upper Tribunal or Court of Appeal:

a) Where a tenant has been successful, it would usually follow that an order should be made.[15]

b) Where the tenant has been unsuccessful, it would require some unusual circumstances to justify an order.[16]

c) As most service charge disputes will fall somewhere between these two extremes, there will need to be a consideration of:

   i) the relative success of the parties;[17]

   ii) the proportionality of the reduction achieved as against the costs of the dispute.[18]

d) Where the landlord is a lessee-owned or -controlled body which might be insolvent if it could not recover its costs, that is a factor which leans against an order being made.[19]

e) The conduct of the parties is relevant[20] and a landlord who has behaved unfairly or improperly should not expect to recover his costs associated with such conduct.[21]

---

14 *Avon Estates (London) Ltd v Sinclair Gardens Investments (Kensington) Ltd* [2013] UKUT 264 (LC); *Tenants of Langford Court v Doren* LRX/37/2000; *Church Commissioners v Derdabi* [2011] UKUT 380 (LC).

15 *Iperion Investments v Broadwalk House Residents Ltd* [1995] 2 EGLR 47; (1994) 27 HLR 196; *Holding & Management Ltd v Property Holding & Investment Trust plc* [1989] 1WLR 1313; although *Tenants of Langford Court v Doren* LRX/37/2000 makes clear that this will not automatically follow.

16 *Canary Riverside Pte Ltd v Schilling* LRX/26/2005.

17 *Church Commissioners v Derdabi* [2011] UKUT 380 (LC).

18 *Canary Riverside Pte Ltd v Schilling* LRX/26/2005; *St John's Wood Leases Ltd v O'Neil* [2012] UKUT 374 (LC); see *Island Homes Housing Association v Benet Allen, Claire Louise Keyte* [2013] UKUT 258 (LC) for the clearest example of a 'proportion' order, where the service charges were reduced by c3 per cent, leading to a 3 per cent section 20C order.

19 *Iperion Investments v Broadwalk House Residents Ltd* [1995] 2 EGLR 47; (1994) 27 HLR 196; *Church Commissioners v Derdabi* [2011] UKUT 380 (LC); *Plantation Wharf Management Co Ltd v Jackson* [2011] UKUT 488 (LC); [2012] L&TR 18.

20 *Iperion Investments v Broadwalk House Residents Ltd* [1995] 2 EGLR 47; (1994) 27 HLR 196; *Tenants of Langford Court v Doren* LRX/37/2000; *Church Commissioners v Derdabi* [2011] UKUT 380 (LC).

21 *Tenants of Langford Court v Doren* LRX/37/2000.

f) Whatever order is made, the tenant will still be able to dispute the reasonableness of the costs under LTA 1985 s19.[22]

g) The tribunal should also consider offers of settlement (particularly where the eventual result is less advantageous than a rejected offer).[23]

10.7 On appeal to the Upper Tribunal, it may be appropriate to make an order in favour of an unsuccessful tenant responding to the appeal if the error which occasioned the appeal was due to an error by the tribunal, rather than an argument advanced by the tenant.[24]

Contractual entitlement to costs as an administration charge

10.8 There are two common contractual rights to costs, each of which have been held to be administration charges.[25] Although there is no equivalent of LTA 1985 s20C, the costs must still be reasonable,[26] which necessarily includes a consideration of whether the costs are proportionate.[27]

10.9 The authorities appear to assume, although there is nothing in the statute to suggest this, that a charge may not be both an administration charge and a service charge and that therefore, having found that a charge is an administration charge it cannot also be a service charge and hence cannot be controlled by the tribunal using its powers under LTA 1985 s20C. In our view, this cannot be good law. The Commonhold and Leasehold Reform Act (CLRA) 2002's introduction of control over administration charges cannot –without much clearer wording – have removed protections available for charges that would, before that Act, have clearly been protected under LTA 1985 s20C. See the discussion in chapter 6.

22 *Tenants of Langford Court v Doren* LRX/37/2000; *Church Commissioners v Derdabi* [2011] UKUT 380 (LC).

23 Although the authors cannot find a reported case on this point, this must be right.

24 *Southwark LBC v Bevan* [2013] UKUT 0114 (LC); *Birmingham City Council v Keddie* [2012] UKUT 323 (LC).

25 *Christoforou and others v Standard Apartments Ltd* [2013] UKUT 586 (LC).

26 CLRA 2002 Sch 11.

27 *Christoforou and others v Standard Apartments Ltd* [2013] UKUT 586 (LC).

Forfeiture clauses

10.10   A lease will commonly contain a covenant requiring the tenant to pay to the landlord all fees, costs and expenses incurred or payable by the landlord in connection with any steps taken in contemplation of, or in relation to, forfeiture proceedings. It has been held that such a clause is wide enough to embrace legal costs incurred in either the county court or tribunal in proceedings brought by the landlord for the recovery of service charges (or other determination of breach), on the basis that no forfeiture can occur until it has been determined that the service charge is payable or the breach has occurred.[28] This has the potential to increase significantly the ability of landlords[29] to recover their legal costs incurred in bringing (or, possibly, defending[30]) service charge claims and breach of covenant claims in the tribunal.

Indemnity covenants

10.11   In addition, residential long leases often contain covenants requiring the tenant to indemnify the landlord in respect of legal costs incurred by the landlord in remedying a breach of covenant by the tenant. The costs said to be payable under such covenants are variable administration charges.[31]

---

28   *Freeholds of 69 Marina v Oram* [2011] EWCA Civ 1258; [2012] HLR 12; Housing Act 1996 s81; CLRA 2002 s168; see further chapter 11.

29   But not management companies, as they cannot forfeit leases.

30   See the discussion in *Cussens v Realreed Ltd* [2013] EWHC 1229 (QB), as to the broad range of cases which could satisfy CLRA 2002 s168.

31   *Christoforou v Standard Apartments Ltd* [2013] UKUT 586 (LC).

CHAPTER 11

Forfeiture

Key points

- Leases often contain a provision that allows the landlord to bring the lease to an end if the tenant defaults on any obligation under the lease, including a covenant to pay service charges. This is known as 'forfeiture.'
- A court order is required before a lease can be deemed forfeit.
- In most cases, the landlord is required to prove that the breach has occurred before being able to forfeit. This can be done by proceedings in the tribunal
- The landlord may not forfeit for failure to pay rent, service charges or administration charges where less than £350 has been due for less than 3 years.

Advice for tenants

- Leases often contain a provision that allows the landlord to bring the lease to an end if the tenant defaults on any obligation under the lease, including a covenant to pay service charges. This is known as 'forfeiture'.
- A court order is required before a lease can be deemed forfeit.
- Where the landlord is attempting to forfeit for failure to pay service charges or administration charges, the landlord must first have obtained a determination from the court, the tribunal or an arbitral tribunal that the amount of the service charge or administration charge is payable.
- The landlord may not forfeit for failure to pay rent, service charges or administration charges where less than £350 has been due for less than three years.

Introduction

11.1   Many leases have a provision which allows the landlord[1] to bring the lease to an end if the tenant defaults on any of the covenants in the lease – including covenants to pay rent and service charges. This process is known as 'forfeiture'.

11.2   Forfeiture is a Draconian remedy because, if successful, the tenant will lose their property, which will usually be worth far more than any damage suffered by the landlord.

11.3   For this reason, there a number of statutory provisions intended to make it more difficult for a landlord to forfeit a lease. In outline they are:

a) for premises let as a dwelling, a possession order is required;[2]

b) most breaches of covenant (other than a failure to pay rent) require the landlord to serve a notice giving the tenant an opportunity to remedy the breach before bringing proceedings for forfeiture;[3]

c) for breaches of covenant other than a failure to pay rent, the fact of the breach must first be admitted or proved before any steps may be taken by the landlord.[4]

11.4   The tribunal has a limited role in relation to forfeiture. It does not, for example, deal with possession proceedings. Its primary role is in relation to obtaining a determination of breach as a prelude to forfeiture for covenants other than to pay rent.

11.5   It is impossible to cover the law of forfeiture in this chapter in any detail,[5] but, equally, there needs to be some explanation of the general law in order to understand the role of the tribunal in the process.

---

1 And only the landlord, ie a management company – even as a party to the lease – cannot exercise a right of forfeiture. *Hotley v Scott* (1773) Lofft 316, 319; *Doe d Barney v Adams* (1832) 2 C&J 232 1 LJ Ex 105; *Doe d Barker v Goldsmith* (1832) 2 C&J 674.

2 Protection from Eviction Act (PEA) 1977.

3 Law of Property Act (LPA) 1925 s146.

4 Housing Act (HA) 1996 s81; Commonhold and Leasehold Reform Act (CLRA) 2002 s168.

5 Such treatment would, in any event, be beyond the scope of this work; regard should be had to the usual landlord and tenant textbooks, eg Megarry & Wade, *The law of real property*, 8th edn, Sweet & Maxwell, 2012; Woodfall, *Landlord and tenant*, Sweet & Maxwell, looseleaf.

The right to forfeit

11.6   The most common way in which the right to forfeit arises is if there
has been a breach of covenant which gives rise to a contractual right
to re-enter the property or forfeit the lease. Note that such a clause
will not usually be implied.[6]

11.7   Although it is extremely unusual for a forfeiture clause to be
absent from a lease, tenant advisers should satisfy themselves that
there is such a clause in the lease and that any conditions it imposes
on the exercise of the right have been satisfied.

Waiver of forfeiture

11.8   Upon discovering the breach, the landlord must make a choice (or
'election'): to accept the breach and forfeit the lease; or to waive the
breach and allow the lease to continue.[7]

11.9   A decision to waive the breach need not be communicated in writing to a leaseholder; rather, the law looks to see if the landlord, knowing that there has been a breach of the lease which has given rise to a
right to forfeit, does some act which is only compatible with the lease
continuing.[8]

11.10   A very common situation in which waiver of forfeiture occurs is
when a landlord, knowing of a tenant's breach of covenant, demands
or accepts rent falling due after that breach; such a demand or accept-
ance is, of course, only consistent with the continued existence of
the lease and incompatible with forfeiture, such that the landlord is
likely to lose the right to forfeit.[9]

11.11   Advisers dealing with a forfeiture situation should always assess
very carefully whether a waiver of forfeiture may have arisen.

Exercising the right to forfeit

11.12   In the past, a power to forfeit a lease was often expressed to be exercisable by 're-entry'. All a landlord needed to do was to re-enter the

6   *Re Anderton and Milner's Contract* (1890) 45 Ch D 476.
7   *Mathews v Smallwood* [1910] 1 Ch 777; *Cornillie v Saha* (1996) 72 P&CR 147.
8   See generally *Matthews v Smallwood* [1910] 1 Ch 777.
9   *Expert Clothing Service and Sales Ltd v Hillgate House Ltd* [1986] 1 Ch 340; [1985]
3 WLR 359.

property peaceably and the lease would come to an end, though it could be brought back into existence if the tenant successfully applied to a court for relief against forfeiture.

11.13   In modern times, forfeiture is almost always exercised by applying for an order for possession from a court. For tenants of a dwelling, a court order is compulsory before a lease is forfeit.[10] An attempt to evict a residential tenant unlawfully is (potentially) a breach of contract,[11] a tort[12] and a crime.[13]

Right to relief

11.14   Where there has been a breach of covenant, a tenant will usually retain the right to ask the court to give 'relief' from forfeiture.

11.15   In general terms this permits the tenant either to pay all the arrears of rent, together with the landlord's reasonable costs, or in the case of a breach of a covenant other than one to pay the rent, to take steps to remedy the breach. In granting relief, the court will normally order that, upon the tenant taking the necessary steps, the lease continues as if it the landlord had never attempted to exercise a right to forfeit.

11.16   The specific rules on relief are convoluted since there are different statutory powers depending on whether the breach was of a covenant to pay rent or some other covenant; and whether the claim is proceeding in the High Court or county court, as well as an inherent power to give relief. In some cases a tenant will have a right to relief, while in others the court will have a discretion. Advisers should consult one of the standard landlord and tenant textbooks.[14]

Breach of covenant to pay ground rent

11.17   The rent that is due under long leases (usually called the 'ground rent') is often of a very small amount, perhaps tens of pounds every year. Where a landlord has been inactive, a tenant might well

---

10 PEA 1977 s2.
11 If only of the implied covenant for quiet enjoyment; see generally Arden QC, Chan and Madge-Wyld, *Quiet enjoyment: Arden and Partington's guide to remedies for harassment and illegal eviction*, LAG, 7th edn, 2012.
12 HA 1988 ss27–28.
13 PEA 1977 s1.
14 Eg Woodfall, Megarry & Wade.

inadvertently fail to pay the rent when it falls due. Under common law this amounts to a breach of covenant and gives the landlord the right to forfeit the lease. There is anecdotal evidence that some landlords were deliberately waiting for tenants to pay late in order to threaten forfeiture as a way of extorting money from their tenants.[15]

11.18   The CLRA 2002 introduced two specific protections for tenants under long leases of dwellings. First, rent will not be due until the landlord has notified the tenant that it is;[16] and second, the landlord will not be able to forfeit for a failure to pay a small amount of rent for a short period.[17]

Notification that rent is due

11.19   A tenant under a long lease of a dwelling will not be liable to pay any rent until the landlord has served a notice on the tenant that rent is due.[18] The notice must be in the prescribed form.[19] The effect of this is that the notice must specify:

a) the amount that is due;

b) when it would have been due under the lease;

c) a date for payment of the rent, which must be no earlier than when it would have been due under the lease and between 30 and 60 days (inclusive) after the service of the notice;[20]

d) the name of the leaseholder to whom the notice is given;

e) the period to which the rent demanded is attributable;

f) the name of the person to whom payment is to be made, and the address for payment;

g) the name of the landlord by whom the notice is given and (if not specified as the address for payment given above) the landlord's address;

---

15 *Hansard*, 10 June 1998, col 1000, per Barry Gardner MP.

16 CLRA 2002 s166.

17 CLRA 2002 s167.

18 CLRA 2002 s166(1).

19 CLRA 2002 s166(2); Landlord and Tenant (Notice of Rent) (England) Regulations 2004 SI No 3096; Landlord and Tenant (Notice of Rent) (Wales) Regulations 2005 SI No 1355. Note that the English regulations were amended by way of a correction slip dated 26 April 2011.

20 If this results in the date on which the tenant is liable to pay the rent being later than the lease specifies, no interest or other late payment charges may be levied in respect of this period: CLRA 2002 s166(4).

h) information provided in the notes to the form set out in the Schedule to the regulations (which gives some warning to leaseholders of their legal position).

11.20 The Welsh regulations permit a landlord to serve a notice that is 'substantially to the same effect' as the prescribed form.[21] The English regulations do not.

11.21 The tenant then becomes liable to pay the rent on the date specified in the notice.

11.22 For these purposes, 'rent' does not include service or administration charges[22] even if they are reserved as rent under the lease. These charges have their own, more exacting, requirements for notice.[23]

11.23 If the notice is sent by post, then it must be addressed to the tenant at the dwelling, unless the tenant has notified the landlord of another address (which must be in England or Wales) to which notices that rent is due should be sent, in which case the landlord must send the notice to that other address.[24] In any claim for forfeiture, the landlord must plead and prove compliance with these provisions.[25]

Small amount and short period

11.24 A landlord is also prevented from bringing proceedings for forfeiture of a long lease of a dwelling for failure to pay either rent, service or administration charges (or any combination of them) unless either:[26]

a) the amount owed is more than a 'small amount'; or
b) at least part of the sum owing has been payable for more than a 'short period'.

11.25 Regulations have set the 'small amount' to £350, and the 'short period' to three years.[27]

11.26 The calculation of the amount owed excludes any 'default charge', ie an administration charge imposed for failure to pay rent, service or

21 Landlord and Tenant (Notice of Rent) (Wales) Regulations 2005 reg 3(2).
22 CLRA 2002 s166(7).
23 See chapter 3.
24 CLRA 2002 s166(6).
25 *Chasewood Park Residents Ltd v Kim* [2010] EWHC 579 (Ch).
26 CLRA 2002 s167(1).
27 Rights of Re-entry and Forfeiture (Prescribed Sum and Period) (England) Regulations 2004 SI No 3086; Rights of Re-entry and Forfeiture (Prescribed Sum and Period) (Wales) Regulations 2005 SI No 1352.

administration charges on time[28] otherwise a landlord would be able to avoid the protection given to tenants by imposing default charges that would automatically take any arrears over the specified 'small amount'.

Breach of other covenants (except service and administration charges)

11.27   Where a landlord wishes to forfeit a lease because a tenant has breached a covenant, other than one to pay rent, the landlord will normally be required to serve a notice (under LPA 1925), called a 'section 146 notice', on the tenant.

11.28   The notice must specify the breach of covenant that is complained of and give the tenant a reasonable time in which to remedy it. Only if the tenant fails to remedy the breach within that time, is the landlord permitted to forfeit the lease.[29]

11.29   The landlord is not required to serve a section 146 notice if the breach of covenant by the tenant is not capable of being remedied, the thinking being that since the tenant cannot put the breach right, there is no point in asking them to do so. There is a great deal of case-law as to what does and does not constitute an irremediable breach of covenant which we will not discuss here.

Protection for residential tenants

11.30   CLRA 2002 s168 prevents service of a notice under LPA 1925 s146 in respect of any breach of covenant (other than one relating to service charges or administration charges)[30] unless:

a) the tribunal has determined that the breach has occurred; or
b) the tenant had admitted the breach; or
c) a court or arbitral tribunal has determined that the breach has occurred.

11.31   Save where the tenant had admitted the breach, no notice under section 146 can be served until at least 14 days have passed since the decision became final.[31]

---

28   CLRA 2002 s167(3).
29   LPA 1925 s146.
30   Which are governed by HA 1996 s81; see further CLRA 2002 s169.
31   CLRA 2002 s168(3).

11.32　　The tribunal is limited to deciding whether or not the breach has occurred; it need not be subsisting at the date of the application or hearing.[32] In addition, the tribunal must not go on to consider whether the landlord has suffered any loss or whether relief from forfeiture is likely to be granted.[33] The tribunal may, however, consider whether the landlord has waived the covenant or is estopped from alleging a breach.[34]

11.33　　It has been held that the tribunal has a discretion as to whether to issue a determination: *Beaufort Park Residents Management Ltd v Sabahipour*.[35] The Upper Tribunal found that there had been a breach, but postponed making a determination under section 168 to give the tenant time to remedy. Such postponed order may be familiar to advisers who deal with social housing, and it has obvious practical value in working justice, but the authors doubt that the tribunal actually has such a jurisdiction. Nevertheless, *Sabahipour* remains, at the time of writing, good authority for the possibility that a tribunal may postpone a finding under section 168 in the interests of justice. Unless and until it is overturned, tenant advisers should consider requesting such a postponement where it would benefit the tenant.

11.34　　Section 168 can also be satisfied by making an application to the county court for a declaration that the tenant is in breach of covenant.[36] If the landlord issues proceedings for a declaration in the county court, it is, however, possible for the court to transfer the case to the tribunal.[37]

Breach of covenant to pay service or administration charges

11.35　Some leases are said to 'reserve' payments (which will usually be service or administration charges) as rent. Until recently it was understood that any such reservation gave the payment the 'character

---

32　*Forest House Estates Ltd v Al-Harthi* [2013] UKUT 479 (LC).

33　*Glass v McCready* [2009] UKUT 136 (LC).

34　*Swanston Grange (Luton) Management Ltd v Eileen Langley Essen* [2008] L&TR 20.

35　[2011] UKUT 436 (LC).

36　*Cussens v Realread Ltd* [2013] EWHC 1229 (QB).

37　*Cussens*. See also the discussion at [2013] EWCA Civ 1333 (refusing permission to appeal in *Cussens* about the significance of the different costs regimes in the tribunal and county court and whether the county court should adopt the same approach to costs as in the tribunal).

of rent'[38] with the result that, for the purposes of forfeiture, such payments would be treated as rent payments. If there were no clear reservation, the charge would not be 'rent' for the purposes of LPA 1925 s146.[39]

11.36   One effect of being treated as a payment of rent is that a landlord would not need to serve a section 146 notice before bringing a claim for forfeiture.[40] In such a situation, where a court grants relief against forfeiture by ordering the tenant to pay all arrears of rent and the landlord's costs, the service charges owed will be treated as rent and would form part of the sum that the tenant had to pay.

11.37   This situation has been thrown into doubt by the Court of Appeal's 2011 decision in *Freeholders of 69 Marina v Oram*.[41] The court appears to have held that the effect of section 81 of the HA 1996 (see below) was to modify the effect of LPA 1925 s146 on residential leaseholds so as to require the service of a section 146 notice in all cases of service (or administration) charge arrears, whether they have been reserved as rent or not.

11.38   The reasoning of the court has been widely criticised,[42] and it is the authors' view that it was wrongly decided, not least because it contradicts earlier authority.[43] Despite this view, tenant advisers can properly argue that a landlord is required to serve a section 146 notice in all service and administration charge cases.

Protection for residential tenants

11.39   HA 1996 s81 contains significant restrictions on the rights of a landlord to forfeit for arrears of service charge or administration charges.

11.40   Before a landlord may exercise a right of re-entry or forfeiture[44] for non-payment of service charges or administration charges, the landlord must first have obtained a determination from the court,

---

38   *Escalus Properties v Robinson* [1996] QB 231 per Nourse LJ.
39   *Khar v Delbounty Ltd* (1998) 75 P&CR 232; [1996] EGCS 183.
40   LPA 1925 s146(11).
41   [2011] EWCA Civ 1258.
42   'Reservations on forfeiture', Daniel Dovar, [2012] L&T Review 16(1), 23–26 and 'Freeholders of 69 Marina: judicial reading between the lines ...', Kester Lees, [2012] Conv 6, 498–505.
43   *Escalus Properties v Robinson* [1996] QB 231; *Khar v Delbounty Ltd* (1998) 75 P&CR 232; [1996] EGCS 183; and *Contractreal v Davies* [2001] EWCA Civ 928 at [45] per Arden LJ.
44   Which includes service of an LPA 1925 s146 notice: HA 1996 s81(4A).

the tribunal or an arbitral tribunal that the amount of the service charge or administration charge is payable.[45] In the case of the tribunal, a determination under LTA 1985 s27A and/or CLRA 2002 Sch 11 would clearly be sufficient. Alternatively, the tenant may admit that it is so payable.[46]

11.41 There are conflicting county court decisions on whether a default judgment under Civil Procedure Rules (CPR) Part 12 is a 'determination' for these purposes: In *Church Commissioners for England v Koyale Enterprises*[47] and *Southwark LBC v Tornaritis*[48] it was held that a default judgment was sufficient, whereas in *Hillbrow (Richmond) Ltd v Alogaily*[49] it was held not to be on the basis that a 'determination' requires an actual decision whereas a default judgment is obtained by an administrative act.[50]

11.42 Even after obtaining a determination, the landlord may not exercise a right of re-entry or forfeiture until at least 14 days after the determination became final.[51] A determination becomes final once the time for an appeal has passed or any appeal has been decided or abandoned.[52]

11.43 In *Mohammadi v Anston Investments Ltd*[53] it was suggested (without deciding the point) that landlords should plead and prove compliance with s81 in any claim for forfeiture. It was also suggested that the court would be required to satisfy itself that s81 had been complied with, regardless of the pleading.

---

45 HA 1996 s81(1)(a).
46 HA 1996 s81(1)(b).
47 [2012] L&TR 24.
48 [1999] CLY 3744.
49 [2006] CLY 2707.
50 In the light of *Faizi v Greenside Properties Ltd* [2013] EWCA Civ 1382 and *New Century Media Ltd v Makhlay* [2013] EWHC 3556 (QB), it seems that a default judgment probably is sufficient.
51 HA 1996 s81(2).
52 HA 1996 s81(3), (3A).
53 [2003] EWCA Civ 981; [2004] HLR 8.

CHAPTER 12

Right to buy

Key points

- During the 'right to buy' process, the landlord will serve a notice setting out the service charges expected to be payable in the first five years. Apart from increasing for inflation, the landlord will usually be forced to keep to the terms of this notice in respect of repairs and improvements
- There is a right to a loan from the landlord in order to pay for certain categories of service charge within the first ten years of the lease. There are also additional rights to loans or financial assistance.
- Further, there is government guidance as to when certain costs should or could be waived if funded from public funds.

Advice for tenants

- Properties acquired pursuant to the 'right to buy' come with a number of additional rights and obligations which do not necessarily apply to leaseholders of other properties. The most important of these is a cap on service charges during the initial years of the lease, although other limitations on service charges also exist.
- In addition, tenants should not overlook their right to a loan from the landlord in respect of service charge demands. It will usually be preferable to borrow money from the landlord than from a private company.

Introduction

12.1   The 'right to buy'[1] is a statutory right for certain tenants of social landlords to purchase the leasehold or freehold of their homes. The process by which a tenant exercises this right is beyond the scope of this work,[2] however, in the case of tenants who have purchased the leasehold of their homes, there are a number of important statutory

---

1   See generally Housing Act (HA) 1985 Part 5.
2   See Arden, Partington et al, *Housing law*, Sweet & Maxwell, looseleaf.

provisions that operate in addition to the general law described elsewhere in this book.

Lease construction

12.2   In general terms, the case-law on the construction of service charge clauses in leases has taken a relatively restrictive approach, requiring the landlord to identify clear words in the lease which unambiguously provide for recovery of the items in question.[3] The Lands Tribunal/Upper Tribunal has indicated that a less restrictive approach may be taken with right to buy leases, particularly as regards recovery of management costs.[4] In addition, the terms of a Housing Act (HA) 1985 s125 notice (see below) are relevant when construing the terms of the lease.[5]

12.3   Further, certain terms are implied into the lease by the HA 1985, such that advisers will need to consider both the express terms of the lease and the statutorily implied terms before being able to advise properly.[6]

Section 125 notices

12.4   During the right to buy process, the landlord must serve a notice under section 125 of the HA 1985. While the notice deals primarily with the proposed purchase price, it must also contain details about service charges.[7]

12.5   The exact nature of the notice will vary from case to case. In general terms, it must provide estimates for repairs[8] and improvements[9]

---

3   See generally, chapter 1; *Gilje v Charlegrove Securities Ltd* [2002] 1 EGLR 41.

4   *LB Brent v Hamilton* LRX/51/2005; *Norwich City Council v Marshall* LRX/114/2007; *Palley v Camden LBC* [2010] UKUT 469 (LC); *Southwark LBC v Paul* [2013] UKUT 0375 (LC); *Waverley Borough Council v Kamal Arya* [2013] UKUT 0501 (LC).

5   *Leicester City Council v Masters* LRX/175/2007.

6   See HA 1985 Sch 6. This can make a significant difference, see eg *Sheffield City Council v St Clare Oliver* LRX/146/2007. Note that not all the provisions in HA 1985 Sch 6 are implied; some are merely permissive of what can be included in a lease: *Mihovilovic v Leicester City Council* [2010] UKUT 22 (LC).

7   HA 1985 s125A.

8   HA 1985 s125A(2).

9   HA 1985 s125B.

over a period of five years, starting no later than six months after the service of the section 125 notice.[10]

12.6   The tenant cannot be required to pay service charges for repairs or improvements in excess of those specified in the section 125 notice,[11] although an allowance is made for inflation.[12]

12.7   A section 125 notice does not guarantee that works will be carried out within a particular period, nor that the costs will be incurred during that period,[13] nor is there anything necessarily impermissible in works projects starting during the reference period but continuing after the period ends, so that the leaseholder may be charged in full for those works which fall outside of the reference period.[14] A notice may, however, be used to found an estoppel against an authority to prevent recovery of costs if the facts justify the same.[15]

Administration charges[16]

12.8   Any provision of a lease granted under the right to buy which purports to allow the landlord to charge the tenant a sum for or in connection with the giving or a consent or approval is void.[17]

Consultation provisions[18]

12.9   For the first 30 days of a right-to-buy tenancy the consultation requirements do not apply.[19]

---

10   Called a 'reference period'. While the period of five years from a date no later than six months after the service of the section 125 notice is usual, other periods may be chosen: see HA 1985 s125C.
11   HA 1985 Sch 6 paras 16B and 16C.
12   Housing (Right to Buy) (Service Charges) Order 1986 SI No 2195.
13   *LB Havering v Smith* [2012] UKUT 295 (LC).
14   *LB Havering v Smith* [2012] UKUT 295 (LC).
15   *LB Havering v Smith* [2012] UKUT 295 (LC).
16   See chapter 6.
17   HA 1985 Sch 6 para 6.
18   See chapter 3.
19   Service Charges (Consultation Requirements) (England) Regulations 2003 SI No 1987; Service Charges (Consultation Requirements) (Wales) Regulations 2004 SI No 684 – regs 5 and 7 in each case. See *Mihovilovic v Leicester City Council* [2010] UKUT 22 (LC) for how to calculate the 30-day period.

Equity share purchases

12.10   Both the secretary of state and the Welsh Ministers have power to make regulations providing for a housing authority landlord to purchase an equitable interest in a long lease granted by the authority in exchange for a reduction (in whole or part) in the service charges payable by the tenant.[20] Both have exercised this power.[21]

12.11   The Welsh and English regulations are essentially identical in terms. The power may only be exercised for service charges in respect of repairs or improvements (and hence not management costs) with the consent of the tenant and where the purpose of the purchase is to assist the tenant meeting some or all of the service charge payments. The authority and tenant can agree that part of the purchase price will include the authority's administrative costs. There is no mechanism by which a tenant can 'pay off' the equitable interest by forcing the authority to sell it back.

Loans

12.12   A tenant may have a right to a loan from their local authority landlord in respect of service charges (again, only in respect of repairs and improvements) incurred under leases granted pursuant to the right to buy.[22] In addition, tenants of other categories of leases granted by specified public authorities may be able to apply for loans in respect of their service charges.[23] Detailed provision for such loans are made in statutory instrument.[24]

---

20   HA 1985 s450D.
21   Housing (Purchase of Equitable Interests) (England) Regulations 2009 SI No 601; Housing (Purchase of Equitable Interests) (Wales) Regulations 2011 SI No 1865.
22   HA 1985 s450A.
23   HA 1985 s450B.
24   Housing (Service Charge Loans) Regulations 1992 SI No 1708.

Discretionary reductions

12.13   The secretary of state has power to issue directions to social landlords[25] about service charge recovery in respect of repairs, maintenance or improvement works.[26] Those directions may require or permit the waiver or reduction of charges in specified circumstances.[27]

12.14   Two sets of directions have been issued.[28] Landlords have a discretionary power to reduce or waive service charges for past, current and future works of repair, maintenance or improvement if (a) the total charges exceed £10,000 in a five-year period; or (b) if carried out wholly or partially with the assistance of the Estate Action City Challenge, the Single Regeneration Challenge Fund or the Estates Renewal Challenge Fund, where that funding was applied for before 25 February 1997.[29]

12.15   Landlords are required to reduce service charges for repairs, maintenance or improvements carried out wholly or partially with the assistance of the Single Regeneration Challenge Fund or the Estates Renewal Challenge Fund, where that funding was applied for on or after 25 February 1997 and if the charges will exceed £10,000 in a five-year period.[30] In October 2013, the government proposed extending the scope of these directions to cover additional sources of funding.[31]

12.16   The application of the directions is not something that the tribunal can consider.[32] Further, a tenant cannot obtain relief under the directions unless the tenant first pays the service charge or it is otherwise determined that a sum is payable by them.[33]

---

25 In general terms, a district council, unitary authority or registered social landlord: HA 1996 s219(4).

26 HA 1996 s219.

27 HA 1996 s219(1)(a)–(b).

28 Social Landlords Discretionary Reduction of Service Charges (England) Directions 1997; Social Landlords Mandatory Reduction of Service Charges (England) Directions 1997.

29 Social Landlords Discretionary Reduction of Service Charges (England) Directions 1997.

30 Social Landlords Mandatory Reduction of Service Charges (England) Directions 1997.

31 See *Protecting local authority leaseholders from unreasonable charges*, DCLG, October 2013.

32 *Craighead v Islington LBC* [2010] UKUT 47(LC).

33 *Craighead v Islington LBC* [2010] UKUT 47(LC).

CHAPTER 13

Funding cases

Key points

- It is very unlikely that legal aid will be available for hearings before the tribunal.
- Legal expenses insurance should be explored as a possible source of funding
- Alternatively, there are various pro bono (ie, free) groups who will provide advice, assistance and representation.

Advice for tenants

- It is too simplistic simply to say that tenants can represent themselves before the tribunal. Certain types of proceedings will require expert evidence and, in that case, it will be necessary to instruct a surveyor. In addition, some cases are legally complex and, without legal assistance, tenants will find themselves at a disadvantage.
- Legal aid is only available in truly exceptional circumstances. Tenants need to think innovatively when it comes to securing funding. Insurance policies are worth exploring. It may be possible to obtain pro bono (free) legal advice. Tenants who are unable to fund a case themselves should make full use of these resources.

Introduction

13.1　The tribunal was designed to be a less formal forum for resolving disputes than that provided by the courts. It was intended that parties should be able to represent themselves without needing expert legal advice.

13.2　The reality, however, is more complex. Some disputes involve complex issues of law (eg lease interpretation); others require expert evidence (eg whether premises can be the subject of a right to manage application). Such disputes, involving technical and complex matters, will usually mean that parties are well advised to instruct a surveyor, solicitor and/or barrister.

13.3　As a general rule, legal aid is unlikely to be available for such matters and tenants will need to be aware of other funding options.

Legal aid

13.4   Legal aid is unlikely to be available for proceedings before the tribunal.[1] Any person seeking legal aid in respect of such proceedings is
likely to need to show that they come within the 'exceptional cases'
category.[2] The authors are not aware of any case in which legal aid
has been granted for a case in the tribunal.

Legal expenses insurance

13.5   Many people have legal expenses insurance as part of their motor,
home or contents insurance policies.[3] Some credit cards also provide insurance of this nature. The primary restriction on the use of
this insurance appears to be that very few people are aware that they
have the benefit of this insurance.[4] Solicitors are obliged, as a matter of professional conduct, to discuss with their clients at the outset
whether such insurance could cover the legal costs.[5]

13.6   After-the-event insurance, while theoretically available, does not
sit easily with tribunal litigation, as the limited costs powers of the
tribunal means that there is no real prospect of a leaseholder recovering costs against a landlord, such that, even a successful leaseholder
will be out-of-pocket in the sum of the cost of the insurance policy.

Pro bono services

13.7   There are some pro bono (ie free) providers of legal advice and representation in London, although the rest of the country is less well
served. BPP Law School has a scheme whereby students (those who
are training to be barristers and/or solicitors) advise leaseholders and

---

1 Legal Aid, Sentencing and Punishment of Offenders (LASPO) Act 2012 s9; Sch
1 Part 1.
2 LASPO Act 2012 s10; *Lord Chancellor's exceptional funding guidance (non-
inquests)*, June 2013.
3 The Jackson Review (Right Honourable Lord Justice Jackson, *Review of civil
litigation costs: final report*, December 2009) suggests that between 10 and 15
million householders have such insurance as part of their home or contents
insurance: Jackson Review ch 8 para 5.1.
4 Jackson Review ch 8 para.5.5.
5 Solicitors' Code of Conduct 2007 para 2.03(1)(d)(ii).

represent them in the tribunal. There is, however, no guarantee that everyone who wants representation will be assisted.

13.8   The Bar Pro Bono unit has also arranged representation in some cases. Contact details are found in appendix D.

Freehold charges

Key points

- Freehold charges can arise in a number of different ways and, for the most part, dealt with in the court rather than the tribunal.
- The exception to that is 'estate management schemes' which are regulated in a similar way to administration charges.

Advice for owners

- It is quite common for there to be a mixture of freehold houses and leasehold flats on the same estate. Many 'new build' estates are designed on this basis. Alternatively, the situation may have developed through the exercise of the right to buy. Freehold owners on such estates are commonly required to contribute to certain shared 'estate' costs. There are many fewer controls on the costs imposed on freeholders than those imposed on leaseholders, and so it is important to know exactly what sort of charge one is dealing with in order to identify what rights one might have.
- In addition, the tribunal has a relatively limited role in relation to freehold charges, which means that litigation will be in the county court.

Introduction

14.1   It is commonly the case that freehold owners of houses are required to contribute to shared costs of estate services, such as gardening, maintaining communal car parking facilities, etc. There is some regulation of these charges, but nothing as detailed as exists for leasehold service charges. The tribunal has a limited role to play in disputes around such charges. This chapter deals first with estate management schemes (a limited category of charge over which the tribunal does have jurisdiction) before dealing briefly with charges payable in respect of land previously owned by certain public authorities (such as houses acquired under the right to buy) and rentcharges. The tribunal has no jurisdiction over these last two categories of charge.

Estate management schemes

14.2 Estate management schemes are defined as those imposed by land-lords as a condition of enfranchisement,[1] which, eg require the owners of the newly enfranchised houses to contribute to certain communal estate costs.

14.3 Anyone may apply to the tribunal for a determination as to whether an estate charge is payable and, if it is, who should pay it, to whom, in what sum, by when and/or in what manner.[2]

14.4 An application may be made regardless of whether payment has been made or not, although a tenant who disputes the charge is well-advised to ensure that any payment made is clearly made 'under protest'.[3]

14.5 An application cannot be made in respect of a matter which:[4]

a) has been agreed or admitted;
b) has been or is to be referred to arbitration pursuant to a post-dispute arbitration agreement to which the tenant is a party;
c) has been the subject of a determination by court; or,
d) has been the subject of a determination by an arbitral tribunal pursuant to a post-dispute arbitration agreement.

14.6 Further, the tribunal has no jurisdiction to consider whether particular costs that may or may not be added to a future estate charge are payable or reasonable.[5]

---

1 See Leasehold Reform Act 1967 s19; Leasehold Reform, Housing and Urban Development Act (LRHUDA) 1993 Ch 4 Part 1 s94(6). For more information on enfranchisement see *Hague on leasehold enfranchisement*, Sweet & Maxwell, 5th edn, 2012. Note that it is only charges arising under these schemes which can be the subject of an application, a point which is often missed, eg *Re 113 Church Lane, London, SW17* LON/00BJ/LVE/2007/0002; *Gosling v Mulbury Management Ltd* LON/00BG/LSC/2005/0320; *Re 55 Empire Walk, Dartford* CHI/29UD/LSC/2008/0110; *Lyric Studios Residents Co Ltd v Catalyst Communities Housing Ltd* LON/00AJ/LSC/2011/0860; *QE Park Residents Management Co Ltd v Cartwright* CHI/43UD/LIS/2009/0059.

2 Commonhold and Leasehold Reform Act (CLRA) 2002 s159(6); as to the width of potential applicants, see *Oakfern Properties Ltd v Ruddy* [2006] EWCA Civ 1389; [2007] Ch 335.

3 CLRA 2002 s159(7).

4 CLRA 2002 s159(9). Note that, while payment does not in and of itself amount to an admission, it might be sufficient if taken with other factors, such as the passage of time: *Shersby v Grenehurst Park Residents Co Ltd* [2009] UKUT 241 (LC).

5 *Freeman v Hampstead Garden Suburb Trust Ltd* LON/00AC/LLE/2006/0001.

Variable estate charges

14.7   A variable estate charge is one which is neither specified in the scheme nor calculated in accordance with a formula specified in the scheme.[6] Such charges are only payable to the extent that the amount is reasonable.[7]

14.8   In *Botterill v Hampstead Garden Suburbs Trust Ltd*,[8] the Lands Tribunal held that a provision in an estate management scheme which obliged all owners to contribute an equal proportion of certain costs[9] was a charge calculated in accordance with a formula and, hence, not a variable estate management charge. That approach has not been followed in relation to the similarly worded provisions on administration charges[10] and was subsequently doubted in *Scriven v Calthorpe Estates*.[11]

Non-variable estate charges

14.9   Any person who is obliged to pay an estate charge may apply to the tribunal for an order varying the scheme on the grounds that any estate charge specified in the scheme is unreasonable or any formula specified in the scheme for the calculation of such charges is unreasonable.[12] As the Upper Tribunal noted in *Scriven v Calthorpe Estates*, this definition would appear to exclude variable estate charges from the scope of these provisions.[13]

14.10   If the tribunal agrees that the charge or formula is unreasonable, then it may make an order varying the scheme.[14] This may be a variation as proposed by the applicant or some other variation as the tribunal thinks fit.[15]

---

6   CLRA 2002 s159(2).
7   CLRA 2002 s159(2). There appear to be relatively few challenges to the reasonableness of such charges. For one example, see *Freeman v Hampstead Garden Suburb Trust Ltd* LON/00AC/LLE/2006/0001.
8   LRX/135/2007.
9   Described as 'x/y = z ... where z is the amount certified as payable and y is the number of properties'.
10   See chapter 6.
11   [2013] UKUT 469 (LC).
12   CLRA 2002 s159(3).
13   Although, as noted above, *Botterill* is to the opposite effect and has not, as yet, been overruled.
14   CLRA 2002 s159(4).
15   CLRA 2002 s159(5).

Public sector charges

14.11 Where specified public authorities[16] (including local authorities and other social landlords) have sold the freehold of a house on terms which provides for the recovery of service charges,[17] then those charges are payable only to the extent that they are reasonably incurred and to the extent that the works or services are of a reasonable standard.[18] This is the same protection as is available to leaseholders under Landlord and Tenant Act (LTA) 1985 s19. Unlike with leasehold service charges, however, disputes are resolved in the county court, rather than the tribunal.[19]

14.12 In addition, the paying party may require the service provider to provide a written summary of costs in the previous 12 months, in a similar manner to LTA 1985 s21.[20] There is also a right to inspect the accounts, receipts and other documents, akin to that in LTA 1985 s22.[21] It is a criminal offence to fail to comply with these obligations, subject to a defence of reasonable excuse.[22] The offence cannot be committed by local authorities, development corporations or the Welsh Ministers.[23] Presumably it is not possible to enforce the obligations by injunction.[24]

Rentcharges

14.13 A rentcharge is a perpetual periodic payment made in respect of freehold land by the current freeholder to a third party (often a predecessor in title).[25] The Rentcharges Act 1977 prohibited the creation of new rentcharges, save for in certain limited circumstances.[26] Those

---

16 HA 1985 s45(1), (2A), (2B).
17 Defined as costs which are payable, directly or indirectly, for services, repairs, maintenance, insurance costs of management, the whole or part of which varies or may vary according to the relevant costs: HA 1985 s621 (and the same as LTA 1985 s18).
18 HA 1985 s47(1).
19 HA 1985 s45(3).
20 HA 1985 s48(1)–(3).
21 HA 1985 s48(4)–(5).
22 HA 1985 s50(1).
23 HA 1985 s50(2).
24 See *Di Marco v Morshead Mansions Ltd* [2014] EWCA Civ 96.
25 See generally Megarry & Wade, *The law of real property*, Sweet & Maxwell, 7th edn, para 30-107; Law Commission Report No 68, 1975.
26 Rentcharges Act 1977 s2.

include the creation of 'estate rentcharges', ie charges for purpose of providing services for the benefit of the land affected or to that and other land.[27] Such charges must be reasonable.[28] A charge designed to create a pure profit is unlikely to pass this test.[29] The degree of benefit which the paying party receives is not relevant; rather, the focus is on the provision of services.[30]

14.14   The tribunal has no jurisdiction over these charges and any disputes must be resolved in the court.

27 Rentcharges Act 1977 s2(4)(b); see *Canwell Estate Co Ltd v Smith Brothers Farms Ltd* [2012] EWCA Civ 237; [2012] 1 WLR 2626 for an example of an estate rentcharge.

28 Rentcharges Act 1977 s2(5). It is unclear whether this means that, if an unreasonable charge is levied, only the reasonable amount is payable or, the whole demand is invalidated. See Susan Bright, 'Estate charges and reasonableness', Conv 2002, Sep/Oct, 507–513.

29 *Orchard Trading Estate Management Ltd v Johnson Security Ltd* [2002] EWCA Civ 406.

30 *Canwell Estate Co Ltd v Smith Brothers Farms Ltd* [2012] EWCA Civ 237; [2012] 1 WLR 2626.

CHAPTER 15

Procedure in Wales

continued

Key points

- In Wales, the LVT still has the 'old' procedure regulations from 2004. Whilst the rules are less detailed than those in England, they have the benefit of over 10 years of case-law to assist in their interpretation.
- Cases can be issued in the LVT or transferred from the court. If the latter, the LVT cannot expand or enlarge the scope of the dispute beyond the matters set out in the pleadings. If parties wish to raise new issues, a fresh application is needed.
- Directions will be issued, giving a time-line for the production of evidence and similar, so as to enable a smooth trial. These can be done after an oral hearing or by the LVT considering the matter on paper.
- The LVT can dismiss vexatious or abusive cases, but otherwise has limited powers to enforce its own directions.
- The final hearing will often start with an inspection of the property, followed by an informal hearing at which all parties get to present their case.
- The decision will usually follow in writing within a few weeks.
- Appeals are to the Upper Tribunal (Lands Chamber).

Advice for tenants

- The leasehold valuation tribunal (LVT) is designed to be a more informal and accessible forum than a court. This does not mean, however, that parties can afford to be flippant or cavalier in their preparation of their cases. The LVT is judicial body, and failure to comply with its orders and rules can lead to the case being dismissed or evidence being excluded.
- It is important to be realistic about the time that it will take to prepare a case, collect evidence, etc and, if a problem arises, to make an application to the LVT for more time or for other directions, rather than simply to allow matters to drift.

Introduction

15.1   Until the creation of the First-tier Tribunal (Property Chamber) (FTT(PC)) in England in July 2013, the LVT in England and Wales had almost identical procedural rules. Those rules were widely regarded as, if not inadequate, then at least insufficiently comprehensive. Whilst England has developed more detailed procedural rules (which are considered in detail in the next chapter), Wales has retained its existing rules.

Starting a case

15.2   There are two ways in which a case can come before the LVT: it can be transferred from existing court proceedings or it can be commenced as a free-standing application.

Transfer from the court

15.3   If the court is faced with a question which may also be determined by the LVT, the court may[1] order that the whole or part of the proceedings be transferred to the LVT.[2] The court retains jurisdiction over any additional or ancillary matters, including enforcement of the LVT decision.[3]

15.4   If the case is to be transferred to the LVT, the court should send notice of the transfer to all parties to the claim and send the LVT all the documents relating to the claim together with the order of transfer.[4] Any monies paid in respect of court fees shall be set off against any fees payable to the LVT.[5]

15.5   In determining whether to transfer the case, the court should have regard to the following (non-exhaustive) factors: [6]

---

1   Commonhold and Leasehold Reform Act (CLRA) 2002 Sch 12 para 3. Note that transfer is discretionary: *Staunton v Taylor* [2010] UKUT 270 (LC).
2   CLRA 2002 Sch 12 para 3(1)(a).
3   CLRA 2002 Sch 12 paras 3(1)(b), 2.
4   Civil Procedure Rules (CPR) Part 56 PD15.
5   Leasehold Valuation Tribunals (Fees) (Wales) Regulations ('LVT Fees Regs') 2004 SI No 683 reg 4.
6   *Aylesbond Estates Ltd v MacMillan and others* (2000) 32 HLR 1; [1999] L&TR 127.

a) the LVT, as an expert tribunal, which habitually inspects premises, may well be in a better position to determine service charge disputes than the county court;[7]

b) however, it may not be as well placed as a court to determine complex questions of law;[8]

c) any referral to the LVT will inevitably involve delay and new directions being given;

d) once the county court has given directions for the management of the case – and particularly if those directions have been complied with – any transfer to the LVT will inevitably involve a delay in the dispute being determined, and a corresponding increase in costs;

e) if the LVT is incapable of resolving all the issues in the case, this is a factor which sounds against any transfer, as it is preferable for all the matters to be resolved together at one hearing.

As both the court and the LVT have the same powers to protect a tenant against claims for costs by the landlord[9] this is not a factor that points one way or the other.

15.6 One limitation of the transfer process is that the parties are not permitted to argue matters which have not been raised in the pleadings and the LVT is not entitled to rule on matters which have not been raised in the pleadings.[10] If the parties wish to extend the scope of the dispute, a fresh application must be issued and consolidated with the transferred proceedings.[11]

Applying to the LVT

15.7 The LVT has a number of model application forms for use in the most common cases. These are available online at http://rpt.wales.gov.uk.

15.8 If there is no appropriate form available, the application can properly be made by sending a letter to the LVT, containing the necessary

---

7 In *Phillips v Francis* [2010] L&TR 28, the High Court considered that the tribunal was the appropriate forum for the great majority of cases.

8 See the discussion in *Schilling v Canary Riverside Development PTD Ltd* LRX/26/2005, in the context of when the tribunal should entertain a counterclaim.

9 Landlord and Tenant Act (LTA) 1985 s20C.

10 *Staunton v Taylor* [2010] UKUT 270 (LC).

11 *Lennon v Ground Rents (Regisport) Ltd* [2011] UKUT 330 (LC).

information[12] and a statement that the applicant believes the information in the letter to be true.[13]

Who may apply?

15.9 A question that is often raised by applicants and their advisers is whether a particular individual is entitled to apply to the LVT. The answer will depend on the particular jurisdiction being exercised by the LVT. In some cases there are legislative provisions which restrict who may apply. Even where there is no restriction, an LVT has the power to strike out a frivolous application.[14] A vexatious litigant[15] may be prohibited from issuing proceedings in the tribunal.[16]

15.10 The table covers all the jurisdictions of the LVT covered in this book, and indicates who may apply under that jurisdiction.

---

12 As to which, see para 15.11 below.
13 Leasehold Valuation Tribunals (Procedure) (Wales) Regulations ('LVT Procedure Regs') 2004 SI No 681 reg 3(1)(e).
14 LVT Procedure Regs reg 11.
15 Within the meaning of Senior Courts Act 1981 s42.
16 *Attorney-General v Singer* [2012] EWHC 326 (Admin). Query whether a similar result could be achieved by use of a civil restraint order.

Provision	Description	Applicant
Service charges		
LTA 1985 s27A	Determination of liability to pay service charge	Anyone[a]
LTA 1985 s20ZA	Dispensation from consultation requirements	Anyone
LTA 1985 s21A	Determination that landlord has a reasonable excuse for a failure giving rise to the tenant's right to withhold service charges	Landlord[b] (includes any person who has a right to enforce payment of service charges)[c]
LTA 1985 s20C	Order that costs in connection with LVT proceedings should not be regarded as relevant costs	Tenant[d]
Administration charges		
CLRA 2002 Sch 11 para 3	Variation of administration charge provision in a lease	Any party to the lease[e]
CLRA 2002 Sch 11 para 5	Liability to pay an administration charge	Anyone[f]
Estate charges		
CLRA 2002 s159(3)	Variation of estate charge provisions in an estate management scheme	Any person on whom an obligation to pay an estate charge is imposed by the scheme
CLRA 2002 s159(6)	Determination of payability of an estate charge	Anyone[g]

a   See also *Oakfern Properties Ltd v Ruddy* [2006] EWCA Civ 1389; [2007] Ch 335.
b   If a Right to Manage (RTM) company has acquired the right to manage, the RTM company has the right instead of the landlord: CLRA 2002 Sch 11 para 4(2).
c   LTA 1985 s30.
d   Includes a landlord under a lease of the whole or any part of the premises if an RTM company has acquired the right to manage: CLRA 2002 Sch 11 para 4(3).
e   Includes an RTM company, if it has acquired the right to manage: CLRA 2002 Sch 11 para 16.
f   See, by analogy, *Oakfern Properties Ltd v Ruddy* [2006] EWCA Civ 1389; [2007] Ch 335.
g   See, by analogy, *Oakfern Properties Ltd v Ruddy* [2006] EWCA Civ 1389; [2007] Ch 335.

Provision	Description	Applicant
Variation of leases		
LTA 1987 s35	Application to vary a long lease	A party to the lease[h]
LTA 1987 s36	Application to vary another lease in response to an LTA 1987 s35 application to vary a long lease	A party to the LTA 1987 s35 lease
LTA 1987 s37	Application to vary two or more leases	Landlord or any tenant of the leases
LTA 1987 s39(3)(b)	Application for the cancellation or modification of an order varying a lease	A person on whom a notice was required to be served under LTA 1987 s35(5)
Variation of insurance provisions		
LTA 1987 s40(1)	Variation of the insurance provisions of a dwelling	A party to the lease
Challenge to the landlord's choice of insurer		
LTA 1985 Schedule para 8	Challenge to the landlord's choice of insurer	Landlord[i] or tenant[j]
Appointment of manager		
LTA 1987 s24(1)	Order appointing a manager	Tenant[k]
LTA 1987 s24(9)	Variation or discharge of order appointing a manager	Any person interested
LTA 1987 s22(3)	Order dispensing with requirement to serve a preliminary notice before applying for appointment of a manager	Anyone

h Includes an RTM company, if it has acquired the right to manage: CLRA 2002 Sch 11 para 10.
i If an RTM company has acquired the right to manage in respect of the premises, the RTM company instead of the landlord: CLRA 2002 Sch 11 para 5(2).
j Includes a landlord under a lease of the whole or any part of the premises who is under an obligation to make payments under CLRA 2002 s103 (landlord's contribution to service charges): CLRA 2002 Sch 11 para 5(3).
k Includes a landlord under a lease of the whole or any part of the premises, where an RTM company has acquired the right to manage: CLRA 2002 Sch 11 para 8(3).

Provision	Description	Applicant
Right to Manage		
CLRA 2002 s84(3)	Determination that an RTM company was entitled to acquire the right to manage in response to a counter-notice	The RTM company
CLRA 2002 s85(2)	Order that an RTM company is to acquire the right to manage where the landlord is missing	The RTM company
CLRA 2002 s88(4)	Determination of any question arising in relation to the costs payable by an RTM company	Anyone
CLRA 2002 s94(3)	Determination of amount of payment of accrued uncommitted service charges	(1) Any party, other than a tenant, of a lease of the whole or part of the premises (2) A manager appointed by the LVT (3) The RTM company
CLRA 2002 s99(1)	Determination of whether an approval is to be given under the terms of the lease	The RTM company, landlord, tenant or sub-tenant (where the approval is to be given by a tenant)
CLRA 2002 Sch 6 para 5(3)	Determination that right to manage may be exercised earlier than four years	The RTM company
Forfeiture		
CLRA 2002 s168(4)	Determination that a breach of covenant or other condition in the lease has occurred	Landlord

Information to be included

15.11   All applications must include the following information:[17]

    a) the name and address of the applicant;

    b) the name and address of the respondent;

    c) the name and address of any landlord or tenant of the property to which the application relates;

    d) the address of the premises to which the application relates;

    e) a statement that the applicant believes the facts stated in the application to be true.

15.12   In addition, each application has further specified requirements, as follows.

Service charge, administration charge and estate charge applications[18]

    a) A copy of the lease/estate management scheme must always be included;

    b) if the application is to determine the payability of service charges, the name and address of any recognised tenant's association must be included;

    c) if the application is to vary an administration charge, a draft of the proposed variation must be included.

Estate management schemes[19]

    a) A copy of the existing estate management scheme or proposed estate management scheme must always be included;

    b) a statement that the applicant is either a natural person, a representative body or a relevant authority;

    c) any notice given under Leasehold Reform, Housing and Urban Development Act 1993 s70;

    d) any proposed variation to an estate management scheme must include a description of the proposed variation, including identification of the area by a map or plan;

    e) a copy of any consent given by the National Assembly for Wales under Leasehold Reform, Housing and Urban Development Act 1993 s72.[20]

---

17 LVT Procedure Regs reg 3(1).

18 LVT Procedure Regs Sch 2 para 2.

19 LVT Procedure Regs Sch 2 para 3.

20 Presumably, if the consent was provided by the secretary of state as it pre-dated the establishment of the Assembly, then that should be provided instead.

Right to manage[21]

a) The name and address for service of the RTM company, the name and address of the freeholder, any intermediate landlord; and manager;

b) a copy of the memorandum and articles of association of the RTM company;

c) where the application is by the RTM company to determine whether, following the receipt of a counter notice, it was entitled to acquire the right to manage, a copy of the claim notice and any counter notices must be provided;

d) where the RTM company is unable to trace a landlord and applies to the LVT to determine whether it can acquire the right to manage, a statement must be served showing that the notice inviting participation and the notice of claim were fulfilled and a copy of the notice served on all qualifying tenants must also be provided. The reasons why the landlord cannot be identified and traced should also be set out;

e) where the application relates to uncommitted service charges, an estimate of the value of the accrued but uncommitted service charges must be provided;

f) where the RTM company wishes to grant an approval for works or the like without going through the prescribed process and applies to the LVT for dispensation, a copy of the lease must be provided;

g) where the RTM company applies for a determination that, although the right to manage has lapsed, the RTM company should still be permitted to exercise the right to manage, the RTM company must set out the date and circumstances in which the right to manage ceased.

Appointment of manager[22]

a) Where a preliminary notice was served, a copy of that notice;

b) where the application is to vary an existing management order, a copy of the earlier order must be provided.

Variation of leases[23]

a) The name and address of all persons who were served with notice of proposed variation.

b) a draft of the proposed variation;

c) a copy of the lease.

21 LVT Procedure Regs Sch 2 para 4
22 LVT Procedure Regs Sch 2 para 5.
23 LVT Procedure Regs Sch 2 para 6.

Determination of breach of covenant[24]

a) A statement giving particulars of the alleged breach of covenant;

b) a copy of the lease.

15.13   The LVT may dispense with or relax any of these requirements where no prejudice will be caused or is likely to be caused and the information which is provided is sufficient to enable the application to be determined.[25]

Service of the application

15.14   In all cases other than for the variation of a lease described in chapter seven the LVT shall send a copy of the application to the respondent[26] and any other person that it considers appropriate[27] together with details of how to apply to be joined as a party.[28] In service charge, administration charge and estate management charge cases, the LVT shall also give notice of the application to the secretary of any recognised tenants' association and any person who is likely to be significantly affected by the application.[29] The tribunal has power to make orders for substituted service or to dispense with service.[30]

15.15   Where an application to vary a lease is made in accordance with chapter 7, the applicant must give notice of the application to the respondent and any other person who is known or believed to be likely to be affected.[31] Failure to do so may lead to the variation being set aside and a claim for damages.[32] The tribunal may dispense with the requirement for the applicant to serve the documents.[33]

15.16   The LVT may give notice by placing an advertisement in two local newspapers, at least one of which should be a freely distributed

---

24 LVT Procedure Regs Sch 2 para 7.

25 LVT Procedure Regs reg 3(8); see *Gateway Property Holdings Ltd v 6–10 Montrose Gardens RTM Co Ltd* [2011] UKUT 349 (LC) as to what level of detail and documentation is required.

26 LVT Procedure Regs reg 5(1).

27 LVT Procedure Regs reg 5(3).

28 LVT Procedure Regs reg 5(4).

29 LVT Procedure Regs reg 5(2).

30 LVT Procedure Regs reg 23, as explained in *Tobicon Ltd v Rhiannon Collinson* LRX/117/2011

31 LVT Procedure Regs reg 4.

32 LTA 1987 s39.

33 LVT Procedure Regs reg 3(7)–(8), as explained in *Cleary v Lakeside Developments Ltd* [2011] UKUT 264 (LC).

newspaper.[34] This is likely to be relevant where a very large of number of respondents are involved, for example where a council makes an application concerning all, or a large section of, its leaseholders; or where a party is missing or cannot be found.

Fees

15.17   Some – but not all – applications attract a fee.[35] Any relevant fee must be sent with the application, save that fees incurred as a result of a transfer of proceedings from a court must be paid within 14 days of being requested.[36] The fee must be paid by cheque or postal order, drawn in favour of the National Assembly for Wales.[37]

15.18   Where a fee is due and not paid, the application shall not proceed until the fee is paid.[38] If the fee is still outstanding one month after it became due, the application shall be treated as withdrawn unless there are reasonable grounds for it remaining outstanding.[39]

15.19   The amount payable by way of application fee varies according to the value of the application and the type of application.[40]

15.20   In the following cases, the fee is based on the charge which is the subject of the application:[41]

a) an application to determine the liability to pay a service charge or administration charge;

b) a challenge to insurance premiums;

c) variation of a lease because of an administration charge,

and the following fees apply:

Charge which is the subject of the application	Application fee
Not more than £500	£50
More than £500, but not more than £1,000	£70
More than £1,000, but not more than £5,000	£100
More than £5,000, but not more than 15,000	£200
More than £15,000	£350

34 LVT Procedure Regs reg 5(5)–(6).
35 LVT Fees Regs.
36 LVT Fees Regs reg 6.
37 LVT Fees Regs reg 6(3).
38 LVT Procedure Regs reg 7(1).
39 LVT Procedure Regs reg 7(2).
40 LVT Fees Regs reg 3.
41 LVT Fees Regs reg 3(2).

15.21   In the following cases the fee is based on the number of dwellings which are the subject of the application:[42]

a) an application for dispensation from the consultation provisions;
b) a determination as to the suitability of an insurer;
c) the appointment of a manager or the variation of a lease,

and the following fees apply:

Number of dwellings	Application fee
Five or fewer	£150
Between six and ten	£250
More than ten	£350

15.22   If the application is not listed above, then it attracts no application fee. The most obvious example is the absence of any fee for any disputes arising out of the right to manage.

15.23   Regardless of whether there is an application fee or note, all cases attract a hearing fee of £150.[43] It is payable within 14 days of being demanded.[44]

15.24   Those in receipt of the prescribed welfare benefits (or, exceptionally, a legal aid certificate covering the proceedings) are entitled to have their fees waived.[45]

Pre-trial review and other interim matters

15.25   Unless the application appears straightforward, upon receipt of an application, the tribunal is likely to list a pre-trial review (PTR). A PTR may also be requested by the parties.[46] Unless specifically agreed otherwise, at least 14 days' notice of any such hearing must be given.[47]

15.26   If a PTR is listed, it is important that the parties (or their representatives) attend. One of the key roles of a PTR is to set down dates for the service of evidence and the final hearing itself and it is important for each party to have considered any dates that they wish

---

42   LVT Fees Regs reg 3(3)-(4).
43   LVT Fees Regs reg 5.
44   LVT Fees Regs reg 14(2).
45   LVT Fees Regs reg 8.
46   LVT Procedure Regs reg 12(1).
47   LVT Procedure Regs reg 12(2).

to avoid. Although tribunals are not required to list the final hearing at the convenience of the parties, in practice many attempt to do so.

15.27   The purpose of the PTR is to:[48]

a) give any directions that appear necessary or desirable in order to bring about the just, expeditious and economical disposal of proceedings;
b) secure and record all agreements and admissions that can reasonably be made in the proceedings;
c) record any refusal to make agreements or admissions.

15.28   Directions simply mean the steps that must be taken before the final hearing date. Typically they should include:

a) any amendments to the application;
b) the need for any further statements of case;
c) service of witness statements;
d) provision for any expert evidence and the service of experts reports;
e) disclosure of documents;
f) preparation of final hearing bundles;
g) a date for the hearing and a time estimate.

15.29   One of the major weaknesses in the procedural powers of the LVT is that it has no specific power to force parties to disclose documents as part of the litigation process. It does, however, have a power to serve a notice on any party, requiring them to provide any information that the LVT may specify.[49] Failure to comply with this request is a criminal offence, punishable by a fine.[50]

15.30   If no PTR is considered necessary, the tribunal is likely to send out written directions.

Joinder

15.31   Anyone may request (and at any time) to be joined as a party to the proceedings[51] as either an applicant or respondent.[52] The request can be made by writing a letter, explaining the reasons why the party wishes to be joined, to the LVT.

---

48 LVT Procedure Regs reg 12(3).
49 CLRA 2002 Sch 12 para 4(1).
50 CLRA 2002 Sch 12 paras 4(3)–(4).
51 LVT Procedure Regs reg 6.
52 LVT Procedure Regs reg 6(2)(b).

15.32   Surprisingly, there is no need to inform the existing parties of the request[53] and it does not appear that the parties have the right to comment on the request. The parties (and the person wishing to be joined) must be sent a copy of the decision of the LVT, whether or not the LVT agrees to the request.[54]

15.33   Interestingly, there is no obvious power for a party to apply to the LVT for an order that some other party be joined to the proceedings. It may be that the power of the LVT to give 'any direction that appears to the tribunal necessary or desirable for securing the just, expeditious and economical disposal of proceedings' as part of a pre-trial review is sufficient to achieve this end.[55]

Consolidation and representative applications

15.34   A number of applications might relate to substantially the same matter(s). In those circumstances, it would be wasteful to deal with each application separately, especially if the same or similar evidence were to be called in each case. It would also give rise to the possibility of differently constituted tribunals coming to differing conclusions on similar matters.

15.35   If it appears to the LVT that a number of applications have been made in respect of the same or substantially the same matters, or include some matters which are the same or substantially the same, the LVT may propose to determine only one of the applications, as representative of all the applications.[56]

15.36   If the LVT wishes to take this course, it shall serve a notice on the parties setting out the common matters; specifying which application it proposes to determine as representative and explaining that the findings in the representative application will be binding on all the other cases. It shall invite objections to be submitted, which must be received by the LVT by a specified date.[57]

15.37   Those parties who object (for any reason) will not be treated as being part of the representative application and will continue as if their cases separately. However, the separate case may be heard at the same time as the consolidated cases.[58]

---

53 LVT Procedure Regs reg 6(2)(a).
54 LVT Procedure Regs reg 6(4).
55 LVT Procedure Regs reg 12(3)(a).
56 LVT Procedure Regs reg 8(1).
57 LVT Procedure Regs reg 8(2).
58 LVT Procedure Regs reg 8(4).

15.38   If, after the determination of the representative application, a further application is received from any person which includes any of the common matters, the LVT shall inform the parties of the findings in the representative case and, unless it receives any objections within a specified time, those previous findings will stand in the present case.[59] If an objection is received, the LVT must rule on whether or not to accept the objection or whether the findings in the representative action shall stand in the present case.[60]

Track allocation

15.39   The LVT has developed a practice of allocating a case to one of three tracks; the paper track; fast track or standard track. Applicants are asked to suggest a track on the application form.

15.40   It is possible for a case to be re-allocated between the tracks if it becomes more (or less) complicated with the passage of time.

Paper track

15.41   The paper track is suitable for cases which do not require an oral hearing. A case allocated to the paper track will be dealt with entirely on the basis of written representations and documents, without the need for parties to attend a hearing and make oral representations.

15.42   The LVT shall give the parties not less than twenty eight days' notice in writing of its intention to proceed without an oral hearing.[61] If – at any time before the determination of the case[62] – any party requests a hearing,[63] then the LVT shall list the matter for an oral hearing.[64]

15.43   If the matter is dealt with on the basis of written submissions, the LVT give directions to allow this to take place, including directions for the filing and service of written submissions.[65] In practice, paper track determinations are usually made by a single member of the LVT.[66]

---

59 LVT Procedure Regs regs 9 and 10.
60 LVT Procedure Regs regs 9(3) and 10(3).
61 LVT Procedure Regs reg 13(1)(a).
62 LVT Procedure Regs reg 13(3).
63 LVT Procedure Regs reg 13(1)(b).
64 LVT Procedure Regs reg 13(4).
65 LVT Procedure Regs reg 13(2).
66 LVT Procedure Regs reg 13(5).

Fast track

15.44   Both the fast track and the standard track involve oral hearings, but the fast track is suited to more straightforward disputes. The LVT aims to decide fast track cases within ten weeks of the receipt of an application.

Standard track

15.45   The standard track is most suitable for complex cases with a number of issues involved. It almost always involves a pre-trial review being held and detailed – case-specific – directions being issued.

Dismissal of cases

15.46   The LVT has the power to dismiss an application in whole or part if it appears to the tribunal that the application is 'frivolous, vexatious or otherwise an abuse of process of the tribunal'.[67] A respondent may also request that the LVT dismiss the application for the same reasons.[68]

15.47   Before exercising this power, the LVT must give not less than 21 days' notice to the applicant that it is minded to dismiss the application and grounds upon which it is so minded to act.[69]

15.48   If the applicant does not request a hearing, then the application may be dismissed.[70] If a hearing is requested, then it must be listed and the question of dismissal considered.[71]

15.49   Before dismissing any application, the LVT must:[72]

a) remind itself of the provisions of LVT Procedure Regs reg 11 to ensure that proper notice has been given to the applicant. It must ensure that any hearing required is held;

b) analyse the facts relating to the application under consideration and to reach a conclusion as to whether the application (or some identified part of it) can properly be described as one or more of frivolous or vexatious or an abuse of the process of the tribunal;

---

67 CLRA 2002 Sch 12 para 7; LVT Procedure Regs reg 11(1)(a).
68 LVT Procedure Regs reg 11(1)(b).
69 LVT Procedure Regs reg 11(3).
70 LVT Procedure Regs reg 11(4)(a).
71 LVT Procedure Regs reg 11(4)(b).
72 *Volosinovici v Corvan Properties Ltd* LRX/67/2006 (Lands Tribunal), endorsed in *Schilling v Canary Riverside Estate Management Ltd* LRX 41 2007; see also Joy Akah-Douglas, 'Case commentary', (2007) 11 L&TRev 189.

c) consider whether, if the application can in whole or in part properly be described as frivolous or vexatious or otherwise an abuse of process of the tribunal, the facts are such that the LVT should exercise its discretion to dismiss the application in whole or in part under regulation 11;

d) give clear and sufficient reasons for its conclusions.

15.50 Failure to comply with directions issued by the LVT may, in an appropriate case, justify dismissing an application under this power. The power is, however, discretionary, and the LVT will need to have regard to the reasons for any failure to comply with its directions.[73]

15.51 The Lands Tribunal has also suggested that that low value claims[74] may well also be frivolous, vexatious or otherwise an abuse of process. This does not sit easily with the decision of the Court of Appeal in *Yorkbrooke Investments v Batten*[75] that there is no de minimis rule for service charge disputes.

15.52 The LVT also possesses an inherent jurisdiction to regulate its own procedures so as to prevent an abuse of process.[76] However, it will be a rare case where it is appropriate to exercise this power, given that parliament has seen fit to confer a specific statutory power to the similar effect on the LVT.[77]

15.53 If the tribunal has no jurisdiction to deal with a case, then there is no need to invoke these rules; regulation 11 pre-supposes that there the tribunal has jurisdiction.[78]

73 *Volosinovici v Corvan Properties Ltd*, above; *Villatte v 38 Cleveland Square Management Ltd* [2002] EWCA Civ 1549.

74 On the facts of *Volosinovici v Corvan Properties Ltd*, above only 50p–£1.10 of a number of items on a service charge bill appeared to be challenged.

75 (1986) 18 HLR 25; [1985] 2 EGLR 100; (1986) 52 P&CR 51.

76 *Mean Fiddler Holdings Ltd v Islington LBC* ACQ/29/2001 (Lands Tribunal); *De Campomar v The Trustees of the Pettiward Estate* LRA/29&30/2004 (Lands Tribunal).

77 *Schilling v Canary Riverside Estate Management Ltd* LRX 41 2007; although see *Trafalgar Court RTM Company Ltd v Wells and others*, CAM/33UF/LOA/2005/0001 (LVT) for a case where the power was exercised.

78 *Barbara Helen Glass v Claire McCready* [2009] UKUT 136 (LC), although the LVT would have to give the parties an opportunity to make submissions on the issue of jurisdiction first.

Adjournments

15.54   The LVT has the power to postpone or adjourn a hearing or a pre-final hearing review, either of its own initiative or at the request of any party.[79]

15.55   In considering whether to accede to a request for an adjournment or postponement, the LVT give reasonable notice of any postponement or adjournment to the parties[80] and then it must be convinced that it would be reasonable to adjourn, having regard to:[81]

a) the grounds for the request;
b) the time at which the request is made; and
c) the convenience of the other parties.

Final hearing

15.56   The proper approach to planning and presenting a case before the LVT is beyond the scope of this work and is well covered by general works on advocacy. This section highlights those features which are peculiar to an LVT.

15.57   The LVT is to a great extent free to organise its own procedure so that most of what is said here represents widespread practice. Assuming that inspection(s) (if any) have taken place in the morning,[82] it is usual for the final hearing to start in the afternoon. Parties should make sure they arrive in good time. Final hearings usually take place in public before a three-member panel.[83]

15.58   The Chair, who will sit in the middle, will be legally qualified and be in charge of the conduct of proceedings. The other two members will usually not be lawyers, though it is usual for at least one of them to be a surveyor. It is normal to address any remarks to the Chair unless one is answering a question addressed directly by one of the other members of the tribunal. There is no need to stand when making submissions. Unless otherwise stated, the tribunal members are addressed as 'Sir' or 'Madam' as appropriate.

---

79 LVT Procedure Regs reg 15(1).
80 LVT Procedure Regs reg 15(3).
81 LVT Procedure Regs reg 15(2).
82 See para 15.72 below.
83 LVT Procedure Regs reg 14(6).

15.59　　All parties should have been given 21 days' notice of the final hearing date.[84] If one or more of the parties is not present at the final hearing, and the tribunal is satisfied that they had proper notice, then there is no objection to the final hearing continuing without their attendance.[85]

15.60　　Although there should be an agreed bundle of documents produced in good time for the hearing, it is not uncommon for documents to be produced during the hearing. In such cases, parties have the right to have an adjournment to give them time to consider the new evidence and for advisers to take instruction on it.[86] Such an adjournment is normally offered as a matter of course by the tribunal, though usually for a relatively brief period. Enough time should be given to allow a party sufficient opportunity to deal with the matters in the document.[87]

15.61　　The tribunal may want to deal with one or more preliminary matters first, in particular where there is a question of jurisdiction. It is open to the tribunal to hear argument on that point before going on to the remainder of the final hearing.

15.62　　When a party is presenting their case, the normal structure is very similar to that used in the county court. A party may begin their case by making a short opening speech. This should be used to explain the structure of the case the applicant intends to present, especially if it is complicated. There is no need to say very much if the case is a simple one. The party then calls their witnesses in whatever order they choose. After giving evidence there will be an opportunity for other parties to cross-examine. The tribunal has power to limit the extent and nature of questioning to ensure that only relevant evidence is given.[88]

15.63　　Tribunals are at least partly inquisitorial and they are likely to ask detailed questions of witnesses after cross-examination, though they will frequently ask questions at other times in order to clarify answers that have been given.

15.64　　There is usually a seat set aside from which witnesses will give their evidence, although there is no witness box.

15.65　　It is normal for witnesses to sit when giving evidence and no oath is required. It is common for a tribunal to have read a witness

---

84　LVT Procedure Regs reg 14(3).
85　LVT Procedure Regs reg 14(8).
86　LVT Procedure Regs reg 16(2).
87　LVT Procedure Regs reg 16(2).
88　LVT Procedure Regs reg 14; see also *Earl Cadogan v Betul Erkman* LRA/56/2007; LRA/68/2007.

statement prior to the hearing, so that the witness is not required to read it aloud. The applicant and the tribunal may ask supplementary questions to expand upon any points which might be unclear.

15.66   It is normal practice for the applicant to present their case first, followed by the respondent.

15.67   After all parties have presented their cases, each is usually allowed to make a final submission to the tribunal. The purpose is to summarise the evidence and explain what one's case is in the light of the evidence heard by the tribunal. The nature of the relief sought from the tribunal should also be made clear. The party who presented their case first will usually be permitted to make their submissions last.

15.68   At the end of the hearing the question of costs should be raised. Both parties may wish to make submissions on the reimbursement of fees and how much, if any, of their costs they should be awarded. Tenants should remember to make an application for protection against the landlord's costs, under LTA 1985 s20C.[89]

15.69   The decision of the tribunal may be given orally on the same day,[90] but it is more common for a written decision to be sent to the parties.[91]

15.70   Sometimes, the tribunal will invite further written submissions before making its decision, eg where there was only enough time to finish the oral evidence but the parties did not have time to make final speeches.[92]

15.71   If the decision contains a clerical error, omission, or other minor flaw, the tribunal should be notified as they have the power to remedy such flaws after the decision has been handed down.[93] This power does not permit the tribunal to re-open a decision or otherwise alter the substance.[94]

---

89   See chapter 10.
90   LVT Procedure Regs reg 18(2).
91   LVT Procedure Regs reg 18(3).
92   LVT Procedure Regs reg 13; the Upper Tribunal has previously been prepared to assume that this is a lawful way of proceeding: *Kenney Construction Ltd v Brooke* [2013] UKUT 329 (LC).
93   LVT Procedure Regs reg 18(7). In the case of an obvious error (such as a mathematical error when adding sums together), the Upper Tribunal can also exercise this power to correct the decision: *Earl Cadogan v Cadogan Square Properties Ltd* [2011] UKUT 68 (LC); [2011] RVR 115.
94   *Re Clarise Properties Ltd* [2012] UKUT 4 (LC); [2012] L&TR 20; *Holding & Management (Solitaire) Ltd v Sherwin* [2010] UKUT 412 (LC); [2011] 1 EGLR 29

Inspections

15.72 It is common practice for the LVT to inspect any property forming the subject of the application.[95] The LVT may also inspect any comparable house, premises or area to which its attention is directed although in practice is unlikely to do so unless expressly invited to by one of the parties and told the exact address.[96] This can in some cases be a very useful tactic where similar properties may be relevant. The parties must be given notice of the proposed inspection (which is usually on the morning of the final hearing).[97]

15.73 The parties are entitled to refuse consent for the LVT or the other party to enter their property,[98] although, in practice, a refusal to allow one party to enter a property will mean that the LVT declines to inspect it. There are obvious problems of fairness where one party has been excluded.

15.74 If the LVT decides to inspect a property after the hearing, it may reopen the hearing if there is any matter arising from the inspection which requires comment.[99] Additionally, if the LVT is minded to draw an adverse conclusion from what it sees at the inspection, it must inform the parties of this and invite submissions.[100]

The LVT as an expert tribunal

15.75 The LVT is an expert tribunal and, as such, is entitled to critically evaluate the evidence in light of its own knowledge and experience. However, it must reach its decision on the evidence before it; it must give the parties an opportunity to comment on any matters – such as its 'local knowledge' – which it intends to take into account which have not been part of the evidence (a particularly important matter where it intends to reject expert evidence) and must give reasons for its decisions.[101]

15.76 There has been a tendency on the part of some LVTs to consider that their status as an expert tribunal entitles them to conduct an

---

95 LVT Procedure Regs reg 17(1)(a).
96 LVT Procedure Regs reg 17(1)(b).
97 LVT Procedure Regs reg 17(2).
98 LVT Procedure Regs reg 17(3).
99 LVT Procedure Regs reg 17(8).
100 *R v Paddington Rent Tribunal ex p Bell London Properties Ltd* [1949] 1 KB 666; [1949] 1 All ER 720.
101 *Arrowdell Limited v Coniston Court (North) Ltd* LRA/72/2005; [2007] RVR 39 (Lands Tribunal).

inquisitorial approach to proceedings, raising issue which neither the landlord nor the tenant has sought to litigate. The Upper Tribunal has firmly disapproved of this approach, save in the most exceptional circumstances.[102]

Precedent in the LVT

15.77 The LVT is not a court, and their decisions are not capable of binding each other,[103] although, in practice, the LVT is keen to promote consistency. Despite the fact that the Lands Tribunal was not a 'court of record', the LVT will generally follow the decisions of the Lands Tribunal and it is entirely proper for the Lands Tribunal to give guidance to LVTs.[104] The Upper Tribunal is a superior court of record and its decisions are binding on the LVT.

Costs

15.78 The LVT has very limited powers in respect of costs.

Power to award costs

15.79 The LVT may order any person to pay costs where:[105]

a) it has dismissed an application as frivolous, vexatious, or otherwise an abuse of process;[106] or

b) that person has acted frivolously, vexatiously, abusively, disruptively or otherwise unreasonably in connection with the proceedings.[107]

---

102 *Beitov Properties Ltd v Martin* [2012] UKUT 133 (LC); *Fairhold Mercury Ltd v Merryfield RTM Co Ltd* [2012] UKUT 311 (LC); *Birmingham City Council v Keddie* [2012] UKUT 323 (LC) and *Crosspite Ltd v Sachdev* [2012] UKUT 321 (LC).

103 *West Midland Baptist (Trust) Association (Inc) v Birmingham Corporation* [1968] 2 QB 188.

104 *Earl Cadogan and others v Sportelli and others* [2007] EWCA Civ 1042; [2007] RVR 314.

105 CLRA 2002 Sch 12 para 10(2).

106 See para 15.46.

107 See *Halliard Property Co Ltd v Belmont Hall & Elm Court RTM Co Ltd* LRX/130/2007.

15.80 The LVT may order a party to pay up to £500,[108] although there is no reason why the LVT could not make multiple orders during the course of a case, where, for example, multiple adjournments have been necessitated.

Costs under the lease

15.81 This is discussed in chapter 10.

Reimbursement of fees

15.82 The LVT has the power to require any party to reimburse the other party for the whole or part of any fees paid.[109] This power may not be exercised against a party who would entitled to a waiver of any application fees.[110] A successful party can expect the LVT to exercise this power in their favour.

Enforcement

15.83 Any decision of the LVT may be enforced, with the permission of the county court, in the same way as a normal county court order.[111]

15.84 The application may be made without giving notice to the other party and must (unless the court orders otherwise) be made to the court for the district where the person against whom the award was made resides or carries on business.[112]

15.85 The application must be made on form N322A and must state the name and address of the person against whom it is sought to enforce the award and how much of the award remains unpaid.[113] A copy of the LVT decision must also be filed.[114]

---

108 CLRA 2002 Sch 12 para 10(3)(a).
109 LVT Fees Regs reg 9(1).
110 LVT Fees Regs reg 9(2).
111 CLRA 2002 Sch 10 para 11; LVT Procedure Regs reg 19.
112 CPR 70.4.
113 CPR 70.5; CPR Part 70 PD 4.1–4.2.
114 CPR 70.6; CPR Part 70 PD 4.3.

Appeals

15.86   An appeal from a decision of the LVT is to the Upper Tribunal (Lands Chamber).[115] In an exceptional case, it may be possible to judicially review a decision of the LVT.[116] The LVT has no power to re-open a decision.[117]

Permission

15.87   An appeal may only be made with the permission of the LVT or the Upper Tribunal.[118] The Upper Tribunal has indicated that permission to appeal should only be granted where:[119]

a) the decision shows that the LVT wrongly interpreted or wrongly applied the relevant law;

b) the decision shows that the LVT wrongly applied or misinterpreted or disregarded a relevant principle of valuation or other professional practice;

c) the LVT took account of irrelevant considerations, or failed to take account of relevant considerations or evidence, or there was a substantial procedural defect;

d) the point or points at issue is or are of potentially wide implication.

15.88   In addition, the tribunal should consider whether there is a real prospect of success.[120]

15.89   An application for permission must be served on the LVT and all other parties[121] within 21 days, starting with the date on which the document which records the reasons for the decision.[122] Thus,

---

115 CLRA 2002 s175(1).

116 *Daejan Properties Ltd v London Leasehold Valuation Tribunal* [2001] EWCA Civ 1095; [2002] HLR 23; [2001] 3 EGLR 28 The landlord was seeking an order that the LVT be prevented from hearing parts of the case due to a lack of jurisdiction. Given the possibility of an appeal to the Upper Tribunal, it will be a very rare case where judicial review is the appropriate remedy.

117 *Penman v Upavon Enterprises Ltd* [2002] L&TR 10 (although the First-tier Tribunal (Property Chamber) does: *Scriven v Calthorpe Estates* [2013] UKUT 469 (LC)).

118 CLRA 2002 s175(2).

119 Upper Tribunal Practice Direction para 4.2.

120 *Fairhold Mercury Ltd v HQ (Block 1) Action Management Company Ltd* [2013] UKUT 487 (LC).

121 LVT Procedure Regs reg 20(b).

122 LVT Procedure Regs reg 20(a).

assuming that the decision is sent under cover of letter dated 1 January 2014 (and is posted on that day), then the time for seeking permission to appeal is midnight, 21/22 January 2014.[123] Although the covering letter from the LVT usually states when the deadline for appealing is, it is not unknown for the letter to be wrong.[124]

15.90   The LVT has power to extend the 21-day period, but any application for an extension must be made within the 21-day period.[125] If, however, the application is made after the 21-day period, the LVT may, in the exercise of its discretion, proceed to determine it, albeit that the parties have no right to require it to do so.[126]

123 *Ayres v Roberts* [2012] L&TR 1.
124 As in *Ayres v Roberts*.
125 LVT Procedure Regs reg 24.
126 *Grosvenor Estate Belgravia v Adams* LRA/131/2007; [2008] RVR 173.

Procedure in England

Key points

- In mid-2013, the procedural rules in England changed as a result of the abolition of the LVT and its replacement by the First-tier Tribunal (Property Chamber) (FTT(PC)). The new rules are very much more detailed than the old LVT rules but, being relatively new, are not yet the subject of detailed case-law to assist with their interpretation and application.
- Cases can be issued in the FTT(PC) or transferred from the court. If the latter, the FTT(PC) cannot expand or enlarge the scope of the dispute beyond the matters set out in the pleadings. If parties wish to raise new issues, a fresh application is needed.
- If a case is started in the FTT(PC), but is better dealt with in the court, the FTT(PC) can transfer the case.
- The FTT(PC) has extensive case-management powers akin to those available in the courts, and can punish parties who do not comply with its directions by, for example, striking out their case.
- Directions will be issued, giving a time-line for the production of evidence and similar, so as to enable a smooth trial. These can be done after an oral hearing or by the FTT(PC) considering the matter on paper.
- The final hearing will often start with an inspection of the property, followed by an informal hearing at which all parties get to present their case.
- The decision will usually follow in writing within a few weeks.
- The FTT(PC) has power to review its own decisions and set them aside in certain circumstances.
- Appeals are to the Upper Tribunal (Lands Chamber).

Advice for tenants

- The FTT(PC) has a detailed and comprehensive set of procedural rules. These are much more extensive than the old rules which governed the leasehold valuation tribunal (LVT) (and which continue to apply in Wales).
- While this means that, helpfully, the FTT is likely to have better case-management powers than the LVT, because the rules are so new there is significantly less case-law on the FTT rules than on the LVT rules and it is likely that there will be a continued need to refer to the cases applying the old rules, so as to attempt to understand the new rules.
- The old rules are discussed in detail in the previous chapter.

Introduction

16.1   The rules governing the First-tier Tribunal (Property Chamber) (FTT(PC)) – the Tribunal Procedure (First-tier Tribunal) (Property Chamber) Rules ('FTT Rules') 2013[1] – came into force on 1 July 2013, after a detailed consultation process.[2] The rules must be read with the relevant practice directions which have been made.[3] Many of the specific provisions of the rules are based on other – similar – provisions in the rules relating to other chambers of the FTT,[4] and it is likely that decisions from other chambers will be of relevance when applying the FTT(PC) rules.

16.2   The overriding objective of the 2013 FTT Rules is to enable the tribunal to deal with cases fairly and justly.[5] The tribunal must seek to further this purpose when applying or interpreting the 2013 rules and practice directions.[6] The parties must also help the tribunal to further the overriding objective and co-operate with the tribunal.[7] The tribunal should also seek to encourage the use of alternative dispute resolution.[8]

1   SI No 1169.
2   See *Tribunal Procedure (First-tier Tribunal) (Property Chamber) Rules 2013: consultation*, Tribunal Procedure Committee, June 2012.
3   Available at: www.judiciary.gov.uk/publications-and-reports/practice-directions/tribunals/tribunals-pd.
4   See *Tribunal Procedure (First-tier Tribunal) (Property Chamber) Rules 2013: consultation* paras 22–28.
5   FTT Rules r3.
6   FTT Rules r3(3).
7   FTT Rules r3(4).
8   FTT Rules r4.

Starting a case

16.3   A question that is often raised by applicants and their advisers is whether a particular individual is entitled to apply to the tribunal. The following table summarises the position for the most common applications.

Provision	Description	Applicant
Service charges		
Landlord and Tenant Act (LTA) 1985 s27A	Determination of liability to pay service charge	Anyone[a]
LTA 1985 s20ZA	Dispensation from consultation requirements	Anyone
LTA 1985 s21A	Determination that landlord has a reasonable excuse for a failure giving rise to the tenant's right to withhold service charges	Landlord[b] (includes any person who has a right to enforce payment of service charges)[c]
LTA 1985 s20C	Order that costs in connection with tribunal proceedings should not be regarded as relevant costs	Tenant[d]
Administration charges		
Commonhold and Leasehold Reform Act (CLRA) 2002 Sch 11 para 3	Variation of administration charge provision in a lease	Any party to the lease[e]
CLRA 2002 Sch 11 para 5	Liability to pay an administration charge	Anyone[f]

a   See also *Oakfern Properties Ltd v Ruddy* [2006] EWCA Civ 1389; [2007] Ch 335.
b   If a Right to Manage (RTM) company has acquired the right to manage, the RTM company has the right instead of the landlord: CLRA 2002 Sch 11 para 4(2).
c   LTA 1985 s30.
d   Includes a landlord under a lease of the whole or any part of the premises if an RTM company has acquired the right to manage: CLRA 2002 Sch 11 para 4(3).
e   Includes an RTM company, if it has acquired the right to manage: CLRA 2002 Sch 11 para 16.
f   See, by analogy, *Oakfern Properties Ltd v Ruddy* [2006] EWCA Civ 1389; [2007] Ch 335.

Provision	Description	Applicant
Estate charges		
CLRA 2002 s159(3)	Variation of estate charge provisions in an estate management scheme	Any person on whom an obligation to pay an estate charge is imposed by the scheme
CLRA 2002 s159(6)	Determination of payability of an estate charge	Anyone[g]
Variation of leases		
LTA 1987 s35	Application to vary a long lease	A party to the lease[h]
LTA 1987 s36	Application to vary another lease in response to an LTA 1987 s35 application to vary a long lease	A party to the LTA 1987 s35 lease
LTA 1987 s37	Application to vary two or more leases	Landlord or any tenant of the leases
LTA 1987 s39(3)(b)	application for the cancellation or modification of an order varying a lease	A person on whom a notice was required to be served under LTA 1987 s35(5)
Variation of insurance provisions		
LTA 1987 s40(1)	Variation of the insurance provisions of a dwelling	A party to the lease
Challenge to the landlord's choice of insurer		
LTA 1985 Schedule para 8	Challenge to the landlord's choice of insurer	Landlord[i] or tenant[j]

---

g   See, by analogy, *Oakfern Properties Ltd v Ruddy* [2006] EWCA Civ 1389; [2007] Ch 335.

h   Includes an RTM company, if it has acquired the right to manage: CLRA 2002 Sch 11 para 10.

i   If an RTM company has acquired the right to manage in respect of the premises, the RTM company instead of the landlord: CLRA 2002 Sch 11 para 5(2).

j   Includes a landlord under a lease of the whole or any part of the premises who is under an obligation to make payments under CLRA 2002 s103 (landlord's contribution to service charges): CLRA 2002 Sch 11 para 5(3).

Provision	Description	Applicant
Appointment of manager		
LTA 1987 s24(1)	Order appointing a manager	Tenant[k]
LTA 1987 s24(9)	Variation or discharge of order appointing a manager	Any person interested
LTA 1987 s22(3)	Order dispensing with requirement to serve a preliminary notice before applying for appointment of a manager	Anyone
Right to manage		
CLRA 2002 s84(3)	Determination that an RTM company was entitled to acquire the right to manage in response to a counter-notice	The RTM company
CLRA 2002 s85(2)	Order that an RTM company is to acquire the right to manage where the landlord is missing	The RTM company
CLRA 2002 s88(4)	Determination of any question arising in relation to the costs payable by an RTM company	Anyone
CLRA 2002 s94(3)	Determination of amount of payment of accrued uncommitted service charges	1) Any party, other than a tenant, of a lease of the whole or part of the premises 2) A manager appointed by the LVT 3) The RTM company
CLRA 2002 s99(1)	Determination of whether an approval is to be given under the terms of the lease	The RTM company, landlord, tenant or sub-tenant (where the approval is to be given by a tenant)
CLRA 2002 Sch 6 para 5(3)	Determination that right to manage may be exercised earlier than four years	The RTM company

k   Includes a landlord under a lease of the whole or any part of the premises, where an RTM company has acquired the right to manage: CLRA 2002 Sch 11 para 8(3).

Provision	Description	Applicant
Forfeiture		
CLRA 2002 s168(4)	Determination that a breach of covenant or other condition in the lease has occurred	Landlord

16.4 Proceedings must be started by sending or delivering a notice of application to the tribunal.[9] There are various forms which have been produced by the Courts and Tribunals Service for this purpose.[10] If no form has been produced, then a letter is likely to be sufficient.

16.5 In all cases, the application/letter must be signed and dated and must also give:[11]

a) the name and address of the applicant and any representative;

b) an address where documents may be sent or delivered to the applicant;

c) the name and address of each respondent;

d) the address of the premises or property to which the application relates;

e) details of the applicant's connection with the premises or property;

f) the name and address of any landlord or tenant of the premises to which the application relates;

g) the name and address of every interested party, with reasons for their interest;

h) the result the applicant is seeking;

i) the reasons for making the application;

j) a statement that the applicant believes the facts stated in the application are true.

The application must also be accompanied by the relevant fee.[12]

16.6 Additional requirements are also prescribed in the Practice Direction on Residential Property Cases:[13]

a) An application under LTA 1985 s27A must include the name and address of the secretary of any recognised tenants' association and a copy of the lease.[14]

---

9 FTT Rules r26(1).

10 Available at: http://hmctsformfinder.justice.gov.uk/HMCTS/GetForms. do?court_forms_category=Residential%20Property.

11 FTT Rules r26(2).

12 FTT Rules r26(5); see r11 for the consequences of a failure to pay a fee.

13 9 September 2013.

14 Practice Direction Sch.4.

b) An application to vary an administration charge under CLRA 2002 Sch 11 para 3 must include a copy of the proposed variation and a copy of the lease.[15]

c) Any other service charge or administration charge dispute must include a copy of the lease.[16]

d) All right to manage cases must give the name and address for service of the RTM company, together with the name and address of the freeholder, any intermediate landlord and manager appointed under the LTA 1987 as well as a copy of the memorandum and articles of the RTM company.11

  i) If the application is for a determination that the RTM company is entitled to acquire the right to manage, then the claim notice and counter-notices must also be provided.

  ii) If the application is to dispense with the requirement to serve the landlord, then the application must be accompanied by a statement confirming the entitlement of the company to acquire the right to manage and the reasons why the landlord cannot be identified or traced.

  iii) If the application is to determine the amount of accrued uncommitted service charges, an estimate of the amount.

  iv) If the application is to override a landlord's refusal to consent to proposed works, a description of the approval sought and a copy of the relevant lease.

e) An application to appoint a manager under the LTA 1987 must be accompanied by a copy of the section 22 notice.[17]

f) An application for directions under LTA 1987 s24(9) must be accompanied by a copy of the management order.[18]

g) An application to vary a lease under the LTA 1987 must include the name and address of any person the applicant knows or has reason to believe is likely to be affected by any variation specified in the application, together with a draft of the variation sought and a copy of the lease.[19]

h) A case under CLRA 2002 s168 must be accompanied by a copy of the lease and a statement detailing the alleged breaches of covenant or condition.[20]

---

15 Practice Direction Sch.4.

16 Practice Direction Sch.4.

17 Unless an application is also made for dispensation from the requirement to serve the notice: Practice Direction Sch 7.

18 Practice Direction Sch 7.

19 Practice Direction Sch 8.

20 Practice Direction Sch 9.

16.7 The tribunal will serve a copy of the application on the respondent and any interested party.[21]

Transferred cases

16.8 Where proceedings have begun in a court and involve a question that would otherwise fall within the jurisdiction of the FTT, the court may transfer so much of the proceedings as relate to that question or questions, to the FTT.[22]

16.9 In determining whether to transfer any part of the proceedings, the court should have regard to the following (non-exhaustive) factors:[23]

a) the FTT, as an expert tribunal, which habitually inspects premises, may well be in a better position to determine service charge disputes than the county court;[24]

b) however, it may not be as well placed as a court to determine complex questions of law;[25]

c) any referral to the FTT will inevitably involve delay and new directions being given;

d) once the county court has given directions for the management of the case – and particularly if those directions have been complied with – any transfer to the FTT will inevitably involve a delay in the dispute being determined, and a corresponding increase in costs;

e) if the FTT is incapable of resolving all the issues in the case, this is a factor against any transfer, as it is preferable for all the matters to be resolved together at one hearing.

---

21 FTT Rules r29. Interestingly, this appears to apply even to lease variation cases which, under the 'old' LVT rules, required the applicant to serve the respondent and interested parties, presumably because failure to serve such a person entitled them to apply to set the variation aside under LTA 1987 s39. It may be considered good practice for applicants to continue to serve such applications, notwithstanding rule 29.

22 CLRA 2002 s176A.

23 *Aylesbond Estates Ltd v MacMillan and others* (2000) 32 HLR 1; [1999] L&TR 127.

24 In *Phillips v Francis* [2010] L&TR 28, the High Court considered that the tribunal was the appropriate forum for the great majority of cases.

25 See the discussion in *Schilling v Canary Riverside Development PTD Ltd* LRX/26/2005, in the context of when the tribunal should entertain a counterclaim.

As both the court and the FTT have the same powers to protect a tenant against claims for costs by the landlord,[26] this is not a factor that points one way or the other.

16.10   One limitation of the transfer process is that the parties are not permitted to argue matters which have not been raised in the pleadings and the FTT is not entitled to rule on matters which have not been raised in the pleadings.[27] If the parties wish to extend the scope of the dispute, a fresh application must be issued and consolidated with the transferred proceedings.[28]

16.11   Upon receipt of transferred proceedings, the FTT will provide the parties with written notice of the date on which it received the matter and the names and known addresses of the parties to the proceedings.[29] The parties may be directed to provide copies of the court order which transferred the matter.[30]

Fees

16.12   Some – but not all – applications attract a fee.[31] Any relevant fee must be sent with the application.[32] If the case has been transferred from the court, any court fee already paid will be credited towards the fee due in the tribunal.[33]

16.13   In the following cases the fees payable are based on the sum in dispute:[34]

a) an application to determine the liability to pay a service charge or administration charge;

b) a challenge to insurance premiums;

c) variation of a lease because of an administration charge,

and the following fees apply:

---

26   LTA 1985 s20C.
27   *Staunton v Taylor* [2010] UKUT 270 (LC).
28   *Lennon v Ground Rents (Regisport) Limited* [2011] UKUT 330 (LC).
29   FTT Rules r28(3).
30   FTT Rules r28(5).
31   First-tier Tribunal (Property Chamber) Fees Order ('FTT Fees Order') 2013 SI No 1179.
32   FTT Fees Order art 4.
33   FTT Fees Order art 5.
34   FTT Fees Order Sch 1.

Charge which is the subject of the application	Application fee
Not more than £500	£65
More than £500, but not more than £1,000	£90
More than £1,000, but not more than £5,000	£125
More than £5,000, but not more than 15,000	£250
More than £15,000	£440

16.14   In the following cases the fee is based on the number of dwellings which are the subject of the application:[35]

a) an application for dispensation from the consultation provisions;

b) a determination as to the suitability of an insurer;

c) the appointment of a manager or the variation of a lease,

and the following fees apply:

Number of dwellings	Application fee
Five or fewer	£190
Between six and ten	£315
More than ten	£440

16.15   If the application is not listed above, then it attracts no application fee. The most obvious example is the absence of any fee for any disputes arising out of the right to manage.

16.16   Regardless of whether there is an application fee or note, all cases attract a hearing fee of £190.[36] It is payable within 14 days of being demanded.[37]

16.17   There is a complicated fee reduction and remission scheme, having regard to the disposable capital and monthly income available to an applicant.[38]

---

35 FTT Fees Order Sch 1.

36 FTT Fees Order Sch 1.

37 FTT Fees Order art 5.

38 FTT Fees Order Sch 2

Case management powers

16.18   The FTT has extensive case management powers.[39] It also possesses an inherent jurisdiction to regulate its own procedures so as to prevent an abuse of process.[40] However, it will be a rare case where it is appropriate to exercise this power, given that parliament has seen fit to create procedure rules.[41]

16.19   Once an application has been received by the FTT, directions will be issued.[42] Directions may be given by the FTT of its own initiative or at the application of one or more of the parties.[43] Directions may include:

a) adding, substituting and removing parties;[44]
b) provision for disclosure and exchange of evidence;[45]
c) controlling the use of expert evidence;[46]
d) identifying 'lead cases' where a number of cases raise common or related issues;[47] and,
e) transferring appropriate cases into the Upper Tribunal.[48]

16.20   The FTT may issue a witness summons, and may require evidence to be given under oath.[49]

Failure to comply with rules

16.21   A failure to comply with the rules, practice directions or directions of the FTT does not affect the validity of the proceedings – rather, the tribunal may take such action as it considers just, including waiving the requirement, requiring it to be remedied, striking out a case or barring or restricting a party from participating further in proceedings.[50]

---

39   FTT Rules r6.
40   *Mean Fiddler Holdings Ltd v Islington LBC* ACQ/29/2001 (Lands Tribunal); *De Campomar v The Trustees of the Pettiward Estate* LRA/29&30/2004 (Lands Tribunal).
41   See *Schilling v Canary Riverside Estate Management Ltd* LRX 41 2007.
42   FTT Rules r7.
43   FTT Rules r7.
44   FTT Rules r10.
45   FTT Rules r18.
46   FTT Rules r19.
47   FTT Rules r23.
48   FTT Rules r25.
49   FTT Rules rr18, 20.
50   FTT Rules r8.

Striking out

16.22   A case must be struck out to the extent that the FTT has no jurisdiction to deal with it and the case cannot be transferred to another court or tribunal.[51]

16.23   The FTT may strike out a case in whole or part:[52]

a) pursuant to an 'unless' order;
b) where a party has failed to co-operate with the tribunal such that the tribunal cannot deal with the case fairly and justly;
c) if the case arises out of facts which are similar or substantially the same as a case that had already been decided by the FTT;
d) if the case (or the manner in which it is being conducted) is frivolous, vexatious or otherwise an abuse of process; or
e) there is no reasonable prospect of success.

16.24   Unless struck out pursuant to an 'unless' order, the parties must be given the opportunity to make representations.[53] It is possible to re-instate proceedings which have been struck out.[54]

Final hearings

16.25   The general rule is that the tribunal must hold a hearing before making a decision which disposes of the case.[55] The parties may, however, consent to the case being determined on the basis of written submissions alone.[56] Consent may be express or, in certain cases, deemed.[57]

16.26   Parties must be given reasonable notice[58] of the time and place of the hearing.[59] The FTT may hear a case in the absence of one party so long as that party has been given sufficient notice and it is in the interests of justice to proceed.[60] There will usually be a site inspection.[61]

---

51 FTT Rules r9(2).
52 FTT Rules r9(1)–(3).
53 FTT Rules r9(4).
54 FTT Rules r9(5).
55 FTT Rules r31.
56 FTT Rules r31(2).
57 FTT Rules r31(3).
58 Fourteen days, unless consent is given for a shorter period or there are urgent or exceptional circumstances: FTT Rules r32(2).
59 FTT Rules r32(1).
60 FTT Rules r34.
61 FTT Rules r21.

16.27   Hearings should generally be held in public,[62] although there is power to hold some or all of a hearing in private.[63] If a case is heard in private, the FTT may determine who is permitted to attend the hearing or any part of it.[64]

16.28   Decisions may be given orally but, more commonly, are given in writing a few weeks after the hearing.[65]

Role as an expert tribunal

16.29   The FTT is an expert tribunal and, as such, is entitled to critically evaluate the evidence in light of its own knowledge and experience. However, it must reach its decision on the evidence before it; it must give the parties an opportunity to comment on any matters – such as its 'local knowledge' – which it intends to take into account which have not been part of the evidence (a particularly important matter where it intends to reject expert evidence) and must give reasons for its decisions.[66]

16.30   There has been a tendency on the part of some tribunals to consider that their status as an expert tribunal entitles them to conduct an inquisitorial approach to proceedings, raising issues which neither the landlord nor the tenant has sought to litigate. The Upper Tribunal has firmly disapproved of this approach, save in the most exceptional circumstances. [67]

Precedent in the FTT

16.31   The FTT is not a court and its decisions are not capable of binding each other,[68] although, in practice, the FTT is keen to promote consistency. Despite the fact that the Lands Tribunal was not a 'court of record', the FTT will generally follow the decisions of the Lands Tribunal and it was entirely proper for the Lands Tribunal to give

---

62 FTT Rules r33.
63 FTT Rules r33(2).
64 FTT Rules r33.
65 FTT Rules r36.
66 *Arrowdell Ltd v Coniston Court (North) Limited* LRA/72/2005; [2007] RVR 39 (Lands Tribunal).
67 *Beitov Properties Ltd v Martin* [2012] UKUT 133 (LC); *Fairhold Mercury Ltd v Merryfield RTM Co Ltd* [2012] UKUT 311 (LC); *Birmingham City Council v Keddie* [2012] UKUT 323 (LC) and *Crosspite Ltd v Sachdev* [2012] UKUT 321 (LC).
68 *West Midland Baptist (Trust) Association (Inc) v Birmingham Corporation* [1968] 2 QB 188.

guidance to lower tribunals.[69] The Upper Tribunal is a superior court of record and its decisions are binding on the FTT.

Costs

16.32   The FTT has limited powers in respect of costs, albeit more extensive than the LVT.

Power to award costs

16.33   The FTT has two separate powers to award costs.

16.34   The first is a 'wasted costs' jurisdiction,[70] whereby costs arising out of negligent or unreasonable behaviour can be disallowed (or reimbursed). There is a considerable amount of law on when it is appropriate to make such an award and readers are referred to the relevant specialist works.[71] There is no 'cap' on the amount which can be awarded.

16.35   The second, and probably more likely to be relevant, is where a party has acted unreasonably in bringing, defending or conducting proceedings.[72] There is an obvious similarity with the rules governing costs in small claims trials.[73]

16.36   The tribunal may award costs of its own initiative or in response to an application from a party.[74] A party must be given a chance to respond before any award can be made against them.[75] The tribunal may assess the quantum of costs on a summary or detailed assessment basis and may order a payment on account.[76] Again, there is no 'cap' on the amount that can be awarded.

Costs under the lease

16.37   This is discussed in chapter 10.

---

69 *Earl Cadogan and others v Sportelli and others* [2007] EWCA Civ 1042; [2007] RVR 314.
70 FTT Rules r13; Tribunals, Courts and Enforcement Act 2007 s29(4).
71 Eg *Cook on costs 2014*, Lexis Nexis.
72 FTT Rules r13.
73 CPR 27.14.
74 FTT Rules r13.
75 FTT Rules r13.
76 FTT Rules r13.

Reimbursement of fees

16.38   The tribunal may require any party to reimburse another for the value of any fees paid to the tribunal.[77]

Enforcement

16.39   Any decision of the FTT may be enforced, with the permission of the county court, in the same way as a normal county court order.[78]

16.40   The application may be made without giving notice to the other party and must (unless the court orders otherwise) be made to the court for the district where the person against whom the award was made resides or carries on business.[79]

16.41   The application must be made on form N322A and must state the name and address of the person against whom it is sought to enforce the award and how much of the award remains unpaid.[80] A copy of the FTT decision must also be filed.[81]

Clerical errors

16.42   The tribunal may, at any time, correct any clerical mistake or other accidental slip or omission in any decision, direction or other document.[82]

Setting aside a final decision

16.43   The tribunal may set aside (in whole or part) and remake any decision which disposes of proceedings if it is in the interests of justice to do so and either:[83]

---

77 FTT Rules r13.
78 Tribunals, Courts and Enforcement Act 2007 s27.
79 CPR 70.4.
80 CPR 70.5; CPR Part 70 PD 4.1–4.2.
81 CPR 70.6; CPR Part 70 PD 4.3.
82 FTT Rules r50. See *Re: Clarise Properties Ltd* [2012] UKUT 4 (LC); [2012] L&TR 20, for the limits of this power.
83 FTT Rules r51, thus meaning that cases such as *Earl Cadogan v Chehab* [2009] EWHC 3297 (Admin) could be remedied at first instance and not require an appeal.

a) a document relating to the proceedings was not sent to (or received) by a party, a party's representative, or the tribunal; or

b) a party was not present at a hearing related to the proceedings; or

c) there had been some other procedural irregularity.

16.44 Any application to set aside a decision or party of a decision must be made in writing to the tribunal and received within 28 days after the date on which the tribunal sent notice of the decision (or, if later, the reasons) to the parties.[84]

Appeals to the Upper Tribunal

16.45 Anyone seeking to appeal must first seek permission from the FTT.[85] The application must be received by the tribunal within 28 days after the date on which the tribunal sent its reasons, amended or corrected reasons or refusal to set aside the decision.[86] The tribunal may extend time for lodging an application for permission to appeal and may do so before or after the time limit has expired.[87] If an extension of time is sought, reasons must be given for the delay.[88]

16.46 The application for permission to appeal must identify the decision to which it relates, state the grounds of appeal and the result that the appellant seeks.[89]

16.47 The Upper Tribunal (Lands Chamber) Practice Direction[90] indicates that permission to appeal may be granted where:

a) the tribunal wrongly interpreted or wrongly applied the relevant law;

b) the decision shows that the tribunal wrongly applied or misinterpreted or disregarded a relevant principle of valuation or other professional practice;

c) the tribunal took account of irrelevant considerations, or failed to take account of relevant considerations or evidence, or there was a substantial procedural defect;

d) the point(s) at issue are potentially of wide implication.

---

84 FTT Rules r51(3).
85 FTT Rules r52(1).
86 FTT Rules r52(2).
87 FTT Rules r6(3).
88 FTT Rules r52(4).
89 FTT Rules r52(5).
90 Upper Tribunal (Lands Chamber) Practice Direction para 4.2.

16.48   It has been suggested by the Upper Tribunal that the FTT should not grant permission to appeal unless there is a 'real' or 'realistic' prospect of success, and that permission should be granted more sparingly for 'technical' arguments.[91]

16.49   When considering an application for permission to appeal, the FTT must first consider whether to review – and set aside – its own decision.[92] It may do so only if it is satisfied that a ground of appeal is likely to be successful.[93] The purpose of this power is to correct 'clear errors' where the FTT decision is 'clearly wrong'.[94]

16.50   If the FTT decides not to review the decision – or reviews it and upholds its original decision – the FTT must consider whether to grant permission to appeal and must notify the parties of its decision as soon as possible.[95] If permission to appeal is refused, then reasons must be given, together with details of how to renew the application to the Upper Tribunal.[96] Permission may be granted in whole or in part, but not, it seems, on terms.[97]

Stay pending appeal

16.51   Both the FTT and the Upper Tribunal have power to grant a stay pending the outcome of an appeal.[98]

91 *Fairhold Mercury Ltd v HQ (Block 1) Action Management Company Ltd* [2013] UKUT 487 (LC).
92 FTT Rules rr53, 55.
93 FTT Rules r55.
94 *Scriven v Calthorpe Estates* [2013] UKUT 469 (LC).
95 FTT Rules r53(3).
96 FTT Rules r53(4).
97 FTT Rules r53(5).
98 FTT Rules r54; Tribunal Procedure (Upper Tribunal) (Lands Chamber) Rules 2010 SI No 2600 r5.

Procedure in the Upper Tribunal

Key points

- The Upper Tribunal (Lands Chamber) (UT(LC)) deals with appeals from the leasehold valuation tribunal (LVT) and First-tier Tribunal (Property Chamber) (FTT(PC)). In certain circumstances it can also hear cases as a first-instance tribunal.
- In order for there to be an appeal in the UT(LC), either the LVT/FTT(PC) or UT(LC) must have granted permission to appeal.
- If permission is not granted, it is possible to seek judicial review of that decision in the High Court.
- The UT(LC) will usually not hear new evidence, but will review the decision of the lower tribunal and deal with the case on the basis of legal argument only.
- The decisions of the UT(LC) can be appealed to the Court of Appeal, although permission to appeal is required from either the UT(LC) or the Court of Appeal.

Advice for tenants

- Anecdotally, relatively few tenants bring appeals against decisions of the First-tier Tribunal/leasehold valuation tribunal (FTT/LVT). It is difficult to know why that is. The Upper Tribunal has the same costs powers as the FTT/LVT, so there is only a very limited additional costs 'risk' in appealing.
- It costs nothing to ask the FTT/LVT for permission to appeal and there is no harm in doing so. Even if permission to appeal is granted, there is no requirement to pursue the appeal.

Introduction

17.1   Appeals from the First-tier Tribunal/leasehold valuation tribunal (FTT/LVT) are to the Upper Tribunal (Lands Chamber) (UT(LC)). Permission to appeal is required, but either the FTT/LVT or Upper Tribunal can grant permission. Appeals and related procedure in the UT(LC) is a book in itself, and what follows here is only intended to be a general overview. Similarly, there is only a limited discussion of the procedure governing further appeals (ie to the Court of Appeal) and of judicial review of the Upper Tribunal.

Permission to appeal

17.2 Appeals are from the FTT/LVT to the Upper Tribunal and, in all cases, require the permission of either the FTT/LVT or the Upper Tribunal itself.[1] There are a number of standard forms for use in the UT(LC).[2] Note that there are fees payable in connection with proceedings in the Upper Tribunal.[3]

Permission granted by FTT/LVT

17.3 If the FTT/LVT has granted permission to appeal, the appellant must issue a notice of appeal at the Upper Tribunal which must be received within one month after the date on which permission to appeal was sent to the appellant.[4]

Permission refused by FTT/LVT

17.4 If the FTT/LVT has refused permission to appeal, or otherwise refused to deal with the application as it was made out-of-time, then the appellant must issue an application for permission to appeal at the Upper Tribunal, which must be received no later than 14 days after the date on which the FTT/LVT sent notice of its refusal of permission or refusal to deal with the application.[5] The Upper Tribunal may extend the 14-day period, whether or not it has expired.[6]

17.5 The Upper Tribunal has indicated that permission to appeal should only be granted where:[7]

a) the decision shows that the LVT wrongly interpreted or wrongly applied the relevant law;

b) the decision shows that the LVT wrongly applied or misinterpreted or disregarded a relevant principle of valuation or other professional practice;

---

1 Commonhold and Leasehold Reform Act (CLRA) 2002 ss175, 176B; Tribunals, Courts and Enforcement Act 2007 s11.
2 Available here: http://hmctsformfinder.justice.gov.uk/HMCTS/GetForms. do?court_forms_category=Lands%20Chamber%20-%20Upper%20Tribunal.
3 Upper Tribunal (Lands Chamber) Fees Order 2009 SI No 1114.
4 Tribunal Procedure (Upper Tribunal) (Lands Chamber) Rules ('UT Rules') 2010 SI No 2600 r24.
5 UT Rules r21.
6 UT Rules r21(5).
7 Upper Tribunal Practice Direction para 4.2.

    c) the LVT took account of irrelevant considerations, or failed to take account of relevant considerations or evidence, or there was a substantial procedural defect;

    d) the point or points at issue is or are of potentially wide implication.

17.6   Additionally, if the FTT/LVT refused to deal with the application because it was late, the Upper Tribunal cannot grant permission to appeal unless it is in the interests of justice to do so.[8]

17.7   A respondent may make submissions in relation to whether or not permission should be granted and, if so, whether permission is sought to cross-appeal.[9]

17.8   The tribunal will then issue a written decision on permission to appeal (which can be on terms, or limited to certain issues).[10] If permission is granted, then there will follow directions for the substantive appeal, in the same way as if the FTT/LVT had granted permission to appeal. Grounds of appeal may be amended, including adding a new ground of appeal, with the permission of the Upper Tribunal.[11]

17.9   If permission is refused, there is no right of appeal against that decision,[12] but the refusal of permission to appeal may be the subject of a claim for judicial review.[13] To succeed in such an application, it must be shown that the case involves an important point of principle or practice or that there is some other compelling reason to compel the Upper Tribunal to hear the appeal.[14] The Upper Tribunal has no jurisdiction to reconsider a refusal to grant permission to appeal.[15]

---

8 UT Rules r21(6).

9 UT Rules r22; note that, even if permission to cross-appeal is not sought here, it is still open to the Upper Tribunal to hear a cross-appeal at a later stage: *Avon Estates (London) Ltd v Sinclair Gardens Investments (Kensington) Ltd* [2013] UKUT 264 (LC); *Arrowdell Ltd v Coniston Court (North) Hove Ltd* LRA/72/2005.

10 UT Rules r23. Note that it would not normally be appropriate to grant permission on terms relating to costs: Upper Tribunal Practice Direction para.4.3.

11 *Christoforou and others v Standard Apartments Ltd* [2013] UKUT 586 (LC).

12 Tribunals Courts and Enforcement Act 2007 s13; *Wellcome Trust Ltd v 19–22 Onslow Gardens Freehold* [2012] EWCA Civ 1024; [2012] RVR 342.

13 *R (Cart) v Upper Tribunal* [2011] UKSC 28; [2012] 1 AC 663; [2011] 3 WLR 107. Note also the strict time limits and procedural rules in Civil Procedure Rules (CPR) 54.7A.

14 *R (Cart) v Upper Tribunal* [2011] UKSC 28; [2012] 1 AC 663; [2011] 3 WLR 107.

15 *Samuda v Secretary of State* [2014] EWCA Civ 1.

Procedure on appeal

17.10 Once permission to appeal has been obtained, the Upper Tribunal will usually issue directions, making provision for a statement of case from the appellant and a reply from the respondent.[16] A respondent who does not file any reply will cease to be a party to the proceedings.[17]

Review or re-hearing

17.11 Prior to the 2002 reforms, a hearing in the Lands Tribunal was a rehearing, with the effect that the whole case – evidence and submissions – was conducted afresh.[18]

17.12 However, with the introduction of the requirement to obtain permission to appeal, this is no longer the case. Now, the applicant must make clear whether or not he or she is seeking

a) an appeal by way of review;
b) an appeal by way of review which, if successful, will involve a consequential re-hearing; or
c) an appeal by way of re-hearing.

17.13 The majority of appeals are by way of review, ie no new evidence can be presented.

The appeal

17.14 The Upper Tribunal may decide to determine the appeal on the basis of written submissions only[19] or at a hearing.[20] It may deal with a case in the absence of one or more parties if the tribunal is satisfied that the party has been notified of the hearing or that reasonable steps have been taken to notify the party of the hearing; and it is in the interests of justice to proceed with the hearing.[21]

17.15 Decisions may be given orally but, more commonly, are in writing. In any event, a written record of the decision must be produced

---

16 Directions, see UT Rules r6; statement of case, r24; reply, r25; the applicant may produce a further reply, r26.
17 UT Rules r25(2).
18 *Re London and Winchester Properties Ltd's Appeal* (1983) 45 P&CR 429 (Lands Tribunal); *Wellcome Trust v Romines* [1999] 3 EGLR 229 (Lands Tribunal).
19 UT Rules r46.
20 UT Rules rr47, 48.
21 UT Rules r49.

unless the parties consent to the tribunal dispensing with written reasons.[22] The tribunal may correct clerical errors in its decisions.[23] There is also a limited power to set aside a decision.[24]

17.16 The tribunal has no wider power to award costs than that applicable in the FTT/LVT.[25]

Appeals to the Court of Appeal

17.17 Appeals from the Upper Tribunal are to the Court of Appeal. Either the tribunal or the Court of Appeal can grant permission if satisfied that the proposed appeal would raise some important point of principle or practice; or there is some other compelling reason for the relevant appellate court to hear the appeal.[26]

17.18 Many litigants are deterred from appealing to the Court of Appeal by the potential costs involved and, more importantly, the risk that they will be responsible for the costs of the other side. Since 1 April 2013, the Court of Appeal has been able to decide that, when hearing an appeal from the FTT/LVT, it will exercise only the same limited costs rules which apply in that tribunal.[27]

The first instance jurisdiction of the Upper Tribunal

17.19 The FTT (but not the LVT) has power to transfer cases into the Upper Tribunal for trial.[28] In such cases, the FTT rules apply.[29]

---

22 UT Rules r 51.
23 UT Rules r53.
24 UT Rules r54.
25 Tribunals, Courts and Enforcement Act 2007 s29; Upper Tribunal Practice Direction paras 12 and 12.6.
26 Appeals from the Upper Tribunal to the Court of Appeal Order 2008 SI No 2834.
27 CPR 52.9A.
28 Tribunal Procedure (First-tier Tribunal) (Property Chamber) Rules 2013 SI No 1169 r25; see eg *Ninety Broomfield Road RTM Co Ltd v Triplerose Ltd* [2013] UKUT 606 (LC).
29 UT Rules r44A.

APPENDICES

APPENDIX A

Legislation (extracts)

LANDLORD AND TENANT ACT 1985

Meaning of 'service charge' and *'relevant costs'*

18 (1) In the following provisions of this Act *'service charge'* means an amount payable by a tenant of a dwelling as part of or in addition to the rent–

    (a) which is payable, directly or indirectly, for services, repairs, maintenance, improvements or insurance or the landlord's costs of management, and

    (b) the whole or part of which varies or may vary according to the relevant costs.

  (2) The relevant costs are the costs or estimated costs incurred or to be incurred by or on behalf of the landlord, or a superior landlord, in connection with the matters for which the service charge is payable.

  (3) For this purpose–

    (a) *'costs'* includes overheads, and

    (b) costs are relevant costs in relation to a service charge whether they are incurred, or to be incurred, in the period for which the service charge is payable or in an earlier or later period.

Limitation of service charges: reasonableness

19 (1) Relevant costs shall be taken into account in determining the amount of a service charge payable for a period–

    (a) only to the extent that they are reasonably incurred, and

    (b) where they are incurred on the provision of services or the carrying out of works, only if the services or works are of a reasonable standard;

    and the amount payable shall be limited accordingly.

  (2) Where a service charge is payable before the relevant costs are incurred, no greater amount than is reasonable is so payable, and after the relevant costs have been incurred any necessary adjustment shall be made by repayment, reduction or subsequent charges or otherwise.

(3)–(5) ...

Limitation of service charges: consultation requirements

20 (1) Where this section applies to any qualifying works or qualifying long term agreement, the relevant contributions of tenants are limited in accordance with subsection (6) or (7) (or both) unless the consultation requirements have been either–

    (a) complied with in relation to the works or agreement, or

    (b) dispensed with in relation to the works or agreement by (or on appeal from) the appropriate tribunal.

  (2) In this section *'relevant contribution'*, in relation to a tenant and any works or agreement, is the amount which he may be required under the terms of his lease to contribute (by the payment of service charges) to relevant costs incurred on carrying out the works or under the agreement.

  (3) This section applies to qualifying works if relevant costs incurred on carrying out the works exceed an appropriate amount.

  (4) The Secretary of State may by regulations provide that this section applies to a qualifying long term agreement–

    (a) if relevant costs incurred under the agreement exceed an appropriate amount, or

    (b) if relevant costs incurred under the agreement during a period prescribed by the regulations exceed an appropriate amount.

(5) An appropriate amount is an amount set by regulations made by the Secretary of State; and the regulations may make provision for either or both of the following to be an appropriate amount–

(a) an amount prescribed by, or determined in accordance with, the regulations, and

(b) an amount which results in the relevant contribution of any one or more tenants being an amount prescribed by, or determined in accordance with, the regulations.

(6) Where an appropriate amount is set by virtue of paragraph (a) of subsection (5), the amount of the relevant costs incurred on carrying out the works or under the agreement which may be taken into account in determining the relevant contributions of tenants is limited to the appropriate amount.

(7) Where an appropriate amount is set by virtue of paragraph (b) of that subsection, the amount of the relevant contribution of the tenant, or each of the tenants, whose relevant contribution would otherwise exceed the amount prescribed by, or determined in accordance with, the regulations is limited to the amount so prescribed or determined.

Consultation requirements: supplementary

20ZA(1)Where an application is made to the appropriate tribunal for a determination to dispense with all or any of the consultation requirements in relation to any qualifying works or qualifying long term agreement, the tribunal may make the determination if satisfied that it is reasonable to dispense with the requirements.

(2) In section 20 and this section–

'*qualifying works*' means works on a building or any other premises, and

'*qualifying long term agreement*' means (subject to subsection (3)) an agreement entered into, by or on behalf of the landlord or a superior landlord, for a term of more than twelve months.

(3) The Secretary of State may by regulations provide that an agreement is not a qualifying long term agreement–

(a) if it is an agreement of a description prescribed by the regulations, or

(b) in any circumstances so prescribed.

(4) In section 20 and this section '*the consultation requirements*' means requirements prescribed by regulations made by the Secretary of State.

(5) Regulations under subsection (4) may in particular include provision requiring the landlord–

(a) to provide details of proposed works or agreements to tenants or the recognised tenants' association representing them,

(b) to obtain estimates for proposed works or agreements,

(c) to invite tenants or the recognised tenants' association to propose the names of persons from whom the landlord should try to obtain other estimates,

(d) to have regard to observations made by tenants or the recognised tenants' association in relation to proposed works or agreements and estimates, and

(e) to give reasons in prescribed circumstances for carrying out works or entering into agreements.

(6) Regulations under section 20 or this section—
(a) may make provision generally or only in relation to specific cases, and
(b) may make different provision for different purposes.
(7) Regulations under section 20 or this section shall be made by statutory instrument which shall be subject to annulment in pursuance of a resolution of either House of Parliament.

Limitation of service charges: time limit on making demands

20B(1) If any of the relevant costs taken into account in determining the amount of any service charge were incurred more than 18 months before a demand for payment of the service charge is served on the tenant, then (subject to subsection (2)), the tenant shall not be liable to pay so much of the service charge as reflects the costs so incurred.
(2) Subsection (1) shall not apply if, within the period of 18 months beginning with the date when the relevant costs in question were incurred, the tenant was notified in writing that those costs had been incurred and that he would subsequently be required under the terms of his lease to contribute to them by the payment of a service charge.

Limitation of service charges: costs of proceedings

20C(1) A tenant may make an application for an order that all or any of the costs incurred, or to be incurred, by the landlord in connection with proceedings before a court, residential property tribunal or leasehold valuation tribunal or the First-tier Tribunal, or the Upper Tribunal , or in connection with arbitration proceedings, are not to be regarded as relevant costs to be taken into account in determining the amount of any service charge payable by the tenant or any other person or persons specified in the application.
(2) The application shall be made—
(a) in the case of court proceedings, to the court before which the proceedings are taking place or, if the application is made after the proceedings are concluded, to a county court;
(aa) in the case of proceedings before a residential property tribunal, to a leasehold valuation tribunal;
(b) in the case of proceedings before a leasehold valuation tribunal, to the tribunal before which the proceedings are taking place or, if the application is made after the proceedings are concluded, to any leasehold valuation tribunal;
(ba) in the case of proceedings before the First-tier Tribunal, to the tribunal;
(c) in the case of proceedings before the Upper Tribunal, to the tribunal;
(d) in the case of arbitration proceedings, to the arbitral tribunal or, if the application is made after the proceedings are concluded, to a county court.
(3) The court or tribunal to which the application is made may make such order on the application as it considers just and equitable in the circumstances.

Request for summary of relevant costs

21 (1) A tenant may required the landlord in writing to supply him with a written summary of the costs incurred—
(a) if the relevant accounts are made up for periods of twelve months, in the last such period ending not later than the date of the request, or

(b) if the accounts are not so made up, in the period of twelve months ending with the date of the request,
and which are relevant costs in relation to the service charges payable or demanded as payable in that or any other period.

(2) If the tenant is represented by a recognised tenants' association and he consents, the request may be made by the secretary of the association instead of by the tenant and may then be for the supply of the summary to the Secretary.

(3) A request is duly served on the landlord if it is served on–
   (a) an agent of the landlord named as such in the rent book or similar document, or
   (b) the person who receives the rent on behalf of the landlord;
   and a person on whom a request is so served shall forward it as soon as may be to the landlord.

(4) The landlord shall comply with the request within one month of the request or within six months of the end of the period referred to in subsection (1)(a) or (b) whichever is the later.

(5) The summary shall state whether any of the costs relate to works in respect of which a grant has been or is to be paid under section 523 of the Housing Act 1985 (assistance for provision of separate service pipe for water supply) or any provision of Part I of the Housing Grants, Construction and Regeneration Act 1996 (grants, etc for renewal of private sector housing) or any corresponding earlier enactment and set out the costs in a way showing how they have been or will be reflected in demands for service charges and, in addition, shall summarise each of the following items, namely–
   (a) any of the costs in respect of which no demand for payment was received by the landlord within the period referred to in subsection (1)(a) or (b),
   (b) any of the costs in respect of which–
      (i) a demand for payment was so received, but
      (ii) no payment was made by the landlord within that period, and
   (c) any of the costs in respect of which–
      (i) a demand for payment was so received, and
      (ii) payment was made by the landlord within that period,
   and specify the aggregate of any amounts received by the landlord down to the end of that period on account of service charges in respect of relevant dwellings and still standing to the credit of the tenants of those dwellings at the end of that period

(5A) In subsection (5) '*relevant dwelling*' means a dwelling whose tenant is either–
   (a) the person by or with the consent of whom the request was made, or
   (b) a person whose obligations under the terms of his lease as regards contributing to relevant costs relate to the same costs as the corresponding obligations of the person mentioned in paragraph (a) above relate to.

(5B) The summary shall state whether any of the costs relate to works which are included in the external works specified in a group repair scheme, within the meaning of Chapter II of Part I of the Housing Grants, Construction and Regeneration Act 1996 or any corresponding earlier enactment, in which the landlord participated or is participating as an assisted participant.

(6) If the service charges in relation to which the costs are relevant costs as

mentioned in subsection (1) are payable by the tenants of more than four dwellings, the summary shall be certified by a qualified accountant as–

(a) in his opinion a fair summary complying with the requirements of subsection (5), and

(b) being sufficiently supported by accounts, receipts and other documents which have been produced to him.

Notice to accompany demands for service charges

21B(1) A demand for the payment of a service charge must be accompanied by a summary of the rights and obligations of tenants of dwellings in relation to service charges.

(2) The Secretary of State may make regulations prescribing requirements as to the form and content of such summaries of rights and obligations.

(3) A tenant may withhold payment of a service charge which has been demanded from him if subsection (1) is not complied with in relation to the demand.

(4) Where a tenant withholds a service charge under this section, any provisions of the lease relating to non-payment or late payment of service charges do not have effect in relation to the period for which he so withholds it.

(5) Regulations under subsection (2) may make different provision for different purposes.

(6) Regulations under subsection (2) shall be made by statutory instrument which shall be subject to annulment in pursuance of a resolution of either House of Parliament.

Request to inspect supporting accounts etc

22 (1) This section applies where a tenant, or the secretary of a recognised tenants' association, has obtained such a summary as is referred to in section 21(1) (summary of relevant costs), whether in pursuance of that section or otherwise.

(2) The tenant, or the secretary with the consent of the tenant, may within six months of obtaining the summary require the landlord in writing to afford him reasonable facilities–

(a) for inspecting the accounts, receipts and other documents supporting the summary, and

(b) for taking copies or extracts from them.

(3) A request under this section is duly served on the landlord if it is served on–

(a) an agent of the landlord named as such in the rent book or similar document, or

(b) the person who receives the rent on behalf of the landlord;

and a person on whom a request is so served shall forward it as soon as may be to the landlord.

(4) The landlord shall make such facilities available to the tenant or secretary for a period of two months beginning not later than one month after the request is made.

(5) The landlord shall–

(a) where such facilities are for the inspection of any documents, make them so available free of charge;

(b) where such facilities are for the taking of copies or extracts, be entitled to make them so available on payment of such reasonable charge as he may determine.

(6) The requirement imposed on the landlord by subsection (5)(a) to make any facilities available to a person free of charge shall not be construed as precluding the landlord from treating as part of his costs of management any costs incurred by him in connection with making those facilities so available.

Request relating to information held by superior landlord

23 (1) If a request under section 21 (request for summary of relevant costs) relates in whole or in part to relevant costs incurred by or on behalf of a superior landlord, and the landlord to whom the request is made is not in possession of the relevant information–

(a) he shall in turn make a written request for the relevant information to the person who is his landlord (and so on, if that person is not himself the superior landlord),

(b) the superior landlord shall comply with that request within a reasonable time, and

(c) the immediate landlord shall then comply with the tenant's or secretary's request, or that part of it which relates to the relevant costs incurred by or on behalf of the superior landlord, within the time allowed by section 21 or such further time, if any, as is reasonable in the circumstances.

(2) If a request under section 22 (request for facilities to inspect supporting accounts, etc) relates to a summary of costs incurred by or on behalf of a superior landlord–

(a) the landlord to whom the request is made shall forthwith inform the tenant or secretary of that fact and of the name and address of the superior landlord, and

(b) section 22 shall then apply to the superior landlord as it applies to the immediate landlord.

Effect of assignment on request

24 The assignment of a tenancy does not affect the validity of a request made under section 21, 22 or 23 before the assignment; but a person is not obliged to provide a summary or make facilities available more than once for the same dwelling and for the same period.

Failure to comply with ss21 22, or 23 an offence

25 (1) It is a summary offence for a person to fail, without reasonable excuse, to perform a duty imposed on him by section 21, 22 or 23.

(2) A person committing such an offence is liable on conviction to a fine not exceeding level 4 on the standard scale.

Liability to pay service charges: jurisdiction

27A(1) An application may be made to the appropriate tribunal for a determination whether a service charge is payable and, if it is, as to–

(a) the person by whom it is payable,

(b) the person to whom it is payable,

(c) the amount which is payable,

(d) the date at or by which it is payable, and

(e) the manner in which it is payable.

(2) Subsection (1) applies whether or not any payment has been made.

(3) An application may also be made to the appropriate tribunal for a determination whether, if costs were incurred for services, repairs, maintenance,

improvements, insurance or management of any specified description, a service charge would be payable for the costs and, if it would, as to–

(a) the person by whom it would be payable,

(b) the person to whom it would be payable,

(c) the amount which would be payable,

(d) the date at or by which it would be payable, and

(e) the manner in which it would be payable.

(4) No application under subsection (1) or (3) may be made in respect of a matter which–

(a) has been agreed or admitted by the tenant,

(b) has been, or is to be, referred to arbitration pursuant to a post-dispute arbitration agreement to which the tenant is a party,

(c) has been the subject of determination by a court, or

(d) has been the subject of determination by an arbitral tribunal pursuant to a post-dispute arbitration agreement.

(5) But the tenant is not to be taken to have agreed or admitted any matter by reason only of having made any payment.

(6) An agreement by the tenant of a dwelling (other than a post-dispute arbitration agreement) is void in so far as it purports to provide for a determination–

(a) in a particular manner, or

(b) on particular evidence,

of any question which may be the subject of an application under subsection (1) or (3).

(7) The jurisdiction conferred on the appropriate tribunal in respect of any matter by virtue of this section is in addition to any jurisdiction of a court in respect of the matter.

Schedule 1

1   In this Schedule–

'*landlord*', in relation to a tenant by whom a service charge is payable which includes an amount payable directly or indirectly for insurance, includes any person who has a right to enforce payment of that service charge;

'*relevant policy*', in relation to a dwelling, means any policy of insurance under which the dwelling is insured (being, in the case of a flat, a policy covering the building containing it); and

'*tenant*' includes a statutory tenant.

2 (1) Where a service charge is payable by the tenant of a dwelling which consists of or includes an amount payable directly or indirectly for insurance, the tenant may by notice in writing require the landlord to supply him with a written summary of the insurance for the time being effected in relation to the dwelling.

(2) If the tenant is represented by a recognised tenants' association and he consents, the notice may be served by the secretary of the association instead of by the tenant and may then be for the supply of the summary to the secretary.

(3) A notice under this paragraph is duly served on the landlord if it is served on–

(a) an agent of the landlord named as such in the rent book or similar document, or

(b) the person who receives the rent on behalf of the landlord;

and a person on whom such a notice is so served shall forward it as soon as may be to the landlord.

(4) The landlord shall, within the period of twenty-one days beginning with the day on which he receives the notice, comply with it by supplying to the tenant or the secretary of the recognised tenants' association (as the case may require) such a summary as is mentioned in sub-paragraph (1), which shall include–

(a) the insured amount or amounts under any relevant policy, and

(b) the name of the insurer under any such policy, and

(c) the risks in respect of which the dwelling or (as the case may be) the building containing it is insured under any such policy.

(5) In sub-paragraph (4)(a) *'the insured amount or amounts'*, in relation to a relevant policy, means–

(a) in the case of a dwelling other than a flat, the amount for which the dwelling is insured under the policy; and

(b) in the case of a flat, the amount for which the building containing it is insured under the policy and, if specified in the policy, the amount for which the flat is insured under it.

(6) The landlord shall be taken to have complied with the notice if, within the period mentioned in sub-paragraph (4), he instead supplies to the tenant or the secretary (as the case may require) a copy of every relevant policy.

(7) In a case where two or more buildings are insured under any relevant policy, the summary or copy supplied under sub-paragraph (4) or (6) so far as relating to that policy need only be of such parts of the policy as relate–

(a) to the dwelling, and

(b) if the dwelling is a flat, to the building containing it.

3 (1) Where a service charge is payable by the tenant of a dwelling which consists of or includes an amount payable directly or indirectly for insurance, the tenant may by notice in writing require the landlord–

(a) to afford him reasonable facilities for inspecting any relevant policy or associated documents and for taking copies of or extracts from them, or

(b) to take copies of or extracts from any such policy or documents and either send them to him or afford him reasonable facilities for collecting them (as he specifies).

(2) If the tenant is represented by a recognised tenants' association and he consents, the notice may be served by the secretary of the association instead of by the tenant (and in that case any requirement imposed by it is to afford reasonable facilities, or to send copies or extracts, to the secretary).

(3) A notice under this paragraph is duly served on the landlord if it is served on–

(a) an agent of the landlord named as such in the rent book or similar document, or

(b) the person who receives the rent on behalf of the landlord;

and a person on whom such a notice is so served shall forward it as soon as may be to the landlord.

(4) The landlord shall comply with a requirement imposed by a notice under this paragraph within the period of twenty-one days beginning with the day on which he receives the notice.

(5) To the extent that a notice under this paragraph requires the landlord to

afford facilities for inspecting documents–

    (a) he shall do so free of charge, but

    (b) he may treat as part of his costs of management any costs incurred by him in doing so.

(6) The landlord may make a reasonable charge for doing anything else in compliance with a requirement imposed by a notice under this paragraph.

(7) In this paragraph–

    '*relevant policy*' includes a policy of insurance under which the dwelling was insured for the period of insurance immediately preceding that current when the notice is served (being, in the case of a flat, a policy covering the building containing it), and

    '*associated documents*' means accounts, receipts or other documents which provide evidence of payment of any premiums due under a relevant policy in respect of the period of insurance which is current when the notice is served or the period of insurance immediately preceding that period.

4 (1) If a notice is served under paragraph 2 in a case where a superior landlord has effected, in whole or in part, the insurance of the dwelling in question and the landlord on whom the notice is served is not in possession of the relevant information–

    (a) he shall in turn by notice in writing require the person who is his landlord to give him the relevant information (and so on, if that person is not himself the superior landlord),

    (b) the superior landlord shall comply with the notice within a reasonable time, and

    (c) the immediate landlord shall then comply with the tenant's or secretary's notice in the manner provided by sub-paragraphs (4) to (7) of paragraph 2 within the time allowed by that paragraph or such further time, if any, as is reasonable in the circumstances.

(2) If, in a case where a superior landlord has effected, in whole or in part, the insurance of the dwelling in question, a notice under paragraph 3 imposes a requirement relating to any policy of insurance effected by the superior landlord–

    (a) the landlord on whom the notice is served shall forthwith inform the tenant or secretary of that fact and of the name and address of the superior landlord, and

    (b) that paragraph shall then apply to the superior landlord in relation to that policy as it applies to the immediate landlord.

4A(1) This paragraph applies where, at a time when a duty imposed on the landlord or a superior landlord by virtue of any of paragraphs 2 to 4 remains to be discharged by him, he disposes of the whole or part of his interest as landlord or superior landlord).

(2) If the landlord or superior landlord is, despite the disposal, still in a position to discharge the duty to any extent, he remains responsible for discharging it to that extent.

(3) If the other person is in a position to discharge the duty to any extent, he is responsible for discharging it to that extent.

(4) Where the other person is responsible for discharging the duty to any extent (whether or not the landlord or superior landlord is also responsible for discharging it to that or any other extent)–

(a) references to the landlord or superior landlord in paragraphs 2 to 4 are to, or include, the other person so far as is appropriate to reflect his responsibility for discharging the duty to that extent, but

(b) in connection with its discharge by that person, paragraphs 2(4) and 3(4) apply as if the reference to the day on which the landlord receives the notice were to the date of the disposal referred to in sub-paragraph (1)...

5   The assignment of a tenancy does not affect any duty imposed by virtue of any of paragraphs 2 to 4A; but a person is not required to comply with more than a reasonable number of requirements imposed by any one person.

6 (1) It is a summary offence for a person to fail, without reasonable excuse, to perform a duty imposed on him by or by virtue of any of paragraphs 2 to 4A.

(2) A person committing such an offence is liable on conviction to a fine not exceeding level 4 on the standard scale.

7 (1) This paragraph applies to any dwelling in respect of which the tenant pays to the landlord a service charge consisting of or including an amount payable directly or indirectly for insurance.

(2) Where–

(a) it appears to the tenant of any such dwelling that damage has been caused–

(i) to the dwelling, or

(ii) if the dwelling is a flat, to the dwelling or to any other part of the building containing it,

in respect of which a claim could be made under the terms of a policy of insurance, and

(b) it is a term of that policy that the person insured under the policy should give notice of any claim under it to the insurer within a specified period,

the tenant may, within that specified period, serve on the insurer a notice in writing stating that it appears to him that damage has been caused as mentioned in paragraph (a) and describing briefly the nature of the damage.

(3) Where–

(a) any such notice is served on an insurer by a tenant in relation to any such damage, and

(b) the specified period referred to in sub-paragraph (2)(b) would expire earlier than the period of six months beginning with the date on which the notice is served,

the policy in question shall have effect as regards any claim subsequently made in respect of that damage by the person insured under the policy as if for the specified period there were substituted that period of six months.

(4) Where the tenancy of a dwelling to which this paragraph applies is held by joint tenants, a single notice under this paragraph may be given by any one or more of those tenants.

(5) The Secretary of State may by regulations prescribe the form of notices under this paragraph and the particulars which such notices must contain.

(6) Any such regulations–

(a) may make different provision with respect to different cases or descriptions of case, including different provision for different areas, and

(b) shall be made by statutory instrument.

8 (1) This paragraph applies where a tenancy of a dwelling requires the tenant to insure the dwelling with an insurer nominated or approved by the landlord.

(2) The tenant or landlord may apply to a county court or the appropriate tribunal for a determination whether–
  (a) the insurance which is available from the nominated or approved insurer for insuring the tenant's dwelling is unsatisfactory in any respect, or
  (b) the premiums payable in respect of any such insurance are excessive.
(3) No such application may be made in respect of a matter which–
  (a) has been agreed or admitted by the tenant,
  (b) under an arbitration agreement to which the tenant is a party is to be referred to arbitration, or
  (c) has been the subject of determination by a court or arbitral tribunal.
(4) On an application under this paragraph the court or tribunal may make–
  (a) an order requiring the landlord to nominate or approve such other insurer as is specified in the order, or
  (b) an order requiring him to nominate or approve another insurer who satisfies such requirements in relation to the insurance of the dwelling as are specified in the order.
(5) ...
(6) An agreement by the tenant of a dwelling (other than an arbitration agreement) is void in so far as it purports to provide for a determination in a particular manner, or on particular evidence, of any question which may be the subject of an application under this paragraph.
9 (1) Paragraphs 2 to 8 do not apply to a tenant of–
  a local authority,
  a National Park authority, or
  a new town corporation, ...
  unless the tenancy is a long tenancy, in which case paragraphs 2 to 5 and 7 and 8 apply but paragraph 6 does not.
(2) Subsections (2) and (3) of section 26 shall apply for the purposes of sub-paragraph (1) as they apply for the purposes of subsection (1) of that section.

LANDLORD AND TENANT ACT 1987

Tenant's right to apply to court for appointment of manager

21 (1) The tenant of a flat contained in any premises to which this Part applies may, subject to the following provisions of this Part, apply to the appropriate tribunal for an order under section 24 appointing a manager to act in relation to those premises.

(2) Subject to subsection (3), this Part applies to premises consisting of the whole or part of a building if the building or part contains two or more flats.

(3) This Part does not apply to any such premises at a time when–

(a) the interest of the landlord in the premises is held by–

(i) an exempt landlord or a resident landlord, or

(ii) the Welsh Ministers in their new towns residuary capacity,

(b) the premises are included within the functional land of any charity.

(3A) But this Part is not prevented from applying to any premises because the interest of the landlord in the premises is held by a resident landlord if at least one-half of the flats contained in the premises are held on long leases which are not tenancies to which Part 2 of the Landlord and Tenant Act 1954 applies.

(4) An application for an order under section 24 may be made–

(a) jointly by tenants of two or more flats if they are each entitled to make such an application by virtue of this section, and

(b) in respect of two or more premises to which this Part applies;

and, in relation to any such joint application as is mentioned in paragraph (a), references in this Part to a single tenant shall be construed accordingly.

(5) Where the tenancy of a flat contained in any such premises is held by joint tenants, an application for an order under section 24 in respect of those premises may be made by any one or more of those tenants.

(6) An application to the court for it to exercise in relation to any premises any jurisdiction to appoint a receiver or manager shall not be made by a tenant (in his capacity as such) in any circumstances in which an application could be made by him for an order under section 24 appointing a manager to act in relation to those premises.

(7) References in this Part to a tenant do not include references to a tenant under a tenancy to which Part II of the Landlord and Tenant Act 1954 applies.

(8) For the purposes of this Part, *'appropriate tribunal'* means–

(a) in relation to premises in England, the First-tier Tribunal or, where determined by or under Tribunal Procedure Rules, the Upper Tribunal; and

(b) in relation to premises in Wales, a leasehold valuation tribunal.

Preliminary notice by tenant

22 (1) Before an application for an order under section 24 is made in respect of any premises to which this Part applies by a tenant of a flat contained in those premises, a notice under this section must (subject to subsection (3)) be served by the tenant on–

(i) the landlord, and

(ii) any person (other than the landlord) by whom obligations relating to the management of the premises or any part of them are owed to the tenant under his tenancy.

(2) A notice under this section must–

(a) specify the tenant's name, the address of his flat and an address in England and Wales (which may be the address of his flat) at which any person on whom the notice is served may serve notices, including notices in proceedings, on him in connection with this Part;

(b) state that the tenant intends to make an application for an order under section 24 to be made by the appropriate tribunal in respect of such premises to which this Part applies as are specified in the notice, but (if paragraph (d) is applicable) that he will not do so if the requirement specified in pursuance of that paragraph is complied with;

(c) specify the grounds on which the court would be asked to make such an order and the matters that would be relied on by the tenant for the purpose of establishing those grounds;

(d) where those matters are capable of being remedied by any person on whom the notice is served, require him, within such reasonable period as is specified in the notice, to take such steps for the purpose of remedying them as are so specified; and

(e) contain such information (if any) as the Secretary of State may by regulations prescribe.

(3) The appropriate tribunal may (whether on the hearing of an application for an order under section 24 or not) by order dispense with the requirement to serve a notice under this section on a person in a case where it is satisfied that it would not be reasonably practicable to serve such a notice on the person, but the tribunal may, when doing so, direct that such other notices are served, or such other steps are taken, as it thinks fit.

(4) In a case where–

(a) a notice under this section has been served on the landlord, and

(b) his interest in the premises specified in pursuance of subsection (2)(b) is subject to a mortgage, the landlord shall, as soon as is reasonably practicable after receiving the notice, serve on the mortgagee a copy of the notice.

Application to court for appointment of manager

23 (1) No application for an order under section 24 shall be made to the appropriate tribunal unless–

(a) in a case where a notice has been served under section 22, either–

(i) the period specified in pursuance of paragraph (d) of subsection (2) of that section has expired without the person required to take steps in pursuance of that paragraph having taken them, or

(ii) that paragraph was not applicable in the circumstances of the case; or

(b) in a case where the requirement to serve such a notice has been dispensed with by an order under subsection (3) of that section, either–

(i) any notices required to be served, and any other steps required to be taken, by virtue of the order have been served or (as the case may be) taken, or

(ii) no direction was given by the tribunal when making the order.

Appointment of manager by a tribunal

24 (1) The appropriate tribunal may, on an application for an order under this section, by order (whether interlocutory or final) appoint a manager to carry out

in relation to any premises to which this Part applies–

   (a) such functions in connection with the management of the premises, or

   (b) such functions of a receiver,

   or both, as the tribunal thinks fit.

(2) The appropriate tribunal may only make an order under this section in the following circumstances, namely–

   (a) where the tribunal is satisfied–

      (i) that any relevant person either is in breach of any obligation owed by him to the tenant under his tenancy and relating to the management of the premises in question or any part of them or (in the case of an obligation dependent on notice) would be in breach of any such obligation but for the fact that it has not been reasonably practicable for the tenant to give him the appropriate notice, and

      (ii) ...

      (iii) that it is just and convenient to make the order in all the circumstances of the case;

   (ab) where the tribunal is satisfied–

      (i) that unreasonable service charges have been made, or are proposed or likely to be made, and

      (ii) that it is just and convenient to make the order in all the circumstances of the case;

   (aba) where the tribunal is satisfied–

      (i) that unreasonable variable administration charges have been made, or are proposed or likely to be made, and

      (ii) that it is just and convenient to make the order in all the circumstances of the case;

   (ac) where the tribunal is satisfied–

      (i) that any relevant person has failed to comply with any relevant provision of a code of practice approved by the Secretary of State under section 87 of the Leasehold Reform, Housing and Urban Development Act 1993 (codes of management practice), and

      (ii) that it is just and convenient to make the order in all the circumstances of the case; or

   (b) where the tribunal is satisfied that other circumstances exist which make it just and convenient for the order to be made.

(2ZA) In this section *'relevant person'* means a person–

   (a) on whom a notice has been served under section 22, or

   (b) in the case of whom the requirement to serve a notice under that section has been dispensed with by an order under subsection (3) of that section.

(2A) For the purposes of subsection (2)(ab) a service charge shall be taken to be unreasonable–

   (a) if the amount is unreasonable having regard to the items for which it is payable,

   (b) if the items for which it is payable are of an unnecessarily high standard, or

   (c) if the items for which it is payable are of an insufficient standard with the result that additional service charges are or may be incurred.

In that provision and this subsection *'service charge'* means a service charge within the meaning of section 18(1) of the Landlord and Tenant Act 1985, other than one excluded from that section by section 27 of that Act (rent of dwelling registered and not entered as variable).

(2B) In subsection (2)(aba) *'variable administration charge'* has the meaning given by paragraph 1 of Schedule 11 to the Commonhold and Leasehold Reform Act 2002.

(3) The premises in respect of which an order is made under this section may, if the tribunal 1 thinks fit, be either more or less extensive than the premises specified in the application on which the order is made.

(4) An order under this section may make provision with respect to–

   (a) such matters relating to the exercise by the manager of his functions under the order, and

   (b) such incidental or ancillary matters,

   as the tribunal thinks fit; and, on any subsequent application made for the purpose by the manager, the tribunal may give him directions with respect to any such matters.

(5) Without prejudice to the generality of subsection (4), an order under this section may provide–

   (a) for rights and liabilities arising under contracts to which the manager is not a party to become rights and liabilities of the manager;

   (b) for the manager to be entitled to prosecute claims in respect of causes of action (whether contractual or tortious) accruing before or after the date of his appointment;

   (c) for remuneration to be paid to the manager by any relevant person, or by the tenants of the premises in respect of which the order is made or by all or any of those persons;

   (d) for the manager's functions to be exercisable by him (subject to subsection (9)) either during a specified period or without limit of time.

(6) Any such order may be granted subject to such conditions as the tribunal thinks fit, and in particular its operation may be suspended on terms fixed by the tribunal.

(7) In a case where an application for an order under this section was preceded by the service of a notice under section 22 , the tribunal may, if it thinks fit, make such an order notwithstanding–

   (a) that any period specified in the notice in pursuance of subsection (2)(d) of that section was not a reasonable period, or

   (b) that the notice failed in any other respect to comply with any requirement contained in subsection (2) of that section or in any regulations applying to the notice under section 54(3).

(8) The Land Charges Act 1972 and the Land Registration Act 2002 shall apply in relation to an order made under this section as they apply in relation to an order appointing a receiver or sequestrator of land.

(9) The appropriate tribunal may, on the application of any person interested, vary or discharge (whether conditionally or unconditionally) an order made under this section; and if the order has been protected by an entry registered under the Land Charges Act 1972 or the Land Registration Act 2002, the tribunal may by order direct that the entry shall be cancelled.

(9A) The tribunal shall not vary or discharge an order under subsection (9) on the application of any relevant person unless it is satisfied–

(a) that the variation or discharge of the order will not result in a recurrence of the circumstances which led to the order being made, and

(b) that it is just and convenient in all the circumstances of the case to vary or discharge the order.

(10) An order made under this section shall not be discharged by the appropriate tribunal by reason only that, by virtue of section 21(3), the premises in respect of which the order was made have ceased to be premises to which this Part applies.

(11) References in this Part to the management of any premises include references to the repair, maintenance , improvement or insurance of those premises.

Application by party to lease for variation of lease

35 (1) Any party to a long lease of a flat may make an application to the appropriate tribunal for an order varying the lease in such manner as is specified in the application.

(2) The grounds on which any such application may be made are that the lease fails to make satisfactory provision with respect to one or more of the following matters, namely–

(a) the repair or maintenance of–
   (i) the flat in question, or
   (ii) the building containing the flat, or
   (iii) any land or building which is let to the tenant under the lease or in respect of which rights are conferred on him under it;

(b) the insurance of the building containing the flat or of any such land or building as is mentioned in paragraph (a)(iii);

(c) the repair or maintenance of any installations (whether they are in the same building as the flat or not) which are reasonably necessary to ensure that occupiers of the flat enjoy a reasonable standard of accommodation;

(d) the provision or maintenance of any services which are reasonably necessary to ensure that occupiers of the flat enjoy a reasonable standard of accommodation (whether they are services connected with any such installations or not, and whether they are services provided for the benefit of those occupiers or services provided for the benefit of the occupiers of a number of flats including that flat);

(e) the recovery by one party to the lease from another party to it of expenditure incurred or to be incurred by him, or on his behalf, for the benefit of that other party or of a number of persons who include that other party;

(f) the computation of a service charge payable under the lease;

(g) such other matters as may be prescribed by regulations made by the Secretary of State.

(3) For the purposes of subsection (2)(c) and (d) the factors for determining, in relation to the occupiers of a flat, what is a reasonable standard of accommodation may include–

(a) factors relating to the safety and security of the flat and its occupiers and of any common parts of the building containing the flat; and

(b) other factors relating to the condition of any such common parts.

(3A) For the purposes of subsection (2)(e) the factors for determining, in relation to a service charge payable under a lease, whether the lease makes satisfactory provision include whether it makes provision for an amount to be payable (by way of interest or otherwise) in respect of a failure to pay the service charge by the due date.

(4) For the purposes of subsection (2)(f) a lease fails to make satisfactory provision with respect to the computation of a service charge payable under it if–

(a) it provides for any such charge to be a proportion of expenditure incurred, or to be incurred, by or on behalf of the landlord or a superior landlord; and

(b) other tenants of the landlord are also liable under their leases to pay by way of service charges proportions of any such expenditure; and

(c) the aggregate of the amounts that would, in any particular case, be payable by reference to the proportions referred to in paragraphs (a) and (b) would either exceed or be less than 3 the whole of any such expenditure.

(5) Procedure regulations under Schedule 12 to the Commonhold and Leasehold Reform Act 2002 and Tribunal Procedure Rules shall make provision–

(a) for requiring notice of any application under this Part to be served by the person making the application, and by any respondent to the application, on any person who the applicant, or (as the case may be) the respondent, knows or has reason to believe is likely to be affected by any variation specified in the application, and

(b) for enabling persons served with any such notice to be joined as parties to the proceedings.

(6) For the purposes of this Part a long lease shall not be regarded as a long lease of a flat if–

(a) the demised premises consist of or include three or more flats contained in the same building; or

(b) the lease constitutes a tenancy to which Part II of the Landlord and Tenant Act 1954 applies.

(8) In this section '*service charge*' has the meaning given by section 18(1) of the 1985 Act.

(9) For the purposes of this section and sections 36 to 39, '*appropriate tribunal*' means–

(a) if one or more of the long leases concerned relates to property in England, the First-tier Tribunal or, where determined by or under Tribunal Procedure Rules, the Upper Tribunal; and

(b) if one or more of the long leases concerned relates to property in Wales, a leasehold valuation tribunal.

Application by respondent for variation of other leases

36 (1) Where an application ('the original application') is made under section 35 by any party to a lease, any other party to the lease may make an application to the tribunal asking it, in the event of its deciding to make an order effecting any variation of the lease in pursuance of the original application, to make an order which effects a corresponding variation of each of such one or more other leases as are specified in the application.

(2) Any lease so specified–

(a) must be a long lease of a flat under which the landlord is the same person as the landlord under the lease specified in the original application; but

(b) need not be a lease of a flat which is in the same building as the flat let under that lease, nor a lease drafted in terms identical to those of that lease.

(3) The grounds on which an application may be made under this section are–

   (a) that each of the leases specified in the application fails to make satisfactory provision with respect to the matter or matters specified in the original application; and

   (b) that, if any variation is effected in pursuance of the original application, it would be in the interests of the person making the application under this section, or in the interests of the other persons who are parties to the leases specified in that application, to have all of the leases in question (that is to say, the ones specified in that application together with the one specified in the original application) varied to the same effect.

Application by majority of parties for variation of leases

37 (1) Subject to the following provisions of this section, an application may be made to the appropriate tribunal in respect of two or more leases for an order varying each of those leases in such manner as is specified in the application.

  (2) Those leases must be long leases of flats under which the landlord is the same person, but they need not be leases of flats which are in the same building, nor leases which are drafted in identical terms.

  (3) The grounds on which an application may be made under this section are that the object to be achieved by the variation cannot be satisfactorily achieved unless all the leases are varied to the same effect.

  (4) An application under this section in respect of any leases may be made by the landlord or any of the tenants under the leases.

  (5) Any such application shall only be made if–

   (a) in a case where the application is in respect of less than nine leases, all, or all but one, of the parties concerned consent to it; or

   (b) in a case where the application is in respect of more than eight leases, it is not opposed for any reason by more than 10 per cent. of the total number of the parties concerned and at least 75 per cent. of that number consent to it.

  (6) For the purposes of subsection (5)–

   (a) in the case of each lease in respect of which the application is made, the tenant under the lease shall constitute one of the parties concerned (so that in determining the total number of the parties concerned a person who is the tenant under a number of such leases shall be regarded as constituting a corresponding number of the parties concerned); and

   (b) the landlord shall also constitute one of the parties concerned.

Orders varying leases

38 (1) If, on an application under section 35 , the grounds on which the application was made are established to the satisfaction of the tribunal, the tribunal may (subject to subsections (6) and (7)) make an order varying the lease specified in the application in such manner as is specified in the order.

  (2) If–

   (a) an application under section 36 was made in connection with that application, and

   (b) the grounds set out in subsection (3) of that section are established to the satisfaction of the tribunal with respect to the leases specified in the application under section 36, the tribunal may (subject to subsections (6) and (7)) also make an order varying each of those leases in such manner as is specified in the order.

(3) If, on an application under section 37, the grounds set out in subsection (3) of that section are established to the satisfaction of the tribunal with respect to the leases specified in the application, the tribunal may (subject to subsections (6) and (7)) make an order varying each of those leases in such manner as is specified in the order.

(4) The variation specified in an order under subsection (1) or (2) may be either the variation specified in the relevant application under section 35 or 36 or such other variation as the tribunal thinks fit.

(5) If the grounds referred to in subsection (2) or (3) (as the case may be) are established to the satisfaction of the tribunal with respect to some but not all of the leases specified in the application, the power to make an order under that subsection shall extend to those leases only.

(6) A tribunal shall not make an order under this section effecting any variation of a lease if it appears to the tribunal –

(a) that the variation would be likely substantially to prejudice–
  (i) any respondent to the application, or
  (ii) any person who is not a party to the application,
and that an award under subsection (10) would not afford him adequate compensation, or
(b) that for any other reason it would not be reasonable in the circumstances for the variation to be effected.

(7) A tribunal shall not, on an application relating to the provision to be made by a lease with respect to insurance, make an order under this section effecting any variation of the lease–

(a) which terminates any existing right of the landlord under its terms to nominate an insurer for insurance purposes; or
(b) which requires the landlord to nominate a number of insurers from which the tenant would be entitled to select an insurer for those purposes; or
(c) which, in a case where the lease requires the tenant to effect insurance with a specified insurer, requires the tenant to effect insurance otherwise than with another specified insurer.

(8) A tribunal may, instead of making an order varying a lease in such manner as is specified in the order, make an order directing the parties to the lease to vary it in such manner as is so specified; and accordingly any reference in this Part (however expressed) to an order which effects any variation of a lease or to any variation effected by an order shall include a reference to an order which directs the parties to a lease to effect a variation of it or (as the case may be) a reference to any variation effected in pursuance of such an order.

(9) A tribunal may by order direct that a memorandum of any variation of a lease effected by an order under this section shall be endorsed on such documents as are specified in the order.

(10) Where a tribunal makes an order under this section varying a lease the tribunal may, if it thinks fit, make an order providing for any party to the lease to pay, to any other party to the lease or to any other person, compensation in respect of any loss or disadvantage that the tribunal considers he is likely to suffer as a result of the variation.

Effect of orders varying leases: applications by third parties

39 (1) Any variation effected by an order under section 38 shall be binding not only on the parties to the lease for the time being but also on other persons (including any predecessors in title of those parties), whether or not they were parties to the proceedings in which the order was made or were served with a notice by virtue of section 35(5).

(2) Without prejudice to the generality of subsection (1), any variation effected by any such order shall be binding on any surety who has guaranteed the performance of any obligation varied by the order; and the surety shall accordingly be taken to have guaranteed the performance of that obligation as so varied.

(3) Where any such order has been made and a person was, by virtue of section 35(5), required to be served with a notice relating to the proceedings in which it was made, but he was not so served, he may–

(a) bring an action for damages for breach of statutory duty against the person by whom any such notice was so required to be served in respect of that person's failure to serve it;

(b) apply to the appropriate tribunal for the cancellation or modification of the variation in question.

(4) A tribunal may, on an application under subsection (3)(b) with respect to any variation of a lease–

(a) by order cancel that variation or modify it in such manner as is specified in the order, or

(b) make such an order as is mentioned in section 38(10) in favour of the person making the application,

as it thinks fit.

(5) Where a variation is cancelled or modified under paragraph (a) of subsection (4)–

(a) the cancellation or modification shall take effect as from the date of the making of the order under that paragraph or as from such later date as may be specified in the order, and

(b) the tribunal may by order direct that a memorandum of the cancellation or modification shall be endorsed on such documents as are specified in the order;

and, in a case where a variation is so modified, subsections (1) and (2) above shall, as from the date when the modification takes effect, apply to the variation as modified.

Application for variation of insurance provisions of lease of dwelling other than a flat

40 (1) Any party to a long lease of a dwelling may make an application to the appropriate tribunal for an order varying the lease, in such manner as is specified in the application, on the grounds that the lease fails to make satisfactory provision with respect to any matter relating to the insurance of the dwelling, including the recovery of the costs of such insurance.

(2) Sections 36 and 38 shall apply to an application under subsection (1) subject to the modifications specified in subsection (3).

(3) Those modifications are as follows–

(a) in section 36–

(i) in subsection (1), the reference to section 35 shall be read as a reference to subsection (1) above, and

(ii) in subsection (2), any reference to a flat shall be read as a reference to a dwelling; and

(b) in section 38–

(i) any reference to an application under section 35 shall be read as a reference to an application under subsection (1) above, and

(ii) any reference to an application under section 36 shall be read as a reference to an application under section 36 as applied by subsection (2) above.

(4) For the purposes of this section, a long lease shall not be regarded as a long lease of a dwelling if–

(a) the demised premises consist of three or more dwellings; or

(b) the lease constitutes a tenancy to which Part II of the Landlord and Tenant Act 1954 applies.

(4A) Without prejudice to subsection (4), an application under sub-section (1) may not be made by a person who is a tenant under a long lease of a dwelling if, by virtue of that lease and one or more other long leases of dwellings, he is also a tenant from the same landlord of at least two other dwellings.

(4B) For the purposes of subsection (4A), any tenant of a dwelling who is a body corporate shall be treated as a tenant of any other dwelling held from the same landlord which is let under a long lease to an associated company, as defined in section 20(1).

(5) In this section '*dwelling*' means a dwelling other than a flat.

(6) For the purposes of subsection (1), '*appropriate tribunal*' means–

(a) if one or more of the dwellings concerned is in England, the First-tier Tribunal or, where determined by or under Tribunal Procedure Rules, the Upper Tribunal; and

(b) if one or more of the dwellings concerned is in Wales, a leasehold valuation tribunal.

Service charge contributions to be held in trust

42 (1) This section applies where the tenants of two or more dwellings may be required under the terms of their leases to contribute to the same costs, or the tenant of a dwelling may be required under the terms of his lease to contribute to costs to which no other tenant of a dwelling may be required to contribute, by the payment of service charges; and in this section–

'*the contributing tenants*' means those tenants and '*the sole contributing tenant*' means that tenant;

'*the payee*' means the landlord or other person to whom any such charges are payable by those tenants, or that tenant, under the terms of their leases, or his lease;

'*relevant service charges*' means any such charges;

'*service charge*'has the meaning given by section 18(1) of the 1985 Act, except that it does not include a service charge payable by the tenant of a dwelling the rent of which is registered under Part IV of the Rent Act 1977, unless the amount registered is, in pursuance of section 71(4) of that Act, entered as a variable amount;

'*tenant*'does not include a tenant of an exempt landlord; and '*trust fund*' means the fund, or (as the case may be) any of the funds, mentioned in subsection (2) below.

(2) Any sums paid to the payee by the contributing tenants, or the sole contributing tenant, by way of relevant service charges, and any investments representing those sums, shall (together with any income accruing thereon) be held by the payee either as a single fund or, if he thinks fit, in two or more separate funds.

(3) The payee shall hold any trust fund–

    (a) on trust to defray costs incurred in connection with the matters for which the relevant service charges were payable (whether incurred by himself or by any other person), and

    (b) subject to that, on trust for the persons who are the contributing tenants for the time being, or the person who is the sole contributing tenant for the time being.

(4) Subject to subsections (6) to (8), the contributing tenants shall be treated as entitled by virtue of subsection (3)(b) to such shares in the residue of any such fund as are proportionate to their respective liabilities to pay relevant service charges or the sole contributing tenant shall be treated as so entitled to the residue of any such fund.

(5) If the Secretary of State by order so provides, any sums standing to the credit of any trust fund may, instead of being invested in any other manner authorised by law, be invested in such manner as may be specified in the order; and any such order may contain such incidental, supplemental or transitional provisions as the Secretary of State considers appropriate in connection with the order.

(6) On the termination of the lease of any of the contributing tenants the tenant shall not be entitled to any part of any trust fund, and (except where subsection (7) applies) any part of any such fund which is attributable to relevant service charges paid under the lease shall accordingly continue to be held on the trusts referred to in subsection (3).

(7) On the termination of the lease of the last of the contributing tenants, or of the lease of the sole contributing tenant, any trust fund shall be dissolved as at the date of the termination of the lease, and any assets comprised in the fund immediately before its dissolution shall–

    (a) if the payee is the landlord, be retained by him for his own use and benefit, and

    (b) in any other case, be transferred to the landlord by the payee.

(8) Subsections (4), (6) and (7) shall have effect in relation to any of the contributing tenants, or the sole contributing tenant, subject to any express terms of his lease (whenever it was granted) which relate to the distribution, either before or (as the case may be) at the termination of the lease, of amounts attributable to relevant service charges paid under its terms (whether the lease was granted before or after the commencement of this section).

(9) Subject to subsection (8), the provisions of this section shall prevail over the terms of any express or implied trust created by a lease so far as inconsistent with those provisions, other than an express trust so created, in the case of a lease of any of the contributing tenants, before the commencement of this section or, in the case of the lease of the sole contributing tenant, before the

commencement of paragraph 15 of Schedule 10 to the Commonhold and Leasehold Reform Act 2002.

Landlord's name and address to be contained in demands for rent etc

47 (1) Where any written demand is given to a tenant of premises to which this Part applies, the demand must contain the following information, namely–

(a) the name and address of the landlord, and

(b) if that address is not in England and Wales, an address in England and Wales at which notices (including notices in proceedings) may be served on the landlord by the tenant.

(2) Where–

(a) a tenant of any such premises is given such a demand, but

(b) it does not contain any information required to be contained in it by virtue of subsection (1),

then (subject to subsection (3)) any part of the amount demanded which consists of a service charge or an administration charge ('the relevant amount') shall be treated for all purposes as not being due from the tenant to the landlord at any time before that information is furnished by the landlord by notice given to the tenant.

(3) The relevant amount shall not be so treated in relation to any time when, by virtue of an order of any court or tribunal, there is in force an appointment of a receiver or manager whose functions include the receiving of service charges or (as the case may be) administration charges from the tenant.

(4) In this section '*demand*' means a demand for rent or other sums payable to the landlord under the terms of the tenancy.

Notification by landlord of address for service of notices

48 (1) A landlord of premises to which this Part applies shall by notice furnish the tenant with an address in England and Wales at which notices (including notices in proceedings) may be served on him by the tenant.

(2) Where a landlord of any such premises fails to comply with subsection (1), any rent , service charge or administration charge otherwise due from the tenant to the landlord shall (subject to subsection (3)) be treated for all purposes as not being due from the tenant to the landlord at any time before the landlord does comply with that subsection.

(3) Any such rent , service charge or administration charge shall not be so treated in relation to any time when, by virtue of an order of any court or tribunal, there is in force an appointment of a receiver or manager whose functions include the receiving of rent , service charges or (as the case may be) administration charges from the tenant.

COMMONHOLD AND LEASEHOLD REFORM ACT 2002

The right to manage

71 (1) This Chapter makes provision for the acquisition and exercise of rights in relation to the management of premises to which this Chapter applies by a company which, in accordance with this Chapter, may acquire and exercise those rights (referred to in this Chapter as a RTM company).

(2) The rights are to be acquired and exercised subject to and in accordance with this Chapter and are referred to in this Chapter as the right to manage.

Premises to which Chapter applies

72 (1) This Chapter applies to premises if–
   (a) they consist of a self-contained building or part of a building, with or without appurtenant property,
   (b) they contain two or more flats held by qualifying tenants, and
   (c) the total number of flats held by such tenants is not less than two-thirds of the total number of flats contained in the premises.

(2) A building is a self-contained building if it is structurally detached.

(3) A part of a building is a self-contained part of the building if–
   (a) it constitutes a vertical division of the building,
   (b) the structure of the building is such that it could be redeveloped independently of the rest of the building, and
   (c) subsection (4) applies in relation to it.

(4) This subsection applies in relation to a part of a building if the relevant services provided for occupiers of it–
   (a) are provided independently of the relevant services provided for occupiers of the rest of the building, or
   (b) could be so provided without involving the carrying out of works likely to result in a significant interruption in the provision of any relevant services for occupiers of the rest of the building.

(5) Relevant services are services provided by means of pipes, cables or other fixed installations.

(6) Schedule 6 (premises excepted from this Chapter) has effect.

RTM companies

73 (1) This section specifies what is a RTM company.

(2) A company is a RTM company in relation to premises if–
   (a) it is a private company limited by guarantee, and
   (b) its articles of association state that its object, or one of its objects, is the acquisition and exercise of the right to manage the premises.

(3) But a company is not a RTM company if it is a commonhold association (within the meaning of Part 1).

(4) And a company is not a RTM company in relation to premises if another company is already a RTM company in relation to the premises or to any premises containing or contained in the premises.

(5) If the freehold of any premises is transferred to a company which is a RTM company in relation to the premises, or any premises containing or contained in the premises, it ceases to be a RTM company when the transfer is executed.

RTM companies: membership and regulations

74 (1) The persons who are entitled to be members of a company which is a RTM company in relation to premises are–

(a) qualifying tenants of flats contained in the premises, and

(b) from the date on which it acquires the right to manage (referred to in this Chapter as the '*acquisition date*'), landlords under leases of the whole or any part of the premises.

(2) The appropriate national authority shall make regulations about the content and form of the articles of association of RTM companies.

(3) A RTM company may adopt provisions of the regulations for its articles.

(4) The regulations may include provision which is to have effect for a RTM company whether or not it is adopted by the company.

(5) A provision of the articles of a RTM company has no effect to the extent that it is inconsistent with the regulations.

(6) The regulations have effect in relation to articles–

(a) irrespective of the date of the articles, but

(b) subject to any transitional provisions of the regulations.

(7) Section 20 of the Companies Act 2006 (default application of model articles) does not apply to a RTM company.

Qualifying tenants

75 (1) This section specifies whether there is a qualifying tenant of a flat for the purposes of this Chapter and, if so, who it is.

(2) Subject as follows, a person is the qualifying tenant of a flat if he is tenant of the flat under a long lease.

(3) Subsection (2) does not apply where the lease is a tenancy to which Part 2 of the Landlord and Tenant Act 1954 (c. 56) (business tenancies) applies.

(4) Subsection (2) does not apply where–

(a) the lease was granted by sub-demise out of a superior lease other than a long lease,

(b) the grant was made in breach of the terms of the superior lease, and

(c) there has been no waiver of the breach by the superior landlord.

(5) No flat has more than one qualifying tenant at any one time; and subsections (6) and (7) apply accordingly.

(6) Where a flat is being let under two or more long leases, a tenant under any of those leases which is superior to that held by another is not the qualifying tenant of the flat.

(7) Where a flat is being let to joint tenants under a long lease, the joint tenants shall (subject to subsection (6)) be regarded as jointly being the qualifying tenant of the flat.

Long leases

76 (1) This section and section 77 specify what is a long lease for the purposes of this Chapter.

(2) Subject to section 77, a lease is a long lease if–

(a) it is granted for a term of years certain exceeding 21 years, whether or not it is (or may become) terminable before the end of that term by notice given by or to the tenant, by re-entry or forfeiture or otherwise,

(b) it is for a term fixed by law under a grant with a covenant or obligation for perpetual renewal (but is not a lease by sub-demise from one which is not a long lease),

(c) it takes effect under section 149(6) of the Law of Property Act 1925 (leases terminable after a death or marriage or the formation of a civil partnership),

(d) it was granted in pursuance of the right to buy conferred by Part 5 of the Housing Act 1985 or in pursuance of the right to acquire on rent to mortgage terms conferred by that Part of that Act,

(e) it is a shared ownership lease, whether granted in pursuance of that Part of that Act or otherwise, where the tenant's total share is 100 per cent., or

(f) it was granted in pursuance of that Part of that Act as it has effect by virtue of section 17 of the Housing Act 1996 (the right to acquire).

(3) *'Shared ownership lease'* means a lease–

(a) granted on payment of a premium calculated by reference to a percentage of the value of the demised premises or the cost of providing them, or

(b) under which the tenant (or his personal representatives) will or may be entitled to a sum calculated by reference, directly or indirectly, to the value of those premises.

(4) *'Total share'*, in relation to the interest of a tenant under a shared ownership lease, means his initial share plus any additional share or shares in the demised premises which he has acquired.

Long leases: further provisions

77 (1) A lease terminable by notice after a death, a marriage or the formation of a civil partnership is not a long lease if–

(a) the notice is capable of being given at any time after the death or marriage of , or the formation of a civil partnership by, the tenant,

(b) the length of the notice is not more than three months, and

(c) the terms of the lease preclude both its assignment otherwise than by virtue of section 92 of the Housing Act 1985 (assignments by way of exchange) and the sub-letting of the whole of the demised premises.

(2) Where the tenant of any property under a long lease, on the coming to an end of the lease, becomes or has become tenant of the property or part of it under any subsequent tenancy (whether by express grant or by implication of law), that tenancy is a long lease irrespective of its terms.

(3) A lease–

(a) granted for a term of years certain not exceeding 21 years, but with a covenant or obligation for renewal without payment of a premium (but not for perpetual renewal), and

(b) renewed on one or more occasions so as to bring to more than 21 years the total of the terms granted (including any interval between the end of a lease and the grant of a renewal),

is to be treated as if the term originally granted had been one exceeding 21 years.

(4) Where a long lease–

(a) is or was continued for any period under Part 1 of the Landlord and Tenant Act 1954 or under Schedule 10 to the Local Government and Housing Act 1989, or

(b) was continued for any period under the Leasehold Property (Temporary Provisions) Act 1951,

it remains a long lease during that period.

(5) Where in the case of a flat there are at any time two or more separate leases, with the same landlord and the same tenant, and–

(a) the property comprised in one of those leases consists of either the flat or a part of it (in either case with or without appurtenant property), and

(b) the property comprised in every other lease consists of either a part of the flat (with or without appurtenant property) or appurtenant property only,

there shall be taken to be a single long lease of the property comprised in such of those leases as are long leases.

Notice inviting participation

78 (1) Before making a claim to acquire the right to manage any premises, a RTM company must give notice to each person who at the time when the notice is given–

(a) is the qualifying tenant of a flat contained in the premises, but

(b) neither is nor has agreed to become a member of the RTM company.

(2) A notice given under this section (referred to in this Chapter as a '*notice of invitation to participate*') must–

(a) state that the RTM company intends to acquire the right to manage the premises,

(b) state the names of the members of the RTM company,

(c) invite the recipients of the notice to become members of the company, and

(d) contain such other particulars (if any) as may be required to be contained in notices of invitation to participate by regulations made by the appropriate national authority.

(3) A notice of invitation to participate must also comply with such requirements (if any) about the form of notices of invitation to participate as may be prescribed by regulations so made.

(4) A notice of invitation to participate must either–

(a) be accompanied by a copy of the articles of association of the RTM company, or

(b) include a statement about inspection and copying of the articles of association of the RTM company.

(5) A statement under subsection (4)(b) must–

(a) specify a place (in England or Wales) at which the articles of association may be inspected,

(b) specify as the times at which they may be inspected periods of at least two hours on each of at least three days (including a Saturday or Sunday or both) within the seven days beginning with the day following that on which the notice is given,

(c) specify a place (in England or Wales) at which, at any time within those seven days, a copy of the articles of association may be ordered, and

(d) specify a fee for the provision of an ordered copy, not exceeding the reasonable cost of providing it.

(6) Where a notice given to a person includes a statement under subsection (4)(b), the notice is to be treated as not having been given to him if he is not

allowed to undertake an inspection, or is not provided with a copy, in accordance with the statement.

(7) A notice of invitation to participate is not invalidated by any inaccuracy in any of the particulars required by or by virtue of this section.

Notice of claim to acquire right

79 (1) A claim to acquire the right to manage any premises is made by giving notice of the claim (referred to in this Chapter as a *'claim notice'*); and in this Chapter the *'relevant date'*, in relation to any claim to acquire the right to manage, means the date on which notice of the claim is given.

(2) The claim notice may not be given unless each person required to be given a notice of invitation to participate has been given such a notice at least 14 days before.

(3) The claim notice must be given by a RTM company which complies with subsection (4) or (5).

(4) If on the relevant date there are only two qualifying tenants of flats contained in the premises, both must be members of the RTM company.

(5) In any other case, the membership of the RTM company must on the relevant date include a number of qualifying tenants of flats contained in the premises which is not less than one-half of the total number of flats so contained.

(6) The claim notice must be given to each person who on the relevant date is–
   (a) landlord under a lease of the whole or any part of the premises,
   (b) party to such a lease otherwise than as landlord or tenant, or
   (c) a manager appointed under Part 2 of the Landlord and Tenant Act 1987 (referred to in this Part as *'the 1987 Act'*) to act in relation to the premises, or any premises containing or contained in the premises.

(7) Subsection (6) does not require the claim notice to be given to a person who cannot be found or whose identity cannot be ascertained; but if this subsection means that the claim notice is not required to be given to anyone at all, section 85 applies.

(8) A copy of the claim notice must be given to each person who on the relevant date is the qualifying tenant of a flat contained in the premises.

(9) Where a manager has been appointed under Part 2 of the 1987 Act to act in relation to the premises, or any premises containing or contained in the premises, a copy of the claim notice must also be given to the tribunal or court by which he was appointed.

Contents of claim notice

80 (1) The claim notice must comply with the following requirements.

(2) It must specify the premises and contain a statement of the grounds on which it is claimed that they are premises to which this Chapter applies.

(3) It must state the full name of each person who is both–
   (a) the qualifying tenant of a flat contained in the premises, and
   (b) a member of the RTM company,
   and the address of his flat.

(4) And it must contain, in relation to each such person, such particulars of his lease as are sufficient to identify it, including–
   (a) the date on which it was entered into,
   (b) the term for which it was granted, and
   (c) the date of the commencement of the term.

(5) It must state the name and registered office of the RTM company.

(6) It must specify a date, not earlier than one month after the relevant date, by which each person who was given the notice under section 79(6) may respond to it by giving a counter-notice under section 84.

(7) It must specify a date, at least three months after that specified under subsection (6), on which the RTM company intends to acquire the right to manage the premises.

(8) It must also contain such other particulars (if any) as may be required to be contained in claim notices by regulations made by the appropriate national authority.

(9) And it must comply with such requirements (if any) about the form of claim notices as may be prescribed by regulations so made.

Claim notice: supplementary

81 (1) A claim notice is not invalidated by any inaccuracy in any of the particulars required by or by virtue of section 80.

(2) Where any of the members of the RTM company whose names are stated in the claim notice was not the qualifying tenant of a flat contained in the premises on the relevant date, the claim notice is not invalidated on that account, so long as a sufficient number of qualifying tenants of flats contained in the premises were members of the company on that date; and for this purpose a 'sufficient number' is a number (greater than one) which is not less than one-half of the total number of flats contained in the premises on that date.

(3) Where any premises have been specified in a claim notice, no subsequent claim notice which specifies–

(a) the premises, or

(b) any premises containing or contained in the premises,

may be given so long as the earlier claim notice continues in force.

(4) Where a claim notice is given by a RTM company it continues in force from the relevant date until the right to manage is acquired by the company unless it has previously–

(a) been withdrawn or deemed to be withdrawn by virtue of any provision of this Chapter, or

(b) ceased to have effect by reason of any other provision of this Chapter.

Right to obtain information

82 (1) A company which is a RTM company in relation to any premises may give to any person a notice requiring him to provide the company with any information–

(a) which is in his possession or control, and

(b) which the company reasonably requires for ascertaining the particulars required by or by virtue of section 80 to be included in a claim notice for claiming to acquire the right to manage the premises.

(2) Where the information is recorded in a document in the person's possession or control, the RTM company may give him a notice requiring him–

(a) to permit any person authorised to act on behalf of the company at any reasonable time to inspect the document (or, if the information is recorded in the document in a form in which it is not readily intelligible, to give any such person access to it in a readily intelligible form), and

(b) to supply the company with a copy of the document containing the information in a readily intelligible form on payment of a reasonable fee.

(3) A person to whom a notice is given must comply with it within the period of 28 days beginning with the day on which it is given.

Right of access

83 (1) Where a RTM company has given a claim notice in relation to any premises, each of the persons specified in subsection (2) has a right of access to any part of the premises if that is reasonable in connection with any matter arising out of the claim to acquire the right to manage.

(2) The persons referred to in subsection (1) are–
  (a) any person authorised to act on behalf of the RTM company,
  (b) any person who is landlord under a lease of the whole or any part of the premises and any person authorised to act on behalf of any such person,
  (c) any person who is party to such a lease otherwise than as landlord or tenant and any person authorised to act on behalf of any such person, and
  (d) any manager appointed under Part 2 of the 1987 Act to act in relation to the premises, or any premises containing or contained in the premises, and any person authorised to act on behalf of any such manager.

(3) The right conferred by this section is exercisable, at any reasonable time, on giving not less than ten days' notice–
  (a) to the occupier of any premises to which access is sought, or
  (b) if those premises are unoccupied, to the person entitled to occupy them.

Counter-notices

84 (1) A person who is given a claim notice by a RTM company under section 79(6) may give a notice (referred to in this Chapter as a '*counter-notice*') to the company no later than the date specified in the claim notice under section 80(6).

(2) A counter-notice is a notice containing a statement either–
  (a) admitting that the RTM company was on the relevant date entitled to acquire the right to manage the premises specified in the claim notice, or
  (b) alleging that, by reason of a specified provision of this Chapter, the RTM company was on that date not so entitled,
  and containing such other particulars (if any) as may be required to be contained in counter-notices, and complying with such requirements (if any) about the form of counter-notices, as may be prescribed by regulations made by the appropriate national authority.

(3) Where the RTM company has been given one or more counter-notices containing a statement such as is mentioned in subsection (2)(b), the company may apply to the appropriate tribunal for a determination that it was on the relevant date entitled to acquire the right to manage the premises.

(4) An application under subsection (3) must be made not later than the end of the period of two months beginning with the day on which the counter-notice (or, where more than one, the last of the counter-notices) was given.

(5) Where the RTM company has been given one or more counter-notices containing a statement such as is mentioned in subsection (2)(b), the RTM company does not acquire the right to manage the premises unless–
  (a) on an application under subsection (3) it is finally determined that the company was on the relevant date entitled to acquire the right to manage the premises, or

(b) the person by whom the counter-notice was given agrees, or the persons by whom the counter-notices were given agree, in writing that the company was so entitled.

(6) If on an application under subsection (3) it is finally determined that the company was not on the relevant date entitled to acquire the right to manage the premises, the claim notice ceases to have effect.

(7) A determination on an application under subsection (3) becomes final–
    (a) if not appealed against, at the end of the period for bringing an appeal, or
    (b) if appealed against, at the time when the appeal (or any further appeal) is disposed of.

(8) An appeal is disposed of–
    (a) if it is determined and the period for bringing any further appeal has ended, or
    (b) if it is abandoned or otherwise ceases to have effect.

Landlords etc. not traceable

85 (1) This section applies where a RTM company wishing to acquire the right to manage premises–
    (a) complies with subsection (4) or (5) of section 79, and
    (b) would not have been precluded from giving a valid notice under that section with respect to the premises,
    but cannot find, or ascertain the identity of, any of the persons to whom the claim notice would be required to be given by subsection (6) of that section.

(2) The RTM company may apply to the appropriate tribunal for an order that the company is to acquire the right to manage the premises.

(3) Such an order may be made only if the company has given notice of the application to each person who is the qualifying tenant of a flat contained in the premises.

(4) Before an order is made the company may be required to take such further steps by way of advertisement or otherwise as is determined proper for the purpose of tracing the persons who are–
    (a) landlords under leases of the whole or any part of the premises, or
    (b) parties to such leases otherwise than as landlord or tenant.

(5) If any of those persons is traced–
    (a) after an application for an order is made, but
    (b) before the making of an order,
    no further proceedings shall be taken with a view to the making of an order.

(6) Where that happens–
    (a) the rights and obligations of all persons concerned shall be determined as if the company had, at the date of the application, duly given notice under section 79 of its claim to acquire the right to manage the premises, and
    (b) the tribunal may give such directions as it thinks fit as to the steps to be taken for giving effect to their rights and obligations, including directions modifying or dispensing with any of the requirements imposed by or by virtue of this Chapter.

(7) An application for an order may be withdrawn at any time before an order is made and, after it is withdrawn, subsection (6)(a) does not apply.

(8) But where any step is taken for the purpose of giving effect to subsection

(6)(a) in the case of any application, the application shall not afterwards be withdrawn except–

(a) with the consent of the person or persons traced, or

(b) by permission of the tribunal.

(9) And permission shall be given only where it appears just that it should be given by reason of matters coming to the knowledge of the RTM company in consequence of the tracing of the person or persons traced.

Withdrawal of claim notice

86 (1) A RTM company which has given a claim notice in relation to any premises may, at any time before it acquires the right to manage the premises, withdraw the claim notice by giving a notice to that effect (referred to in this Chapter as a '*notice of withdrawal*').

(2) A notice of withdrawal must be given to each person who is–

(a) landlord under a lease of the whole or any part of the premises,

(b) party to such a lease otherwise than as landlord or tenant,

(c) a manager appointed under Part 2 of the 1987 Act to act in relation to the premises, or any premises containing or contained in the premises, or

(d) the qualifying tenant of a flat contained in the premises.

Deemed withdrawal

87 (1) If a RTM company has been given one or more counter-notices containing a statement such as is mentioned in subsection (2)(b) of section 84 but either–

(a) no application for a determination under subsection (3) of that section is made within the period specified in subsection (4) of that section, or

(b) such an application is so made but is subsequently withdrawn,

the claim notice is deemed to be withdrawn.

(2) The withdrawal shall be taken to occur–

(a) if paragraph (a) of subsection (1) applies, at the end of the period specified in that paragraph, and

(b) if paragraph (b) of that subsection applies, on the date of the withdrawal of the application.

(3) Subsection (1) does not apply if the person by whom the counter-notice was given has, or the persons by whom the counter-notices were given have, (before the time when the withdrawal would be taken to occur) agreed in writing that the RTM company was on the relevant date entitled to acquire the right to manage the premises.

(4) The claim notice is deemed to be withdrawn if–

(a) a winding-up order is made, or a resolution for voluntary winding-up is passed, with respect to the RTM company, or the RTM company enters administration,

(b) a receiver or a manager of the RTM company's undertaking is duly appointed, or possession is taken, by or on behalf of the holders of any debentures secured by a floating charge, of any property of the RTM company comprised in or subject to the charge,

(c) a voluntary arrangement proposed in the case of the RTM company for the purposes of Part 1 of the Insolvency Act 1986 is approved under that Part of that Act, or

(d) the RTM company's name is struck off the register under section 1000, 1001 or 1003 of the Companies Act 2006.

Costs: general

88 (1) A RTM company is liable for reasonable costs incurred by a person who is–
  (a) landlord under a lease of the whole or any part of any premises,
  (b) party to such a lease otherwise than as landlord or tenant, or
  (c) a manager appointed under Part 2 of the 1987 Act to act in relation to the premises, or any premises containing or contained in the premises,
  in consequence of a claim notice given by the company in relation to the premises.

  (2) Any costs incurred by such a person in respect of professional services rendered to him by another are to be regarded as reasonable only if and to the extent that costs in respect of such services might reasonably be expected to have been incurred by him if the circumstances had been such that he was personally liable for all such costs.

  (3) A RTM company is liable for any costs which such a person incurs as party to any proceedings under this Chapter before the appropriate tribunal only if the tribunal dismisses an application by the company for a determination that it is entitled to acquire the right to manage the premises.

  (4) Any question arising in relation to the amount of any costs payable by a RTM company shall, in default of agreement, be determined by the appropriate tribunal.

Costs where claim ceases

89 (1) This section applies where a claim notice given by a RTM company–
  (a) is at any time withdrawn or deemed to be withdrawn by virtue of any provision of this Chapter, or
  (b) at any time ceases to have effect by reason of any other provision of this Chapter.

  (2) The liability of the RTM company under section 88 for costs incurred by any person is a liability for costs incurred by him down to that time.

  (3) Each person who is or has been a member of the RTM company is also liable for those costs (jointly and severally with the RTM company and each other person who is so liable).

  (4) But subsection (3) does not make a person liable if–
  (a) the lease by virtue of which he was a qualifying tenant has been assigned to another person, and
  (b) that other person has become a member of the RTM company.

  (5) The reference in subsection (4) to an assignment includes–
  (a) an assent by personal representatives, and
  (b) assignment by operation of law where the assignment is to a trustee in bankruptcy or to a mortgagee under section 89(2) of the Law of Property Act 1925 (foreclosure of leasehold mortgage).

The acquisition date

90 (1) This section makes provision about the date which is the acquisition date where a RTM company acquires the right to manage any premises.

  (2) Where there is no dispute about entitlement, the acquisition date is the date specified in the claim notice under section 80(7).

(3) For the purposes of this Chapter there is no dispute about entitlement if–
   (a) no counter-notice is given under section 84, or
   (b) the counter-notice given under that section, or (where more than one is so given) each of them, contains a statement such as is mentioned in subsection (2)(a) of that section.

(4) Where the right to manage the premises is acquired by the company by virtue of a determination under section 84(5)(a), the acquisition date is the date three months after the determination becomes final.

(5) Where the right to manage the premises is acquired by the company by virtue of subsection (5)(b) of section 84, the acquisition date is the date three months after the day on which the person (or the last person) by whom a counter-notice containing a statement such as is mentioned in subsection (2)(b) of that section was given agrees in writing that the company was on the relevant date entitled to acquire the right to manage the premises.

(6) Where an order is made under section 85, the acquisition date is (subject to any appeal) the date specified in the order.

Notices relating to management contracts

91 (1) Section 92 applies where–
   (a) the right to manage premises is to be acquired by a RTM company (otherwise than by virtue of an order under section 85), and
   (b) there are one or more existing management contracts relating to the premises.

(2) A management contract is a contract between–
   (a) an existing manager of the premises (referred to in this Chapter as the *'manager party'*), and
   (b) another person (so referred to as the *'contractor party'*),
   under which the contractor party agrees to provide services, or do any other thing, in connection with any matter relating to a function which will be a function of the RTM company once it acquires the right to manage.

(3) And in this Chapter *'existing management contract'* means a management contract which–
   (a) is subsisting immediately before the determination date, or
   (b) is entered into during the period beginning with the determination date and ending with the acquisition date.

(4) An existing manager of the premises is any person who is–
   (a) landlord under a lease relating to the whole or any part of the premises,
   (b) party to such a lease otherwise than as landlord or tenant, or
   (c) a manager appointed under Part 2 of the 1987 Act to act in relation to the premises, or any premises containing or contained in the premises.

(5) In this Chapter *'determination date'* means–
   (a) where there is no dispute about entitlement, the date specified in the claim notice under section 80(6),
   (b) where the right to manage the premises is acquired by the company by virtue of a determination under section 84(5)(a), the date when the determination becomes final, and
   (c) where the right to manage the premises is acquired by the company by virtue of subsection (5)(b) of section 84, the day on which the person (or the last person) by whom a counter-notice containing a statement such

as is mentioned in subsection (2)(b) of that section was given agrees in writing that the company was on the relevant date entitled to acquire the right to manage the premises.

Duties to give notice of contracts

92 (1) The person who is the manager party in relation to an existing management contract must give a notice in relation to the contract–
   (a) to the person who is the contractor party in relation to the contract (a 'contractor notice'), and
   (b) to the RTM company (a 'contract notice').

(2) A contractor notice and a contract notice must be given–
   (a) in the case of a contract subsisting immediately before the determination date, on that date or as soon after that date as is reasonably practicable, and
   (b) in the case of a contract entered into during the period beginning with the determination date and ending with the acquisition date, on the date on which it is entered into or as soon after that date as is reasonably practicable.

(3) A contractor notice must–
   (a) give details sufficient to identify the contract in relation to which it is given,
   (b) state that the right to manage the premises is to be acquired by a RTM company,
   (c) state the name and registered office of the RTM company,
   (d) specify the acquisition date, and
   (e) contain such other particulars (if any) as may be required to be contained in contractor notices by regulations made by the appropriate national authority,
   and must also comply with such requirements (if any) about the form of contractor notices as may be prescribed by regulations so made.

(4) Where a person who receives a contractor notice (including one who receives a copy by virtue of this subsection) is party to an existing management sub-contract with another person (the 'sub-contractor party'), the person who received the notice must–
   (a) send a copy of the contractor notice to the sub-contractor party, and
   (b) give to the RTM company a contract notice in relation to the existing management sub-contract.

(5) An existing management sub-contract is a contract under which the sub-contractor party agrees to provide services, or do any other thing, in connection with any matter relating to a function which will be a function of the RTM company once it acquires the right to manage and which–
   (a) is subsisting immediately before the determination date, or
   (b) is entered into during the period beginning with the determination date and ending with the acquisition date.

(6) Subsection (4) must be complied with–
   (a) in the case of a contract entered into before the contractor notice is received, on the date on which it is received or as soon after that date as is reasonably practicable, and
   (b) in the case of a contract entered into after the contractor notice is received,

on the date on which it is entered into or as soon after that date as is reasonably practicable.

(7) A contract notice must–

    (a) give particulars of the contract in relation to which it is given and of the person who is the contractor party, or sub-contractor party, in relation to that contract, and

    (b) contain such other particulars (if any) as may be required to be contained in contract notices by regulations made by the appropriate national authority,

and must also comply with such requirements (if any) about the form of contract notices as may be prescribed by such regulations so made.

Duty to provide information

93 (1) Where the right to manage premises is to be acquired by a RTM company, the company may give notice to a person who is–

    (a) landlord under a lease of the whole or any part of the premises,

    (b) party to such a lease otherwise than as landlord or tenant, or

    (c) a manager appointed under Part 2 of the 1987 Act to act in relation to the premises, or any premises containing or contained in the premises,

requiring him to provide the company with any information which is in his possession or control and which the company reasonably requires in connection with the exercise of the right to manage.

(2) Where the information is recorded in a document in his possession or control the notice may require him–

    (a) to permit any person authorised to act on behalf of the company at any reasonable time to inspect the document (or, if the information is recorded in the document in a form in which it is not readily intelligible, to give any such person access to it in a readily intelligible form), and

    (b) to supply the company with a copy of the document containing the information in a readily intelligible form.

(3) A notice may not require a person to do anything under this section before the acquisition date.

(4) But, subject to that, a person who is required by a notice to do anything under this section must do it within the period of 28 days beginning with the day on which the notice is given.

Duty to pay accrued uncommitted service charges

94 (1) Where the right to manage premises is to be acquired by a RTM company, a person who is–

    (a) landlord under a lease of the whole or any part of the premises,

    (b) party to such a lease otherwise than as landlord or tenant, or

    (c) a manager appointed under Part 2 of the 1987 Act to act in relation to the premises, or any premises containing or contained in the premises,

must make to the company a payment equal to the amount of any accrued uncommitted service charges held by him on the acquisition date.

(2) The amount of any accrued uncommitted service charges is the aggregate of–

    (a) any sums which have been paid to the person by way of service charges in respect of the premises, and

(b) any investments which represent such sums (and any income which has accrued on them),

less so much (if any) of that amount as is required to meet the costs incurred before the acquisition date in connection with the matters for which the service charges were payable.

(3) He or the RTM company may make an application to the appropriate tribunal 1 to determine the amount of any payment which falls to be made under this section.

(4) The duty imposed by this section must be complied with on the acquisition date or as soon after that date as is reasonably practicable.

Introductory

95 Sections 96 to 103 apply where the right to manage premises has been acquired by a RTM company (and has not ceased to be exercisable by it).

Management functions under leases

96 (1) This section and section 97 apply in relation to management functions relating to the whole or any part of the premises.

(2) Management functions which a person who is landlord under a lease of the whole or any part of the premises has under the lease are instead functions of the RTM company.

(3) And where a person is party to a lease of the whole or any part of the premises otherwise than as landlord or tenant, management functions of his under the lease are also instead functions of the RTM company.

(4) Accordingly, any provisions of the lease making provision about the relationship of–

(a) a person who is landlord under the lease, and

(b) a person who is party to the lease otherwise than as landlord or tenant,

in relation to such functions do not have effect.

(5) 'Management functions' are functions with respect to services, repairs, maintenance, improvements, insurance and management.

(6) But this section does not apply in relation to–

(a) functions with respect to a matter concerning only a part of the premises consisting of a flat or other unit not held under a lease by a qualifying tenant, or

(b) functions relating to re-entry or forfeiture.

(7) An order amending subsection (5) or (6) may be made by the appropriate national authority.

Management functions: supplementary

97 (1) Any obligation owed by the RTM company by virtue of section 96 to a tenant under a lease of the whole or any part of the premises is also owed to each person who is landlord under the lease.

(2) A person who is–

(a) landlord under a lease of the whole or any part of the premises,

(b) party to such a lease otherwise than as landlord or tenant, or

(c) a manager appointed under Part 2 of the 1987 Act to act in relation to the premises, or any premises containing or contained in the premises,

is not entitled to do anything which the RTM company is required or empowered to do under the lease by virtue of section 96, except in accordance with an agreement made by him and the RTM company.

(3) But subsection (2) does not prevent any person from insuring the whole or any part of the premises at his own expense.

(4) So far as any function of a tenant under a lease of the whole or any part of the premises–
   (a) relates to the exercise of any function under the lease which is a function of the RTM company by virtue of section 96, and
   (b) is exercisable in relation to a person who is landlord under the lease or party to the lease otherwise than as landlord or tenant,
   it is instead exercisable in relation to the RTM company.

(5) But subsection (4) does not require or permit the payment to the RTM company of so much of any service charges payable by a tenant under a lease of the whole or any part of the premises as is required to meet costs incurred before the right to manage was acquired by the RTM company in connection with matters for which the service charges are payable.

Functions relating to approvals

98 (1) This section and section 99 apply in relation to the grant of approvals under long leases of the whole or any part of the premises; but nothing in this section or section 99 applies in relation to an approval concerning only a part of the premises consisting of a flat or other unit not held under a lease by a qualifying tenant.

(2) Where a person who is–
   (a) landlord under a long lease of the whole or any part of the premises, or
   (b) party to such a lease otherwise than as landlord or tenant,
   has functions in relation to the grant of approvals to a tenant under the lease, the functions are instead functions of the RTM company.

(3) Accordingly, any provisions of the lease making provision about the relationship of–
   (a) a person who is landlord under the lease, and
   (b) a person who is party to the lease otherwise than as landlord or tenant,
   in relation to such functions do not have effect.

(4) The RTM company must not grant an approval by virtue of subsection (2) without having given–
   (a) in the case of an approval relating to assignment, underletting, charging, parting with possession, the making of structural alterations or improvements or alterations of use, 30 days' notice, or
   (b) in any other case, 14 days' notice,
   to the person who is, or each of the persons who are, landlord under the lease.

(5) Regulations increasing the period of notice to be given under subsection (4)(b) in the case of any description of approval may be made by the appropriate national authority.

(6) So far as any function of a tenant under a long lease of the whole or any part of the premises–
   (a) relates to the exercise of any function which is a function of the RTM company by virtue of this section, and
   (b) is exercisable in relation to a person who is landlord under the lease or party to the lease otherwise than as landlord or tenant,
   it is instead exercisable in relation to the RTM company.

(7) In this Chapter *'approval'* includes consent or licence and *'approving'* is to be construed accordingly; and an approval required to be obtained by virtue of a restriction entered on the register of title kept by the Chief Land Registrar is, so far as relating to a long lease of the whole or any part of any premises, to be treated for the purposes of this Chapter as an approval under the lease.

Approvals: supplementary

99 (1) If a person to whom notice is given under section 98(4) objects to the grant of the approval before the time when the RTM company would first be entitled to grant it, the RTM company may grant it only–
(a) in accordance with the written agreement of the person who objected, or
(b) in accordance with a determination of (or on an appeal from) the appropriate tribunal.

(2) An objection to the grant of the approval may not be made by a person unless he could withhold the approval if the function of granting it were exercisable by him (and not by the RTM company).

(3) And a person may not make an objection operating only if a condition or requirement is not satisfied unless he could grant the approval subject to the condition or requirement being satisfied if the function of granting it were so exercisable.

(4) An objection to the grant of the approval is made by giving notice of the objection (and of any condition or requirement which must be satisfied if it is not to operate) to–
(a) the RTM company, and
(b) the tenant,
and, if the approval is to a tenant approving an act of a sub-tenant, to the sub-tenant.

(5) An application to the appropriate tribunal for a determination under subsection (1)(b) may be made by–
(a) the RTM company,
(b) the tenant,
(c) if the approval is to a tenant approving an act of a sub-tenant, the sub-tenant, or
(d) any person who is landlord under the lease.

Enforcement of tenant covenants

100 (1) This section applies in relation to the enforcement of untransferred tenant covenants of a lease of the whole or any part of the premises.

(2) Untransferred tenant covenants are enforceable by the RTM company, as well as by any other person by whom they are enforceable apart from this section, in the same manner as they are enforceable by any other such person.

(3) But the RTM company may not exercise any function of re-entry or forfeiture.

(4) In this Chapter *'tenant covenant'*, in relation to a lease, means a covenant falling to be complied with by a tenant under the lease; and a tenant covenant is untransferred if, apart from this section, it would not be enforceable by the RTM company.

(5) Any power under a lease of a person who is–
(a) landlord under the lease, or
(b) party to the lease otherwise than as landlord or tenant,

to enter any part of the premises to determine whether a tenant is complying with any untransferred tenant covenant is exercisable by the RTM company (as well as by the landlord or party).

Tenant covenants: monitoring and reporting

101 (1) This section applies in relation to failures to comply with tenant covenants of leases of the whole or any part of the premises.

(2) The RTM company must–

    (a) keep under review whether tenant covenants of leases of the whole or any part of the premises are being complied with, and

    (b) report to any person who is landlord under such a lease any failure to comply with any tenant covenant of the lease.

(3) The report must be made before the end of the period of three months beginning with the day on which the failure to comply comes to the attention of the RTM company.

(4) But the RTM company need not report to a landlord a failure to comply with a tenant covenant if–

    (a) the failure has been remedied,

    (b) reasonable compensation has been paid in respect of the failure, or

    (c) the landlord has notified the RTM company that it need not report to him failures of the description of the failure concerned.

Statutory functions

102 (1) Schedule 7 (provision for the operation of certain enactments with modifications) has effect.

(2) Other enactments relating to leases (including enactments contained in this Act or any Act passed after this Act) have effect with any such modifications as are prescribed by regulations made by the appropriate national authority.

Landlord contributions to service charges

103 (1) This section applies where–

    (a) the premises contain at least one flat or other unit not subject to a lease held by a qualifying tenant (an 'excluded unit'),

    (b) the service charges payable under leases of flats contained in the premises which are so subject fall to be calculated as a proportion of the relevant costs, and

    (c) the proportions of the relevant costs so payable, when aggregated, amount to less than the whole of the relevant costs.

(2) Where the premises contain only one excluded unit, the person who is the appropriate person in relation to the excluded unit must pay to the RTM company the difference between–

    (a) the relevant costs, and

    (b) the aggregate amount payable in respect of the relevant costs under leases of flats contained in the premises which are held by qualifying tenants.

(3) Where the premises contain more than one excluded unit, each person who is the appropriate person in relation to an excluded unit must pay to the RTM company the appropriate proportion of that difference.

(4) And the appropriate proportion in the case of each such person is the proportion of the internal floor area of all of the excluded units which is internal floor area of the excluded unit in relation to which he is the appropriate person.

(5) The appropriate person in relation to an excluded unit–
 (a) if it is subject to a lease, is the landlord under the lease,
 (b) if it is subject to more than one lease, is the immediate landlord under whichever of the leases is inferior to all the others, and
 (c) if it is not subject to any lease, is the freeholder.

Cessation of management

105 (1) This section makes provision about the circumstances in which, after a RTM company has acquired the right to manage any premises, that right ceases to be exercisable by it.

 (2) Provision may be made by an agreement made between–
 (a) the RTM company, and
 (b) each person who is landlord under a lease of the whole or any part of the premises,
 for the right to manage the premises to cease to be exercisable by the RTM company.

 (3) The right to manage the premises ceases to be exercisable by the RTM company if–
 (a) a winding-up order is made, or a resolution for voluntary winding-up is passed, with respect to the RTM company, or the RTM company enters administration,
 (b) a receiver or a manager of the RTM company's undertaking is duly appointed, or possession is taken, by or on behalf of the holders of any debentures secured by a floating charge, of any property of the RTM company comprised in or subject to the charge,
 (c) a voluntary arrangement proposed in the case of the RTM company for the purposes of Part 1 of the Insolvency Act 1986 is approved under that Part of that Act, or
 (d) the RTM company's name is struck off the register under section 1000, 1001 or 1003 of the Companies Act 2006.

 (4) The right to manage the premises ceases to be exercisable by the RTM company if a manager appointed under Part 2 of the 1987 Act to act in relation to the premises, or any premises containing or contained in the premises, begins so to act or an order under that Part of that Act that the right to manage the premises is to cease to be exercisable by the RTM company takes effect.

 (5) The right to manage the premises ceases to be exercisable by the RTM company if it ceases to be a RTM company in relation to the premises.

Agreements excluding or modifying right

106   Any agreement relating to a lease (whether contained in the instrument creating the lease or not and whether made before the creation of the lease or not) is void in so far as it–
 (a) purports to exclude or modify the right of any person to be, or do any thing as, a member of a RTM company,
 (b) provides for the termination or surrender of the lease if the tenant becomes, or does any thing as, a member of a RTM company or if a RTM company does any thing, or
 (c) provides for the imposition of any penalty or disability if the tenant

becomes, or does any thing as, a member of a RTM company or if a RTM company does any thing.

Enforcement of obligations

107 (1) A county court may, on the application of any person interested, make an order requiring a person who has failed to comply with a requirement imposed on him by, under or by virtue of any provision of this Chapter to make good the default within such time as is specified in the order.

(2) An application shall not be made under subsection (1) unless–

(a) a notice has been previously given to the person in question requiring him to make good the default, and

(b) more than 14 days have elapsed since the date of the giving of that notice without his having done so.

Application to Crown

108 (1) This Chapter applies in relation to premises in which there is a Crown interest.

(2) There is a Crown interest in premises if there is in the premises an interest or estate–

(a) which is comprised in the Crown Estate,

(b) which belongs to Her Majesty in right of the Duchy of Lancaster,

(c) which belongs to the Duchy of Cornwall, or

(d) which belongs to a government department or is held on behalf of Her Majesty for the purposes of a government department.

(3) Any sum payable under this Chapter to a RTM company by the Chancellor of the Duchy of Lancaster may be raised and paid under section 25 of the Duchy of Lancaster Act 1817 as an expense incurred in improvement of land belonging to Her Majesty in right of the Duchy.

(4) Any sum payable under this Chapter to a RTM company by the Duke of Cornwall (or any other possessor for the time being of the Duchy of Cornwall) may be raised and paid under section 8 of the Duchy of Cornwall Management Act 1863 as an expense incurred in permanently improving the possessions of the Duchy.

Powers of trustees in relation to right

109 (1) Where trustees are the qualifying tenant of a flat contained in any premises, their powers under the instrument regulating the trusts include power to be a member of a RTM company for the purpose of the acquisition and exercise of the right to manage the premises.

(2) But subsection (1) does not apply where the instrument regulating the trusts contains an explicit direction to the contrary.

(3) The power conferred by subsection (1) is exercisable with the same consent or on the same direction (if any) as may be required for the exercise of the trustees' powers (or ordinary powers) of investment.

(4) The purposes–

(a) authorised for the application of capital money by section 73 of the Settled Land Act 1925, and

(b) authorised by section 71 of that Act as purposes for which moneys may be raised by mortgage,

include the payment of any expenses incurred by a tenant for life or statutory owner as a member of a RTM company.

Power to prescribe procedure

110 (1) Where a claim to acquire the right to manage any premises is made by the giving of a claim notice, except as otherwise provided by this Chapter–
(a) the procedure for giving effect to the claim notice, and
(b) the rights and obligations of all parties in any matter arising in giving effect to the claim notice,
shall be such as may be prescribed by regulations made by the appropriate national authority.

(2) Regulations under this section may, in particular, make provision for a person to be discharged from performing any obligations arising out of a claim notice by reason of the default or delay of some other person.

Notices

111 (1) Any notice under this Chapter–
(a) must be in writing, and
(b) may be sent by post.

(2) A company which is a RTM company in relation to premises may give a notice under this Chapter to a person who is landlord under a lease of the whole or any part of the premises at the address specified in subsection (3) (but subject to subsection (4)).

(3) That address is–
(a) the address last furnished to a member of the RTM company as the landlord's address for service in accordance with section 48 of the 1987 Act (notification of address for service of notices on landlord), or
(b) if no such address has been so furnished, the address last furnished to such a member as the landlord's address in accordance with section 47 of the 1987 Act (landlord's name and address to be contained in demands for rent).

(4) But the RTM company may not give a notice under this Chapter to a person at the address specified in subsection (3) if it has been notified by him of a different address in England and Wales at which he wishes to be given any such notice.

(5) A company which is a RTM company in relation to premises may give a notice under this Chapter to a person who is the qualifying tenant of a flat contained in the premises at the flat unless it has been notified by the qualifying tenant of a different address in England and Wales at which he wishes to be given any such notice.

Definitions

112 (1) In this Chapter–
'*appropriate tribunal*' means–
(a) in relation to premises in England, the First-tier Tribunal or, where determined by Tribunal Procedure Rules, the Upper Tribunal; and
(b) in relation to premises in Wales, a leasehold valuation tribunal;
'*appurtenant property*', in relation to a building or part of a building or a flat, means any garage, outhouse, garden, yard or appurtenances belonging to, or usually enjoyed with, the building or part or flat,
'*copy*', in relation to a document in which information is recorded, means anything onto which the information has been copied by whatever means and whether directly or indirectly,

'*document*' means anything in which information is recorded,

'*dwelling*' means a building or part of a building occupied or intended to be occupied as a separate dwelling,

'*flat*' means a separate set of premises (whether or not on the same floor)–

    (a) which forms part of a building,

    (b) which is constructed or adapted for use for the purposes of a dwelling, and

    (c) either the whole or a material part of which lies above or below some other part of the building,

'*relevant costs*' has the meaning given by section 18 of the 1985 Act,

'*service charge*' has the meaning given by that section, and

'*unit*' means–

    (a) a flat,

    (b) any other separate set of premises which is constructed or adapted for use for the purposes of a dwelling, or

    (c) a separate set of premises let, or intended for letting, on a tenancy to which Part 2 of the Landlord and Tenant Act 1954 (business tenancies) applies.

(2) In this Chapter '*lease*' and '*tenancy*' have the same meaning and both expressions include (where the context permits)–

    (a) a sub-lease or sub-tenancy, and

    (b) an agreement for a lease or tenancy (or for a sub-lease or sub-tenancy), but do not include a tenancy at will or at sufferance.

(3) The expressions '*landlord*' and '*tenant*', and references to letting, to the grant of a lease or to covenants or the terms of a lease, shall be construed accordingly.

(4) In this Chapter any reference (however expressed) to the lease held by the qualifying tenant of a flat is a reference to a lease held by him under which the demised premises consist of or include the flat (whether with or without one or more other flats).

(5) Where two or more persons jointly constitute either the landlord or the tenant or qualifying tenant in relation to a lease of a flat, any reference in this Chapter to the landlord or to the tenant or qualifying tenant is (unless the context otherwise requires) a reference to both or all of the persons who jointly constitute the landlord or the tenant or qualifying tenant, as the case may require.

(6) In the case of a lease which derives (in accordance with section 77(5)) from two or more separate leases, any reference in this Chapter to the date of the commencement of the term for which the lease was granted shall, if the terms of the separate leases commenced at different dates, have effect as references to the date of the commencement of the term of the lease with the earliest date of commencement.

Index of defined expressions

113   In this Chapter the expressions listed below are defined by the provisions specified.

Expression	Interpretation provision
Approval (and approving)	Section 98(7)
Appurtenant property	Section 112(1)
Acquisition date	Sections 74(1)(b) and 90
Claim notice	Section 79(1)
Contractor party	Section 91(2)(b)
Copy	Section 112(1)
Counter-notice	Section 84(1)
Date of the commencement of the term of a lease	Section 112(6)
Determination date	Section 91(5)
Document	Section 112(1)
Dwelling	Section 112(1)
Existing management contract	Section 91(3)
Flat	Section 112(1)
Landlord	Section 112(3) and (5)
Lease	Section 112(2) to (4)
Letting	Section 112(3)
Long lease	Sections 76 and 77
Manager party	Section 91(2)(a)
No dispute about entitlement	Section 90(3)
Notice of invitation to participate	Section 78
Notice of withdrawal	Section 86(1)
Premises to which this Chapter applies	Section 72 (and Schedule 6)
Qualifying tenant	Sections 75 and 112(4) and (5)
Relevant costs	Section 112(1)
Relevant date	Section 79(1)
Right to manage	Section 71(2)
RTM company	Sections 71(1) and 73
Service charge	Section 112(1)
Tenancy	Section 112(2)
Tenant	Section 112(3) and (5)
Tenant covenant	Section 100(4)
Unit	Section 112(1)

SCHEDULE 6: PREMISES EXCLUDED FROM THE RIGHT TO MANAGE

Buildings with substantial non-residential parts

1 (1) This Chapter does not apply to premises falling within section 72(1) if the internal floor area–
   (a) of any non-residential part, or
   (b) (where there is more than one such part) of those parts (taken together), exceeds 25 per cent. of the internal floor area of the premises (taken as a whole).

  (2) A part of premises is a non-residential part if it is neither–
   (a) occupied, or intended to be occupied, for residential purposes, nor
   (b) comprised in any common parts of the premises.

  (3) Where in the case of any such premises any part of the premises (such as, for example, a garage, parking space or storage area) is used, or intended for use, in conjunction with a particular dwelling contained in the premises (and accordingly is not comprised in any common parts of the premises), it shall be taken to be occupied, or intended to be occupied, for residential purposes.

  (4) For the purpose of determining the internal floor area of a building or of any part of a building, the floor or floors of the building or part shall be taken to extend (without interruption) throughout the whole of the interior of the building or part, except that the area of any common parts of the building or part shall be disregarded.

Buildings with self-contained parts in different ownership

2 Where different persons own the freehold of different parts of premises falling within section 72(1), this Chapter does not apply to the premises if any of those parts is a self-contained part of a building.

Premises with resident landlord and no more than four units

3 (1) This Chapter does not apply to premises falling within section 72(1) if the premises–
   (a) have a resident landlord, and
   (b) do not contain more than four units.

  (2) Premises have a resident landlord if–
   (a) the premises are not, and do not form part of, a purpose-built block of flats (that is, a building which, as constructed, contained two or more flats),
   (b) a relevant freeholder, or an adult member of a relevant freeholder's family, occupies a qualifying flat as his only or principal home, and
   (c) sub-paragraph (4) or (5) is satisfied.

  (3) A person is a relevant freeholder, in relation to any premises, if he owns the freehold of the whole or any part of the premises.

  (4) This sub-paragraph is satisfied if–
   (a) the relevant freeholder, or
   (b) the adult member of his family,
   has throughout the last twelve months occupied the flat as his only or principal home.

  (5) This sub-paragraph is satisfied if–

(a) immediately before the date when the relevant freeholder acquired his interest in the premises, the premises were premises with a resident landlord, and

(b) he, or an adult member of his family, entered into occupation of the flat during the period of 28 days beginning with that date and has occupied the flat as his only or principal home ever since.

(6) *'Qualifying flat'*, in relation to any premises and a relevant freeholder or an adult member of his family, means a flat or other unit used as a dwelling–

(a) which is contained in the premises, and

(b) the freehold of the whole of which is owned by the relevant freeholder.

(7) Where the interest of a relevant freeholder in any premises is held on trust, the references in sub-paragraphs (2), (4) and (5)(b) to a relevant freeholder are to a person having an interest under the trust (whether or not also a trustee).

(8) A person is an adult member of another's family if he is–

(a) the other's spouse or civil partner,

(b) a son, daughter, son-in-law or daughter-in-law of the other, or of the other's spouse or civil partner, who has attained the age of 18, or

(c) the father or mother of the other or of the other's spouse or civil partner; and *'son'* and *'daughter'* include stepson and stepdaughter (*'son-in-law'* and *'daughter-in-law'* being construed accordingly).

Premises owned by local housing authority

4 (1) This Chapter does not apply to premises falling within section 72(1) if a local housing authority is the immediate landlord of any of the qualifying tenants of flats contained in the premises.

(2) *'Local housing authority'* has the meaning given by section 1 of the Housing Act 1985.

Premises in relation to which rights previously exercised

5 (1) This Chapter does not apply to premises falling within section 72(1) at any time if–

(a) the right to manage the premises is at that time exercisable by a RTM company, or

(b) that right has been so exercisable but has ceased to be so exercisable less than four years before that time.

(2) Sub-paragraph (1)(b) does not apply where the right to manage the premises ceased to be exercisable by virtue of section 73(5).

(3) The appropriate tribunal may, on an application made by a RTM company, determine that sub-paragraph (1)(b) is not to apply in any case if it considers that it would be unreasonable for it to apply in the circumstances of the case.

SCHEDULE 11: ADMINISTRATION CHARGES

1 (1) In this Part of this Schedule *'administration charge'* means an amount payable by a tenant of a dwelling as part of or in addition to the rent which is payable, directly or indirectly–

(a) for or in connection with the grant of approvals under his lease, or applications for such approvals,

(b) for or in connection with the provision of information or documents by or on behalf of the landlord or a person who is party to his lease otherwise than as landlord or tenant,

(c) in respect of a failure by the tenant to make a payment by the due date to the landlord or a person who is party to his lease otherwise than as landlord or tenant, or

(d) in connection with a breach (or alleged breach) of a covenant or condition in his lease.

(2) But an amount payable by the tenant of a dwelling the rent of which is registered under Part 4 of the Rent Act 1977 is not an administration charge, unless the amount registered is entered as a variable amount in pursuance of section 71(4) of that Act.

(3) In this Part of this Schedule *'variable administration charge'* means an administration charge payable by a tenant which is neither–

(a) specified in his lease, nor

(b) calculated in accordance with a formula specified in his lease.

(4) An order amending sub-paragraph (1) may be made by the appropriate national authority.

2 A variable administration charge is payable only to the extent that the amount of the charge is reasonable.

3 (1) Any party to a lease of a dwelling may apply to the appropriate tribunal for an order varying the lease in such manner as is specified in the application on the grounds that–

(a) any administration charge specified in the lease is unreasonable, or

(b) any formula specified in the lease in accordance with which any administration charge is calculated is unreasonable.

(2) If the grounds on which the application was made are established to the satisfaction of the tribunal, it may make an order varying the lease in such manner as is specified in the order.

(3) The variation specified in the order may be–

(a) the variation specified in the application, or

(b) such other variation as the tribunal thinks fit.

(4) The tribunal may, instead of making an order varying the lease in such manner as is specified in the order, make an order directing the parties to the lease to vary it in such manner as is so specified.

(5) The tribunal may by order direct that a memorandum of any variation of a lease effected by virtue of this paragraph be endorsed on such documents as are specified in the order.

(6) Any such variation of a lease shall be binding not only on the parties to the lease for the time being but also on other persons (including any predecessors in title), whether or not they were parties to the proceedings in which the order was made.

4 (1) A demand for the payment of an administration charge must be accompanied by a summary of the rights and obligations of tenants of dwellings in relation to administration charges.

(2) The appropriate national authority may make regulations prescribing requirements as to the form and content of such summaries of rights and obligations.

(3) A tenant may withhold payment of an administration charge which has been demanded from him if sub-paragraph (1) is not complied with in relation to the demand.

(4) Where a tenant withholds an administration charge under this paragraph, any provisions of the lease relating to non-payment or late payment of administration charges do not have effect in relation to the period for which he so withholds it.

5 (1) An application may be made to the appropriate tribunal for a determination whether an administration charge is payable and, if it is, as to–
   (a) the person by whom it is payable,
   (b) the person to whom it is payable,
   (c) the amount which is payable,
   (d) the date at or by which it is payable, and
   (e) the manner in which it is payable.

(2) Sub-paragraph (1) applies whether or not any payment has been made.

(3) The jurisdiction conferred on the appropriate tribunal in respect of any matter by virtue of sub-paragraph (1) is in addition to any jurisdiction of a court in respect of the matter.

(4) No application under sub-paragraph (1) may be made in respect of a matter which–
   (a) has been agreed or admitted by the tenant,
   (b) has been, or is to be, referred to arbitration pursuant to a post-dispute arbitration agreement to which the tenant is a party,
   (c) has been the subject of determination by a court, or
   (d) has been the subject of determination by an arbitral tribunal pursuant to a post-dispute arbitration agreement.

(5) But the tenant is not to be taken to have agreed or admitted any matter by reason only of having made any payment.

(6) An agreement by the tenant of a dwelling (other than a post-dispute arbitration agreement) is void in so far as it purports to provide for a determination–
   (a) in a particular manner, or
   (b) on particular evidence,
of any question which may be the subject matter of an application under sub-paragraph (1).

6 (1) This paragraph applies for the purposes of this Part of this Schedule.

(2) '*Tenant*' includes a statutory tenant.

(3) '*Dwelling*' and '*statutory tenant*' (and '*landlord*' in relation to a statutory tenant) have the same meanings as in the 1985 Act.

(4) '*Post-dispute arbitration agreement*', in relation to any matter, means an arbitration agreement made after a dispute about the matter has arisen.

(5) '*Arbitration agreement*' and '*arbitral tribunal*' have the same meanings as in Part 1 of the Arbitration Act 1996.

(6) '*Appropriate tribunal*' means–
   (a) in relation to premises in England, the First-tier Tribunal or, where determined by or under Tribunal Procedure Rules, the Upper Tribunal; and
   (b) in relation to premises in Wales, a leasehold valuation tribunal.

Useful addresses

Contact Addresses for Tribunal Offices

FTT(PC) London Panel
10 Alfred Place
London WC1E 7LR

Tel: 020 7446 7700
Fax: 020 7637 1250

This office covers all the London boroughs.

FTT (PC) Northern Panel
First Floor
5 New York Street
Manchester
M1 4JB

Tel: 0845 100 2614 / 01612 379491
Fax: 0161 237 3656

This office covers the following Metropolitan districts: Bolton, Bury, Manchester, Oldham, Rochdale, Salford, Stockport, Tameside, Trafford, Wigan, Knowsley, Liverpool, St Helens, Sefton, Wirral, Barnsley, Doncaster, Rotherham, Sheffield, Gateshead, Newcastle upon Tyne, North Tyneside, South Tyneside, Sunderland, Bradford, Calderdale, Kirklees, Leeds and Wakefield.

It also covers the following unitary authorities: Hartlepool, Middlesborough, Redcar and Cleveland, Darlington, Halton, Blackburn with Darwen, Blackpool, Kingston upon Hull, East Riding of Yorkshire, North-east Lincolnshire, North Lincolnshire, Stockton-on-Tees, Warrington and York.

It also covers the following counties: Cheshire, Cumbria, Durham, Lancashire, Lincolnshire

FTT (PC) Midlands Panel
3rd Floor
Temple Court
35 Bull St
Birmingham
B4 6AF

Tel: 0845 100 2615 / 0121 681 3084
Fax: 0121 643 760

This office covers the following metropolitan districts: Birmingham, Coventry, Dudley, Sandwell, Solihull, Walsall, Wolverhampton.

It also covers the following unitary authorities: Derby, Leicester, Rutland, Nottingham, Herefordshire, Telford and Wrekin and Stoke on Trent.

It also covers the following counties: Derbyshire, Leicestershire, Nottinghamshire, Shropshire, Staffordshire, Warwickshire and Worcestershire.

FTT (PC) Eastern Panel
Unit 4C
Quern House
Mill Court
Great Shelford
Cambridge
CB22 5LD

Tel: 0845 100 2616 / 01223 841 524
Fax: 01223 505116

This office covers the following unitary authorities: Bracknell Forest, West Berkshire, Reading, Slough, Windsor and Maidenhead, Wokingham, Luton, Peterborough, Milton Keynes, Southend on Sea, Thurrock.

It also covers the following counties: Bedfordshire, Buckinghamshire, Cambridgeshire, Essex, Hertfordshire, Norfolk, Northamptonshire, Oxfordshire and Suffolk.

FTT (PC) Southern Panel
1st Floor
1 Market Avenue
Chichester
PO19 1JU

Tel: 0845 100 2617 / 01243 779 394
Fax: 01243 779389

This office covers the following unitary authorities: Bath and North-east Somerset, Bristol, North Somerset, South Gloucestershire, Bournemouth, Plymouth, Torbay, Poole, Swindon, Medway, Brighton and Hove, Portsmouth, Southampton and the Isle of Wight.

It also covers the following counties: Cornwall and the Isles of Scilly, Devon, Dorset, East Sussex, Gloucestershire, Hampshire, Kent, Somerset, Surrey, West Sussex and Wiltshire.

LVT (Wales)
1st Floor
West Wing
Southgate House
Wood Street
Cardiff
CF1 1EW

Tel: 02920 922 777

Other useful contact details

Association of Residential Managing Agents (ARMA)
178 Battersea Park Road,
London SW11 4ND

Tel: 020 7978 2607
Fax: 020 7498 6153
Email: info@arma.org.uk
Web: arma.org.uk

Association of Retirement Housing Managers
3rd Floor, 89 Albert Embankment
London SE1 7TP

Tel: 020 7463 0660
Fax: 020 7820 1839
Email: enquiries@arhm.org
Web: www.arhm.org

Companies House
Crown Way
Cardiff
CF14 3UZ

Tel: 0303 1234 500
Email: enquiries@companies-house.gov.uk
Web: www.companieshouse.gov.uk

LVT and FTT decisions (England only)
www.residential-property.judiciary.gov.uk/search/decision_search.jsp

LVT decisions (Wales only)
http://rpt.wales.gov.uk/decisions/index/leasehold-valuation-tribunal/
?lang=eng

Royal Institution of Chartered Surveyors
12 Great George Street (Parliament Square)
London SW1P 3AD
United Kingdom

Tel: 024 7686 8555
Fax: 020 7334 3811
Email: contactrics@rics.org
Web: rics.org

Upper Tribunal (Lands Chamber) decisions
www.landstribunal.gov.uk/Aspx/Default.aspx

Sources of free legal advice and representation

LEASE – the Leasehold Advisory Service
Maple House,
149 Tottenham Court Road,
London W1T 7BN

Tel: 020 7383 9800
Fax: 020 7383 9849
Email: info@lease-advice.org
Web: wwwlease-advice.org

The Bar Pro Bono Unit
The National Pro Bono Centre
48 Chancery Lane
London WC2A 1JF

Tel: 0207 611 9500
Email: enquiries@barprobono.org.uk
Web: www.barprobono.org.uk

Worked examples

1 APPOINTMENT OF A MANAGER

Background

Anderson House is a block of 6 flats, all of which are owned by Ms Broome. She has given long leases of all 6 flats to 6 different tenants. The leases are all substantially similar. Anderson House is managed by Ms Broome personally.

Tenant 1 is dissatisfied with Ms Broome's management. She rarely visits Anderson House, fails to return Tenant 1's phone calls and has failed to consult tenant 1 before having the common areas of Anderson House repainted. Tenant 1's lease expressly required him to be consulted about any internal improvements or repairs.

Pre-application process

Tenant 1 speaks to tenants 2, 3, 4 and 5, all of whom agree with tenant 1's complaints about Ms Broome. Tenant 6 does not wish to get involved.

Tenants 1, 2, 3, 4 and 5 write a joint letter to Ms Broome setting out their complaints. They ask her to contact them within 28 days to discuss the problem. Ms Broome never replies. (See letter 1: letter before action)

Tenants 1, 2, 3, 4 and 5 decide that Ms Broome is not someone they want to be responsible for managing the property. They visit their local Citizens Advice Bureau and discover that the Tribunal may have the power to order that a new manager be appointed.

They check that their property is one over which the Tribunal has power. Their property is one with more than two flats and does not fall within any of the exemptions set out in the Landlord and Tenant Act 1987.

Confident that the Tribunal could grant them the remedy that they want, they write to tenant 6, saying that they want to have a new manager appointed. Tenant 6 replies that he has no firm views and does not want to get involved.

They check to see whether there is anything they must do before applying to the Tribunal. They discover that there is a pre-application process set out in the Landlord and Tenant Act 1987.

Firstly they must send a 'preliminary notice' to the landlord and anyone else who had management duties under the lease. They check their leases and discover that only the landlord, Ms Broome, has management duties, although she has a power to appoint a managing agent if she wants.

They therefore have to send a preliminary notice to the landlord. Luckily, they have her address and send the preliminary notice by recorded delivery. They ask Ms Broome to contact them within 28 days in order to discuss their concerns. (See letter 2: preliminary notice)

Ms Broome replies that she has better things to do than answer endless letters from the tenants and that the common areas clearly needed re-painting. She cannot understand why the tenants are complaining.

The tenants decide that nothing else can be achieved without an order of the Tribunal.

The Tribunal application

The tenants produce a document setting out their case. They complain that Ms Broome is in breach of her management obligations under the lease. She is given the duty to manage the property by the lease and, although she is entitled to appoint a managing agent if she wishes, that duty remains hers. By failing to consult the tenants before having the common areas re-painted, she was in breach of an obligation under the lease.

They also allege that, by failing to answer their letters and return their phone calls, she has been in breach of the Code of Practice of the Royal Institution of Chartered Surveyors (RICS).

The Tribunal receives the application, together with the relevant fee. They inform Ms Broome of the application and list a Pre-Trial Review (PTR). The tenants and Ms Broome are each given at least 14 days notice of the PTR.

The Pre-Trial Review

At the PTR only tenants 1, 2, 3 and 4 can attend. Tenant 5 has work commitments. Ms Broome also attends. Tenant 1 is appointed to speak on behalf of the applicants.

The PTR gives the tenants and Ms Broome dates by which they must serve any evidence, including any witness statements. The tenants are ordered to produce a short-list of three possible managers that they agree on. The case is listed for a final hearing.

The tenants have to pay a hearing fee.

Evidence

The tenants send in the following evidence:
1) witness statements from tenants 1, 2, 3, 4 and 5 setting out their specific complaints against Ms Broome, together with copies of the letters that they say she did not answer;
2) copies of their leases, showing Ms Broome's duty to consult them before painting the common areas;
3) a list of three possible managers. They suggest tenant 1 as their first choice manager, and two professional management companies as second and third choices;
4) a letter from tenant 6 saying that, whilst he is not a part to this application, he has no objection to tenant 1 or a professional manager being appointed.
5) letters from the two professional management companies stating that they would be willing to take over the management of the property and setting out their likely fees.

Ms Broome sends in a witness statement explaining that she has been very busy with other commitments and apologises for not answering the letters. She promises to be a better manager in the future.

The hearing

Tenant 1 speaks on behalf of the other tenants. They all confirm that their witness statements are true and that they want tenant 1 to be the manager for the property.

Ms Broome again apologises for the problems. She complains that having tenant 1 as a manager would not be fair to her as she fears that there is now bad blood between her and the tenants. She says that she wants to be a better manager of her property and promises that these problems would not occur again.

When asked by the Tribunal, she says that, if she could not stay as manager, she would prefer to have a professional manager appointed, rather than tenant 1.

The Tribunal adjourned to consider its decision

The decision

Shortly after the hearing, the tenants and Ms Broome are sent a copy of the Tribunal decision.

The Tribunal referred itself to section 24 of the Landlord and Tenant Act 1987. It found that, by not consulting the tenants before having the common area consulted, Ms Broome had been in breach of a management obligation under the lease. It also accepted that by failing to answer letters and return phone calls, Ms Broome was in breach of the RICS code of property management.

However, it noted that Ms Broome was apparently sincere in her desire to be a better property manager. It noted that tenant 1 had no experience in property management and that neither tenant 6 nor Ms Broome had any objection to a professional manager being appointed. In these circumstances, the Tribunal felt that it would not be 'just and convenient' to appoint tenant 1, but rather appointed one of the companies suggested by the tenants.

The company was appointed for two years and was appointed to carry out all the management duties of Ms Broome, as set out in the lease. As the tenants had been substantially successful, Ms Broome was ordered to refund their application fees.

Letter 1 – Letter before action

Tenants 1, 2, 3, 4, 5
Anderson House
London AB12 3CD

Ms Broome
Landlord Road
London EF45 6GH

20 June 2014

Dear Ms Broome

We are contacting you concerning the following problems arising out of your management of Anderson House.

1) We have each individually attempted to contact you in the recent past to discuss various matters, but have been unable to reach you. It appears that you are unable or unwilling to return our telephone calls or acknowledge our letters

2) Under clause 2(a) of our leases, you are required to consult us before carrying out any internal improvements or repairs. The common areas of our property have recently been repainted without you having consulted us.

We are anxious to discuss matters with you to ensure that these problems do not occur again in the future. Please contact us within 28 days of the date of this letter in order that we might arrange a mutually convenient time to meet and discuss the situation.

Yours sincerely

Tenants of Anderson House

Letter 2 – Preliminary Notice

Tenants 1, 2, 3, 4, 5
Anderson House
London AB12 3CD

Ms Broome
Landlord Road
London EF45 6GH

21 July 2014

Dear Ms Broome

We last contacted you on 20 June 2014 and received no reply. For your convenience, a copy of that letter is enclosed.

This is a preliminary notice under section 22 of the Landlord and Tenant Act 1987. Please address all correspondence to 'Tenants 1, 2, 3, 4, 5, Anderson House, London AB12 3CD.

We intend to make an application for an order that a manager be appointed for Anderson House.

You are currently exercising the management functions. It is our view you have failed to comply with clause 2(a) of our leases. By this clause you are required to consult us before carrying out any internal improvements or repairs. The common areas of our property have recently been repainted without you having consulted us. A copy of the lease is attached to this letter.

In addition, you have failed to return our numerous phone calls and letters relating to our concerns about your management of Anderson House.

We would hope that these matters can be resolved without the need for litigation. To assist in achieving this, we ask that you contact us within 28 days of the date of this letter.

If there is an mortgage secured on Anderson House, you must provide the mortgagee with a copy of this notice.

Yours sincerely

Tenants of Anderson House

2 SERVICE CHARGE DISPUTE

Background

Illingworth Housing Association (HA)has granted a long lease of 1 Blackacre Road to Ms Gill. Service charges are collected each year without any difficulties and are generally in the region of £2,500–£3,000 a year.

In 2004, Ms Gill receives a service charge demand for £10,000. Three items listed on the breakdown of costs provided by Illingworth HA concern her. She has been charged £2,000 for new plants in her garden, £3,000 for cleaning services throughout the year and £1,500 for a new fence to be erected.

She feels that these charges are excessive and complains to Illingworth HA. In reply, Illingworth HA point out that, under the lease, all service charge demands are payable within 28 days. Unless the sums are paid, the HA will bring a case in the County Court to recover the sums owed and may even attempt to forfeit her lease. (See letter 3: letter before action)

Ms Gill takes legal advice and discovers that, in her case, the Tribunal has a power to determine whether or not these service charges are payable by her to Illingworth HA. She writes to Illingworth HA stating that she is willing to discuss payment proposals with them, but, if the dispute cannot be resolved amicably, she will issue proceedings in the Tribunal.

Illingworth HA reply that, in their view, the work billed for has all been done and was all subject to competitive tender. She should therefore pay the sums demanded.

Ms Gill applies to the Tribunal for a determination of the payability of her 2004 service charge bill. She is aware that her lease allows Illingworth HA to recover its legal costs from her, and so asks the Tribunal for an order that this not be allowed to happen, as well as a determination of her service charge dispute.

Ms Gill is in receipt of Job Seeker's Allowance and so has her application fee waived.

The Tribunal contacts Illingworth HA to inform them of the application and lists a Pre-trial Review (PTR).

The PTR gives Ms Gill and Illingworth HA dates by which they must serve any evidence, including any witness statements. Ms Gill, as she was in receipt of Job Seeker's Allowance, was also exempt from any hearing fee.

Evidence

Ms Gill submitted a copy of her lease, along with a witness statement setting out her case.

Illingworth HA submitted evidence of their tendering process, showing that the companies that provided the cleaning services and the new fence had been chosen after a competitive and open tendering process.

The hearing

Ms Gill has submitted her witness statement as requested. Her case is:

(a) £2,000 for new plants is not payable because nowhere in her lease is Illingworth HA given responsibility for tending the gardens. This has always been a tenant's own duty.
(b) £3,000 for cleaning services is excessively expensive. She could get cleaners who would do the job for £1,000.
(c) The fence only cost £1,500 because it had to be replaced. In fact it had been deteriorating for years and if it had been repaired when it first began to show signs of wear, it would have been cheaper.

Illingworth HA have submitted their witness statement. Their case is:
(a) The lease gives them a power to 'improve the general amenity of the property and recover any charges associated in so doing from the tenant.'
(b) £3,000 was a fair rate for commercial cleaners
(c) The Housing Association had a policy of replacing all fences every seven years. There was no evidence that the fence should have been repaired earlier. £1,500 was a fair price for a new fence.

The Tribunal asked for an inspection of Ms Gill's property on the morning of the hearing. This request was accepted by Ms Gill. The Tribunal was particularly interested in comparing Ms Gill's fence to those of her neighbours who had not had their fences replaced.

The hearing resumed in the afternoon. The Tribunal decided to deal with each of the three issues in turn.

Ms Gill explained that tenants had always had responsibility for their own gardens. Illingworth HA accepted that this had been the past practice, but pointed to the clause in the lease.

When asked questions by the Tribunal and Illingworth HA, Ms Gill explained that she had no concerns about the quality of the cleaning but had been told by a friend who did some part-time cleaning, that £1,000 would be a fair figure. Illingworth HA relied on their tendering process, but, when questioned by Ms Gill, accepted that their had been some lower tenders.

On the fence, Ms Gill repeated her allegation that, had the fence been replaced earlier, it would have been cheaper. She accepted that she had no evidence to support this. Illingworth HA again relied on their tendering process and denied that the fence could have been replaced for less if it had been done earlier.

The Tribunal indicated that it would give its decision in writing later. However, it wanted to hear submissions on whether or not to allow Illingworth HA to recover its costs from Ms Gill.

Illingworth HA submitted that they had been put to expense attending and that they should be able to recover this from Ms Gill.

Ms Gill pointed to her early letters, whereby she had offered to negotiate the situation without the need for any Tribunal hearing. Had this been taken up, she said, no costs would have needed to be incurred.

Decision

The Tribunal sent a written decision to Ms Gill and Illingworth HA shortly afterwards. When dealing with the service charge application, the Tribunal reminded itself that it had to determine whether or not the amounts claimed were payable.

(a) On the £2,000 for new plants, the Tribunal found that the lease did not allow Illingworth HA to recover these costs. The clause relied on by Illingworth HA did not expressly refer to the gardens. Clauses of this nature had to be read restrictively. As such, none of the £2,000 was payable.

(b) On the £3,000 for cleaning, the Tribunal noted that Ms Gill had accepted that there was no concern over the quality of the work. Illingworth HA was entitled to use commercial cleaners. It did not have to rely on what independent people might charge for cleaning. In any event, Ms Gill had not provided any documentary evidence to support her figure of £1,000. However, using its own local knowledge, the Tribunal did feel that £3,000 was slightly expensive and substituted a figure of £2,500.

(c) On the £1,500 for the new fence, whilst the Tribunal had some sympathy for the argument that it might have been cheaper had the work been done earlier, there was no evidence at all to support this. £1,500 seemed to be a fair figure based on the evidence available to the Tribunal.

Accordingly, the Tribunal found a total of £4,000 to be payable.

The Tribunal decided to grant Ms Gill protection against having to pay Illingworth HA's costs. It was impressed by her early offer to discuss and negotiate the matter and the fact that Illingworth HA had declined to even explore this opportunity should be held against them.

Letter 3 – Letter before action

Ms S Gill
1 Blackacre Road
Manchester
M78 9JL

Illingworth Housing Association
College Street
Manchester
M10 9PQ

20 June 2014

Dear Sir or Madam,

Re: Service charge demand – your ref: 00897436

I am a long leaseholder of 1 Blackacre Road. I have recently received a demand for service charges from you in respect of my property. The total bill is for £10,000. I have identified three items on the bill that I am unclear about. For your ease of reference, these are:

1) £2,000 for new plants in my garden;
2) £3,000 for cleaning services; and
3) £1,500 for a new fence.

I believe the sums demanded to be excessive. I would appreciate your comments as to how each sum has been calculated. In particular, I would ask for your comments on the following:

1) Tenants have, during the whole of my time as a tenant, been responsible for their own gardens. Why have Illingworth HA now decided (a) to do work in the gardens and (b) to charge for this work?
2) £3,000 is excessively expensive. I have been told that £1,000 is a fair price for cleaning charges and I do not see why I should pay more than this.
3) Had the fence been repaired when problems first became apparent, it would not have cost £1,500 as this is the cost of a new fence.

I look forward to hearing from you at your earliest convenience and, in any event, within 28 days of the date of this letter.

Yours sincerely

Ms S Gill

RPTS guidance on tenants' associations[1]

TENANTS' ASSOCIATIONS: APPLICATION FOR RECOGNITION GUIDANCE ON PROCEDURE

1 What is a Tenants' Association?

A Tenants' Association is a group of tenants (lessees) who hold houses or flats on tenancies/leases from the same landlord upon similar terms which contain provisions for the payment of variable service charges. To be wholly effective an association needs to be formally recognised.

2 Why form a Tenants' Association

A landlord can be required to consult a recognised Association regarding such matters as service charges and management, which would not be so in the case of individual tenants. It should also be helpful to a landlord to consult with an Association rather than to have to go to the greater trouble and expense of dealing with individual tenants.

3 What is the role of a Recognised Tenants' Association?

The members will have come to ether to represent their common interest so that the association can with their consent and on their behalf:

- ask for a summary of costs incurred by their landlord in connection with matters for which they are being required to pay a service charge;
- inspect the relevant accounts and receipts;
- be sent a copy of estimates obtained by the landlord for intended work to their properties;
- propose names of contractors for inclusion in any tender list when the landlord wishes to carry out major works;
- ask for a written summary of the insurance cover and inspect the policy; and
- be consulted about the appointment or re-appointment of the agent managing the services.

4 How does an association become recognised?

There are two ways of seeking recognition. The first of these is for an association to ask the landlord for written notice of recognition. If this is given, then

---

1 © Crown copyright 2009. See www.justice.gov.uk/tribunals/residential-property/tenants-assoc.pdf.

no further steps to establish recognition need be taken. Such recognition cannot be withdrawn by the landlord without first giving at least six months' notice to the association. If however the landlord refuses or withdraws recognition, then the association can apply for recognition to one of the five Rent Assessment Panels which constitute the Residential Property Tribunal Service (RPTS) and in whose region the properties are located. A list of the panels and their addresses is given in the annex to this booklet [not reproduced: see weblink in footnote 1].

5   Who will be eligible for Membership of the Association?

There is no precise definition of tenants' qualifications and each case must be considered on its merits. Basically a Member must be contributing to the payment of a service charge levied by a landlord and which the landlord can, under the terms of similar leases/ tenancies, vary from time to time to meet expenditure incurred or to be incurred in the maintenance, repair or insurance of a block or estate of dwellings in the landlord's ownership. Tenants paying fixed rents, which incorporate a non-variable service charge, will not qualify for full Membership and, although they can become Members, they will have no voting rights.

Membership will not be open to landlords personally or, in the case of company landlords, their employees or directors. A management company (including its directors, employees, Members or shareholders) which has purchased the freehold on behalf of the tenants (lessees) cannot be a Member(s) of a Tenant's Association. This is because on enfranchisement, the company effectively becomes the landlord of the building(s).

Tenants of shops, offices, restaurants or similar business premises (unless their tenancies incorporate residential accommodation) would not usually qualify. Membership of an Association may be extended to other individuals with a common interest (for example sub tenants) but they will not have voting rights and cannot be party to the proceedings of the Association in its role as a Recognised Association.

6   Can an estate have more than one recognised association?

In certain circumstances, more than one Association will be recognised where there is no duplication and the interests of tenants can be seen to differ – for example separate blocks of flats (but not separate Associations representing tenants in the same block).

7   What if there is a change of landlord?

The Association with a current Certificate of Recognition should serve a Notice on the new landlord if it still wishes to be consulted indicating the existence of a Certificate.

8   What will it cost to make the application?

The Panel makes no charge but each party must meet their own costs.

9   How is application for recognition made to a panel?

An application form can be obtained from a panel office. The association will need to supply with its application a copy of its rules and constitution and any relevant correspondence.

10 What form should the Association's rules take?

You may draft your own rules but you should consider taking legal advice on their content. However, you must ensure that they are fair and democratic and that they meet the essential criteria set out in paragraph 11 below.

11 What is meant by fair and democratic?

The panel will need to be satisfied that the rules cover the following matters, among others:

- openness of membership – election of a secretary, chairman and any other officers;
- payment and the amount of the subscription – obligatory annual meetings;
- notices of meetings
- voting arrangements and quorum (only one vote per flat or house will be permitted); and
- independence from the landlord.

12 Who will deal with the matter?

In the first instance, the Case officers who comprise the administrative staff of the Panel will deal with the application. They will deal with all correspondence and will continue to deal with the paperwork until the final decision is reached. Case officers are able to speak to an applicant about the processes and procedures relating to the application. They cannot however give legal advice or advise parties about the law relating to an application. It should be noted that it is the Panels' practice to pass copies of documentation received from a party to any other interested party. It follows that correspondence written 'without prejudice' or 'in confidence' cannot be accepted.

13 When the Panel receives the application what procedure will be followed?

On receipt of the application it will be copied to the landlord and any other interested parties for their comments. Once these comments have been received the Case officers will then place the application and any comments from the landlord and any other interested parties
before a Member of the Panel for consideration.

14 Who will decide whether or not recognition will be granted?

The Member of the Panel, who will have been nominated by the Panel President or by a Vice-President, will consider the application and decide whether or not recognition should be granted. The Member will be a qualified lawyer or a valuer (a surveyor with experience of the management of housing property).

15 Will recognition be granted automatically?

No. The Panel has a discretion as to whether recognition should be granted and will need to be satisfied that the Rules of the Association are fair and democratic – also that the actual Membership of the Association will represent a significant proportion of the potential Membership. As a general rule, the Panel would expect the Membership to be not less than 60% of those qualifying to join the Association. In very exceptional circumstances, if a dispute of fact cannot be resolved by correspondence, the Member may arrange an oral hearing.

16 How is recognition by a Panel given and for how long will it last?

If the Member is satisfied that rules are fair and democratic and that there is no reason why recognition should be refused, he or she will issue a Certificate of Recognition. The length of validity of the Certificate is at the Panel's discretion but will usually be for four years. When the Certificate expires, the Association can apply for renewal. It is open to the Panel to cancel a Certificate at any time if it is considered that for some reason the Association no longer merits recognition.

Index